the MOMMY MOB

Inside the Outrageous World of Mommy Blogging

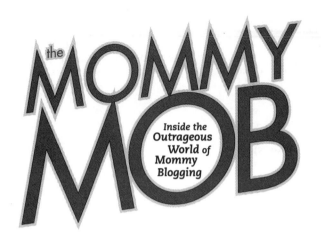

the MOMMY MOB

Inside the
Outrageous
World of
Mommy
Blogging

REBECCA ECKLER

BARLOW

Library and Archives Canada Cataloguing in Publication data available upon request.

ISBN 978-0-9917411-3-7 (book)
ISBN 978-0-9917411-4-4 (ebook)

Printed in Canada

ORDERS:
In Canada:
    Jaguar Book Group
    100 Armstrong Avenue Georgetown, ON L7G 5S4

In the U.S.A.:
    Midpoint Book Sales & Distribution
    27 West 20th Street, Suite 1102, New York, NY 10011

SALES REPRESENTATION:
    Canadian Manda Group
    165 Dufferin Street, Toronto, ON M6K 3H6

Interior and cover design: Kyle Gell Design
Cover imagery: (left) DRB Images, LLC/Getty images; (2nd from left) © iStock/DRB Images, LLC; (3rd from left) © iStock/DRB Images, LLC; (4th from left) DRB Images, LLC/Getty images; (seated woman with laptop) Philipp Nemenz/Getty Images.
Author photograph (page 294): Copyright © Trish Mennell

For more information, visit **www.barlowbookpublishing.com**

Barlow Book Publishing Inc.
77 Douglas Crescent, Toronto, ON, Canada M4W 2E6

BARLOW

For Rowan Joely: You are my inspiration, as always, in every aspect of life. I wish everyone could have your sweet soul. We will always have R and R Land, my favorite spot in the world. I love you.

For Holt: You've made me appreciate the importance of trucks. I love you.

For Jordan: For your support, love, and for always making me feel extraordinary, instead of just ordinary, an important lesson for all our children. I love you.

For All Mothers: We only become mothers when we have children. We are in a not-so-secret club, one that I'm proud to be a member of.

Contents

❦

Introduction

When did so many mothers become so cruel and ruthless? And why? These are the two questions I ask myself daily, along with, Does Baby Brain ever go away?

Let me be blunt: There are no more judgmental people in the world these days than mothers. This is especially the case when it comes to readers of mommy blogs, who, hidden behind their computer screens and fake names, make the effort to comment on parenting blogs. Mothers trolling mommy blogs, broadcasting their opinions, can be the most awful group of intolerant, narrow-minded, and humorless people out there. Not all of them, of course. Some of the women who comment on mommy blogs are actually decent and quite insightful. Other trolls are witty. Others are witty without even knowing they are, like men who walk around with their fly down all day. They don't realize it.

Nowadays, it seems, every mother has her own idea about what is right and wrong when it comes to parenting, and she will let you know it, her words screaming out from the comment sections as loud and clear as if she were yelling into a megaphone. If one mother deviates even slightly from what another mother feels, or if she doesn't agree with how another is raising her children, then a calm discussion can turn swiftly into all-out war, with anonymous mothers attacking the author of the blog post while also attacking other commenters, who will strike back at them. What turns courteous, considerate, civil, and well-mannered women in the real world into maniacal, nasty, and rude Internet trolls in cyberspace?

At home, these ferocious mommy trolls are probably telling their children that swearing and calling people bad names is not cool, while preparing them a wholesome, homemade dinner, and then reading them bedtime stories. This mother, so loving to her children (hopefully) at home, however, becomes a hate-spewing banshee online. It's shocking really. These mothers will read a post I've written about some aspect of parenting—I've been a mommy blogger for a decade now, so I've written thousands—and many just can't seem to help but attack with vitriolic, vicious, and outrageous comments, calling me out as if I were a puppy hater, pedophile, or as if I've just slept with their husband, when they've never even met, spoken to me, or seen me in person!

I've been called by some of these mothers the following:

- cunt
- douche
- whore
- train wreck
- asinine
- conceited bitch
- a horrible excuse for a mother
- retarded

And those deplorable descriptions, written by mothers who simply don't agree with what I write, are becoming the norm in the mommy blogosphere.

Sometimes my ten-year-old daughter will complain about the mean girls in her grade five class. Mean girls in school are fucking *angels* compared to some mothers in the blogosphere, who sometimes post such vulgar and offensive comments, I feel as if I've just been shot with a stun gun. I'm that astounded that these people exist. I've been mean-girled many, many times because of the posts I've written. If my daughter used some of the words these mothers use, either verbally or in written form, she'd be grounded for a year. Then again, I think my daughter may be, or actually is, more mature than many mothers posting comments on mommy blogs these days.

As mothers, or parents, we are supposed to teach our children to play nicely with others. We tell them that if you don't have anything nice to say, then don't say anything at all. Well, HA. HA. HA. HA. Some mothers are too hypocritical for words. Anonymous mothers have also commented after mommy blogs I've written that:

- "I'm glad you're not raising my kids."
- My children "will grow up to have antisocial disorders."
- My children will have "behavioral and emotional difficulties."
- My children are "retarded."
- "You should have kept your legs shut."

Should I just hang myself in the shower or jump out of my second-floor window?

So why do I read the comments? Sometimes they are so outrageous, insane, and disrespectful, that it's better than watching a reality television show. When commenters turn on one another, it's like watching "When Animals Attack." You just can't turn your eyes away no matter how terrifying the spectacle is. When I see there are hundreds of comments posted below a blog I wrote, I usually prepare myself before reading them ... by microwaving up a bowl of popcorn and cozying up in a warm blanket. As disturbing and surprising as these comments are, to me and to others, mommy blogs have become a form of modern, voyeuristic entertainment.

Mostly, I compare reading comments on my mommy blogs to repeatedly opening my refrigerator. Even though I'm not hungry, I still open that door numerous times, hoping that magically a steak sandwich will appear, just as I often hope that, magically, a mommy commenter may write something compassionate and supportive. (Sometimes they do! Not all mommy commenters are nasty and judgmental. Some are sweet, caring, sane, and intelligent.)

Even though I've told myself, over and over again, that maybe I shouldn't read the comments following my mommy blogs, because I am human and not a psychopath, which means I have feelings, I keep on opening that door, and finding milk that expired three months ago. I'm always left with a bad taste in my mouth after reading these uncalled-for attacks. Sometimes they're so foul that, not only do I feel like taking a shower, I think my computer needs one, too.

I constantly come back to the question, Why do mommies become so ill-mannered and irate just because they don't agree with something I, or another mother, wrote? I'm fascinated by the meanness of the comments in much the same way that I'm fascinated by the knowledge that lice can hold their breath for three hours underwater. (When you have kids, you learn these things.)

These days, many mommy commenters are like the Mob. You just don't want to mess with Mob Moms because, no matter how much you try to explain why you did what you did as a parent, or why you think what you think about any aspect of parenting, they still believe that you suck as a mother, and, given the chance, would probably break your thumbs. One commenter actually wrote that she wanted to punch me in the face, all the while probably saying to her child, We do not believe in violence. Such hypocrites! Like the mothers who call me a whore, or cunt, or say that my child is retarded, you have to wonder if they kiss their children with the same mouth that spoke those words.

I look at mothers on the street, holding their toddlers' hands or pushing their baby in a stroller, and think, How sweet! But then I wonder if they go home, put their children down for a nap, rush to their computers to read a mommy blog, and then comment that I'm a douche/cunt/whore. Sigh. There are just too many Mob Moms out there. There are almost four million mommies blogging in North America. That's a heck of a lot of mothers sharing their parenting opinions with the world. And they're all inviting Mob Moms into their virtual homes to comment.

I used to think that once you became a mother, you joined a not-so-secret club, because we do have one thing in common. We all have children. Isn't that enough for us to at least be civil to each other, or respect each other, even though you believe in attachment parenting and I hate school concerts? I've never been so wrong and naïve in my life.

I would take a bullet for my children. I stare at them constantly, more than I used to stare at the poster of Patrick Swayze on my bedroom wall when I was a teenager. (I know. I've always had unique taste in men.) But it doesn't matter how much I love my children. Mob Moms will find fault in anything and everything I write because they can.

I think many mothers are so spiteful and discourteous these days because, when there is a screen to hide behind and their anonymity is guaranteed, it makes it way too easy to be a judgmental bitch. They know I'll never know who they are. They might as well be in the witness protection program. Who knows? With some of these Mob Moms attacking me, *I* may just end up in the witness protection program.

But, because I like to give people the benefit of the doubt, no matter how rude they are, perhaps there is a bit more to be said about the overwhelmingly negative comments seen on mommy blogs today. Perhaps all this repressed anger comes from the sleeplessness that goes with motherhood, the complete change when a baby takes over a mother's life that she can't be prepared for, the guilt that she's not doing the right thing, or the realization that she no longer has the freedom she once enjoyed. Who knows? There could be a plethora of reasons why mothers are so incensed on mommy blogs. Perhaps the mothers who suffer from Judgmental Mother Syndrome just can't bear the thought of the consequences if they're wrong. Perhaps blog commenters feel they need validation for their own approach to parenting, which suggests that they feel insecure, which suggests that they are not getting the kind of support that would make them more tolerant of another mother's viewpoint. Maybe they are attention whores, or just bored. But I'm not a therapist, unlike many Mob Moms, who act as if they are, and as if they know my children better than I do. As Erica Jong once said, "Fame means millions of people have the wrong idea of who you are."

So I often wonder what the heck Mob Moms are thinking when they strike out at me, other bloggers, or other moms. Have they been drinking? Are they desperate to be published in some form? Or did they just have a bad day because their child is teething and was being a cranky little fuck, and they need to vent? We've all had bad days as mothers. But why don't Mob Moms just vent at their spouses and eat an entire box of Oreo cookies, as I do? That's normal! Why, instead, do they post comments implying that the child protection service should take my children away and that I should be arrested? Yes, this *has* happened … often. It's so baffling.

I put my opinions out there, and, yes, the purpose of mommy blogging is to get a conversation going, to encourage a debate, and to promote acceptance of unconventional and more modern views, which I do. But by writing frankly and honestly about motherhood, I'm basically waving a red flag, as if egging on a bull to come after me. When I write, Mob Moms see red!

There was a time, a decade ago, when I loved reading other mothers' comments. That was before the Mob Mommies got onto the Internet and started calling me a cunt as often as they probably use the word *hello*. I really don't want to read advice from, or the opinion of a mother who uses the word *cunt*, especially when she uses it to describe me. Would you? I may not always be Mother of the Year—as many, many Mob Moms have sarcastically commented—but, sarcasm aside, what mother is perfect? Can you honestly say you're a perfect mother?

As I said to a friend, "Every time a child is born, so is a mommy blogger." (Or mommy blog reader.) The number will get larger as new mothers see how easy it is to set up a mommy blog, and then discover the addictive allure of reading blog posts, especially, nowadays, the comments. And they really are addictive.

In this book, I'm offering the most controversial and funniest of my mommy blogs. Even more, I'm including the outrageous comments that followed, some of which are so brutal and amusing you'll be left thinking, "And I thought I had a bad day!" Or, more likely, you won't be able to stop yourself from asking, "Who *are* these people?"

I'm not making fun of the Mob Moms. They don't need me to do that. They do a pretty decent job of making themselves look bad. So get cozy and enjoy the show! And don't forget to make yourself a bowl of popcorn! I would like to sincerely thank the commenters, too. Without you, life as a mommy blogger would be way less entertaining. So thank you, from the bottom of my heart, for your outrageous, sanctimonious, judgmental, vulgar comments ... even if you do think I'm a douche/cunt/whore who should be raising a rock instead of children.

XO
Rebecca

part one

Real Moms

How I Got Away Without Changing a Diaper for ~~Six Weeks~~ Two Months

*She's the one who spread her legs
and brought the baby into the world.*

About a decade ago, there were very few mommy bloggers. Blogging was a fresh new thing. Back when I started blogging as a new parent, I found that many isolated mothers reached out to mommy blogs, including mine, searching for a community that would offer support, friendship, and advice. Other mothers know what it is like to go without a shower for days, and, even better, they can debunk idealistic expectations of what a good mother is. But now, within the infinite boundaries of cyberspace, moms turn to blogs not only to share in the experience of motherhood, but also to use their participatory design, and especially their often un-moderated, anonymous message boards, to tear down mothers whose way of parenting they object to or can't grasp.

Apparently, to these Mob Moms, I'm not a Real Mom. Which, I guess, makes me a Fake Mom. I'm just some sort of imposter who carried around two babies in my stomach for nine months each, gained a combined 130 pounds, went through two C-sections to get them out of me, have stretch marks, and now have a ten-year-old and a fifteen-month-old living in my house. Apparently, in the last few years, I also didn't read, *There's One and Only One Way To Raise Children*, not a real book, but one that Mob Moms all seem to sleep with under their pillows. Judgmental mothers in the blogosphere just love throwing around the phrase *Real Mom*. They use it about as often as Brooke Mueller (mother of Charlie Sheen's twins) ends up in rehab, too many times to count.

In the mommy blogosphere, if you dare to deviate, even slightly, from anyone else's way of parenting, or try to make light of some aspect of parenting—let's say you admit you don't like bath time, or joke you want to fill their sippy cup with vodka and cranberry juice when you take them to the park, or hired a nanny so you can continue your career—they will call you out for not being a Real Mom.

According to Mob Mommies, Real Moms do absolutely everything for their baby, and, not only that, they enjoy every fucking second of it. Sober! As an example, Mob Moms, the ones who use the term *Real Mom*, profess to love changing diapers. The way they describe it, you'd think it was the most amazing experience in the world, and anyone who doesn't share their enthusiasm for diaper-changing is missing out on some sort of once-in-a-lifetime opportunity. You'd think it was akin to meeting the Queen or seeing Madonna in concert. "Real moms change diapers!" wrote one Mob Mom when I admitted I don't like changing diapers. Oh, Mob Mom! You're right. I'm not a Real Mom. I just dreamed I had stretch marks, went to parent–teacher interviews, got up in the middle of the night with a crying baby all those times, and made midnight runs to the nearest drugstore for diapers.

I was definitely called out by Mob Moms when I wrote a post for Mommyish.com about how I got away with not changing my baby's diaper for almost two months. To clarify, my son was not in the same diaper for eight weeks. He was not festering in his own waste. My son was changed as regularly as any baby of a so-called Real Mom. I just wasn't the one doing the actual diaper-changing.

"Wow," wrote one anonymous Mob Mom. "Basically she just confessed to being a manipulative cow!" Actually, I confessed that I managed to get away without changing my son's diaper for a few weeks, not that I'm a manipulative cow.

I wrote that blog post anonymously, rather than under my own name, not because I was embarrassed that I had gotten out of diaper-changing duty for almost two fucking months—I was pleased as punch about that—but because I didn't know if my fiancé, the father of our baby, would read the post. I would so be busted if the post had been written under my name, and he had read it at work, and then come home and said, "I'm onto you. Now I'm not changing a diaper for the next six weeks!" The last thing I wanted was to be caught not changing diapers. I was, after all, on a fucking brilliant roll.

I consider getting out of diaper-changing one of my all time greatest achievements, next to watching three entire seasons of "Breaking Bad" in one weekend. I kept count of the days I didn't change my baby's diaper, all the time wondering when someone in my house would say, "Hey, when is the last time *you* changed his diaper, Rebecca? I don't remember the last time I saw that."

I don't hate changing diapers. I just prefer not to. I was amazed at the responses from mothers who seemed to love it, as if changing diapers didn't mean dealing with a squirming, bawling baby whose adult-sized feces smell like, well, adult-sized feces. Judging by the comments on Mommyish.com following my post, you'd think changing a diaper was as exciting as skydiving or a night out with Adam Levine. After reading the comments, I realized, not for the first time, that true hell-fire is throwing a bunch of anonymous moms into a comment section to discuss diaper-changing. Their views were radical, to say the least. Somehow, over the last decade, mothers have become the worst critics of one another, at least online.

My son has two preteen siblings and one teenage sister, a nanny, a nana who stops by every day, and a father, all of whom are old and capable enough to change a diaper. Last I checked, they all have ten fingers. And they don't mind changing my son's diaper. So why *wouldn't* I take advantage of the people in my household who don't mind changing diapers, some of whom (the siblings) even think it's fun, and ask to do it?

I did sometimes make excuses, saying, for example, "Oh, I just have to make his dinner. Can you change his diaper really quick?" Or, "I just have to go to the washroom. Can you give him a quick diaper change?" Sometimes, I would offer to make a kind of trade, like a good old-fashioned barter system. For example, I'd say to my fiancé, "If you can just change him, then I can prepare his bath!" Or, "I'll run to the store to get the taco seasoning, but you'll have to change his diaper when I'm gone." No one seemed to mind me asking, and so I continued to ask, and ask, and ask. And before I knew it, I hadn't changed a diaper in nearly two months and had eighteen packages of taco seasoning in my kitchen cupboard.

I was amazed! Mostly, I wondered how long I could get away with this. It became a goal, like hitting the gym every day!

Not changing my baby's diaper for so many weeks did not make me feel like a Fake Mom or a manipulative cow. It made me feel like a fucking rock star! It made me feel like I was a magician, as if I had pulled a real live bunny out of my nose. I thought, wrongly of course, that most mothers would think I was nothing less than a fucking mastermind for pulling this off, and for so long, and that they could learn a thing or two from me. I thought I deserved a gold star or medal! In all my years as a mother, let me just say, I have never heard, in real life, another mother say, "Oh, he needs a diaper change. I'm so excited! I can't wait! I love changing diapers! It's the best part of my day!" What I hear is, "Are you fucking kidding me? I just changed her an hour ago!" Or, "Dear God, don't tell me you shat again? This is your fourth diaper change in five hours! I hate my life." Or, "Honey, it's your turn! I did the last one!" No one I know, in person, jumps for joy in anticipation of changing a diaper.

But on the blogosphere, there are actually mothers who do seem to think that diaper changing is the best invention, if you can call it that, since planes, the light bulb, smart phones, or the Internet. For them, the more you change diapers, the more real a mom you are. The fewer you change, the more you are just an imposter, and a fake mom.

Mob Moms, to make matters more laughable, also believe that diaper-changing is a bonding experience—one commenter actually wrote this. These judgmental Mob Mommies must have a different kind of baby than the one I have. My baby's diaper is full of pee and feces … that's it! From the way the Mob Moms commented on my post, you would think their babies shat diamonds, rainbows, puppies, or multimillion-dollar-winning lottery tickets. If so, I want their babies! How, I ask, is wiping urine and feces off your baby's genitals a bonding experience? What am I missing? In fact, I'll give you my address, Mob Moms who worship diaper-changing, and you can bond with my son if you're so adamant that changing diapers is such a bonding experience. You know what my fiancé and I do after changing our son's diaper, especially if I end up getting shit on my hands and my fiancé gets shit on his forehead, the dirty wipe ends up on the carpet, and we are gagging at the stench, so strong that it takes over the entire floor, and we're screaming, "How could something so small make such a disgusting smell?"

Well, of course, we open a bottle of wine, I sit on my fiancé's lap, and then we discuss what a bonding experience we just had changing our baby, and how much closer we feel to him now.

No. We. Don't. We run around like we're going to puke, holding our noses, and argue over who gets to shower first. But, in the mommy blogosphere, you are either a Good Mom or a Bad Mom, or a Real Mom or a Fake Mom. There's rarely that gray area in between.

But, really, is my child going to say to me one day, "Hey, Mom, remember the good old days when you changed my diaper? Those were good times, Mom. Good times"? I truly believe, unless my son's still in diapers when he's five, that he won't remember shit—excuse the pun.

Has any child in history said to their parents, "I just want to thank you for changing my diapers when I was a baby"? If such a child exists, I'd like to meet her. And possibly adopt her.

"I think this is actually sad," wrote a poster who calls herself Too Old-Fashioned, on Mommish.com. "I guess I'm too old-fashioned, but I believe the mom should be the one who changes her babies' diapers." You are correct about one part of your comment, Too Old-Fashioned. You *are* too old-fashioned. I kept it a secret from her that people rarely use fax machines anymore either. Maybe I should have responded, "Hey, Too Old-Fashioned! The '50s called and want you back!" Are you also at the door, Too Old-Fashioned, waiting for your husband to come home, holding a glass of Scotch on the rocks for him and ironing his shirts? And, yet, this Too Old-Fashioned Mob Mom seems to know how to use the Internet and comment on a blog post, so obviously she's not living in the Dark Ages. She may even own a smart phone. Oh my!

Someone named Alice commented that this was "slacking parenting." Well, yeah, of course it is. Duh. Talk about stating the obvious. But is the dad who doesn't do bath time because he hates it, or bedtime because he hates it, a slacker parent? Besides, I'm not sure getting away with not changing my son's diaper for weeks is about slacker parenting, because I do a lot of other parenting, including feeding, bathing, and making sure he stops sticking his finger in light sockets.

I was also called by Mom Mobs a "child abuser" for "guilting my older children into diaper changing." Let me get this straight so you fully understand: I wasn't *guilting* them. I was *maneuvering* them towards the change table. Total fucking difference. There are mothers out there who seriously neglect their children, who beat them, or leave them in locked cars in a heat wave—read the news! Asking other responsible people to change my son's diaper, who don't seem to mind, does not make me a child abuser. Also, can someone really adequately judge my parenting or me by the number of diapers I change? Would two hundred diaper changes be enough to qualify me as a Real Mom? More? Fewer? Exactly how many diapers do I have to change to be a Real Mom? Is it in a parenting rulebook somewhere?

I certainly don't remember signing any contract after giving birth that said that I, as the mother, agreed to change every single diaper. But who knows? I was drugged. Maybe I did sign some sort of diaper-duty contract.

Another Mob Mom suggested that I be reported to the authorities! "Sounds like child abuse and neglect," this poster wrote, adding, "She should be arrested." Arrested! Dear God! I can just picture a police officer coming to my door and saying, "You need to come with me. A blog reader alerted me to the fact you don't really like changing diapers? I'm going to have to put the cuffs on you. It's just part of the procedure." So there are Mob

Moms who believe I should be arrested. To which I can only say, "Please do! Take me to jail!" If I'm locked up, then I really can't change diapers. Being in jail is a perfect excuse for getting out of diaper-changing (or out of a date), and, in fact, a short jail stint will give me a little break from the mayhem at home. I may call the cops on myself, come to think of it.

Incredibly, the Mob Moms didn't stop there. "Is this supposed to make me feel anything other than a need to punch you in the head and scream 'Loser!' at you?" wrote one. Yeah, violence and calling me names: that's appropriate adult behavior. Well, not in real life, but it has totally become acceptable, even the norm, on mommy blogs. And, let's not forget, these mothers are raising children!

So I just need to ask, is this how you speak to your children? Because if so, I'm so super-glad you're not my mother, or my children's mother. It just goes to show that many posts on mommy blogs, even if written with humor, are magnets for mothers to judge away as if it were a spectator sport. What's up with that? Just because you popped out a baby doesn't mean you popped out your sense of humor! Where's the support, Moms?

Another poster wrote, "She's the one who spread her legs and brought the baby into the world," which obviously means that I should be one who changes all diapers all the time. Not. Yes, I had awesome sex to conceive my son, but that's not a reason to slut-shame (another popular phrase on mommy blogs) me over the fact that I didn't change diapers for a few weeks, is it? And, yes, I spread my legs. That's how most babies are conceived. But someone—ahem, my fiancé—had something to do with it, too. But, because I spread my legs, as this Mob Mom poster so eloquently put it, I automatically should like—love—diaper-changing, and find it as irresistible as devouring warm chocolate lava cake?

Another poster wrote that she felt guilty asking her older son to even pass her a baby wipe when she changes her baby. Seriously? If you can't get up the nerve to ask your own child to pass you a wipe, then good luck asking him to do his own laundry, make his own lunch, or clean his bedroom later in life. Good luck to any future girlfriend of your son's, too!

I love my children. But do I love human waste? Absolutely not! Mob Moms seem to believe, too, that getting sprayed in the face with baby pee while changing a diaper is a proud moment for a mother.

And then there are the Mob Moms who think they're therapists, and post comments such as, "She needs mental help." Gee, thanks for your professional opinion, even though I know that 99.9 percent you are *not* professional therapists. Frankly, if you obsessively love diaper-changing, as many Mob Moms assure us they do, then maybe *you're* the ones who need mental help. Another added, "It sounds like this woman doesn't really like being a mom, she may not even like children very much, and her own sound like no exception. She doesn't take joy in all the morning smiles of her baby …" As I said, I love being a mom. I love morning smiles. I don't love human waste. And, are you hiding somewhere in my house, like under my son's crib? How do you know how I feel about morning smiles?

Plus, the two aren't mutually exclusive. When did you have to love feces to become a devoted mother who loves morning smiles? "Guilting your children into taking on parental responsibilities is emotional abuse though …" wrote another, still speculating that what I was doing was neglect. I often wonder if Mob Moms know what true emotional abuse is. The suggestion that I abuse my children is insulting to the millions of children who actually are abused.

Just because Mob Moms think I'm a child abuser, should be arrested, and that I'm not a Real Mom, all because I have the intellect to get out of diaper-changing for almost two months, does not make me a child-hater or abuser. But, according to some, I'm clearly a bad person. "Her pride in how long she's gotten away with it, as well as her goal of seeing how long she can. Truly disgusting," wrote another Mommyish.com commenter. No, what is truly disgusting is a baby's diaper after he's eaten three cobs of corn the previous night. And what's wrong with having pride and setting goals? Isn't that something we're supposed to teach our children?

Another thought I was lazy: "U had the damn kid, now take care of it u lazy bum." Well, it's not like I'm lying on the couch, reading a fashion magazine, and snacking on chocolate, while I demand that someone else change my son's diaper. I'm just doing other parenting things instead of changing diapers.

I finally admitted to my fiancé that I hadn't changed a diaper in weeks, just to see his reaction. And you know what his response was? Shockingly, it was, "I'm not stupid. I know." So maybe I'm not as cunning, or the great mastermind, I thought I was. At least some mothers appreciated my getting out of diaper duty. "Maybe people are responding to what they're interpreting as bragging about neglect? But there's no neglect here, no disrespect for parenting, nor signs that she's a bad mom, just a quirky, cute story about a mom who weaseled out of diaper duty for a few weeks." Thank you! What woman in their right mind would brag about neglect? And it *was* a quirky, cute story about weaseling out of diaper duty! Other moms, in fact, thought I was somewhat of a genius. "Bow down in wonder at this woman," wrote one. "It takes skill and cunning to pull this off." (Actually, it wasn't that hard.) Another poster loved the blog: "This is awesome. I have a six-month-old, and if I can get away for a half day without a diaper change, I feel like I just pulled off the perfect bank heist!" Another even called me a hero. I'm not, obviously, but I like the idea that someone thinks so. "This woman is my hero. I tried to pull this on my husband with the dishes, and he caught on after a day," she wrote. Well, at least your husband is smart, although, in this case, that's unfortunate for you.

Other mothers, who had read the hundreds of comments calling me a child abuser and saying that I should be arrested, loved that I brightened their day. "I read this post yesterday, after it first went up. My initial thought was Anonymous Mom is boring this week. How is getting out of diaper changes even a story? I do it all the time. Guess I'm a bad mom. On the plus side, reading all these seriously batshit comments on here has made my workday fly by! Meanwhile, as I work, other people are changing my kid's dirty bum, and I'm not feeling the least bit guilty, because he's in good hands with his dad. And I'm not even the slightest bit worried that I've ruined his life." And you shouldn't be! What baby, again, remembers who changes him or her? Not one! And I'm glad I made your workday fly by. Other moms agree. One wrote, "There is no neglect, or abuse, or anything else in this case … It's a simple case of a woman being a genius and getting away with not changing a diaper … As a parent, I'd like to cut that part out … as well as bath time … My husband hasn't put our kids to bed for about four weeks now as he hates it. Does that make him a child abuser? Bahahahaha Wow! The idiocy of some people just floors me."

Some posters are considering training their dogs to change diapers. As one funny commenter wrote, "I read an article somewhere about a dog that can drive a car. If that's possible, surely a little diaper change should be no big deal. My dogs need to start pulling their weight around the house." Ha! Yet another mom saw the humor in this post: "So would everyone here react the same way if the mother said, 'I haven't taken the trash out in six weeks!' Or, 'I haven't done the laundry…'

Come on, ladies. I think we're all grown-up enough to realize that there's a tone of humor here, and she's had her fair share of diaper-changing." Yes, I have!

By the way, I haven't taken out the trash in more than six months. I guess that makes me a Fake Mom, too. Call the cops! Or send me to a mental institution. Obviously, I'm a slacker parent and a manipulative cow! Clearly, I'm not fit to be a Real Mom. But, oh! Do I ever want to get t-shirts made with slogans such as, "Real Moms Change Diapers." I think they would be bestsellers. But, in the meantime, don't y'all have a diaper to change? Or, someone to at least try to manipulate into doing it for you?

Yes, I Ditched My Newborn for a Vacation

*Moms who truly want to be moms don't take
vacations, nor feel they* need *a vacation from
their babies … a* real *mother wouldn't want to
miss a minute … being a mom literally means
no vacations from your kids. That's pretty
much the point of being a parent. Duh!*

I once started the mommy war to end all mommy wars by typing a blog of fewer than 800 words.

At least once a month there is a huge mommy war, usually perpetrated by the media, that gets taken up in the blogosphere. It might be a *Time* magazine article about a woman who is still breastfeeding her child who is almost as tall as she is, or a story about a couple called the Duggers, who are pregnant with their eighty-ninth baby. In my case, it was a piece I posted on Mommyish.com about leaving my ten-week-old son behind while I went on vacation in Mexico with my fiancé. (He runs a charity golf tournament there every year.) Because of that post, I found myself all over the news. I followed Prince Harry's *ass* as a lead story on the television program "Inside Edition" after the blog post appeared. The mainstream media, too, is now following mommy blog posts for stories, because they can be so controversial.

I went to Mexico with my fiancé, not to golf, but to lie around and eat guacamole. I had backup: my wonderful nanny, and my son's grandmother who moved into our house for the week. I couldn't read the mind of a two-month-old, I wrote, but I really didn't think he'd miss me all that much. I also wrote that I was teaching him to be independent, by showing him from an early age that he has a lot of people around him who love him and will take care of him. I asked rhetorically if I was a cold-hearted bitch for leaving a ten-week-old infant behind. I answered my own question by saying I'm just super laid-back. Well, I learned that there's no such thing as a rhetorical question in the mommy blogosphere. Everyone will react. Let me remind people: it's not like I ditched him in a dumpster, which is what the press made it look like. My baby son was with his loving grandmother, and nanny, in his own home, for God's sake.

Mob Moms will tell you it takes a village to raise a child. But, in the next breath, they are appalled when a mother dares to leave her baby in other people's hands, even if those hands are more than capable. So which is it? By the way they commented, you'd think that every mother should be chained to her children forever.

"You're famous!" my fiancé's friend told him over the phone when we went out for dinner. "I just saw your mug on 'Inside Edition'!" I was shocked. Not because the fact that I left my baby behind to go on vacation made headlines around the world—even my brother saw it on the news in Israel—but because a forty-two-year-old male friend of my fiancé was watching "Inside Edition" alone. I am still convinced he will get a girlfriend one day.

The Mob Moms were angry and appalled. The emotions were at an all-time high. There were hundreds of comments following my post—so many that it took twenty minutes to download them all, crashing my computer twice. I taped that segment of "Inside Edition," because I knew that they were doing a story on my blog post. When my fiancé and I got home, we settled into bed to watch it. To my horror, the show started with a shot of Prince Harry pulling down his pants in Vegas. A photograph of me, with the host uttering the headline, "Mommy Ditches Baby," followed that sensational lead! "Inside Edition" made it sound as if I had indeed left my baby at a crack house, or with a known pedophile, and not with the most loving grandmother and most capable nanny in the world.

I suppose "Mommy Ditches Baby" is way catchier, and would attract more viewers than "Mommy Leaves Her Baby Behind in Loving Care," which is definitely not as captivating. Just as mommy bloggers feel the need to up the ante when it comes to writing about parenthood (no longer is "my baby's first smile" an interesting post), television, too, needs to up the ante. We all know that viewership is down now that we can get all our celebrity gossip and news online, or our programs on Netflix on our handheld devices. But I was mortified, just the same. I was mortified, not because "Inside Edition" spun the story to make it look like I was the worst mother in the world, but because of the photographs they used. I was still in the midst of losing the seventy pounds I had gained while pregnant. Who the hell wants to be seen on "Inside Edition" forty pounds heavier than their natural weight? Still, my fiancé and I laughed hysterically throughout the show because the way they presented me … Well, let's just say I felt as if my name had been posted on the FBI's Most Wanted list, and I should look into getting a fake passport.

"Do you think a lot of people saw this?" I asked my fiancé. "Only about a million people, or so," he said, as my iPhone kept pinging to signal the onslaught of emails and texts. We had to re-watch the segment, like, twelve times, because we couldn't stop laughing. It was as if we had eaten a plate of pot cookies for dinner. The program also flashed a full-screen photograph of my fiancé and me at a Mexican restaurant, where we looked as if we were on our honeymoon, instead of exhausted new parents, which only added fuel to the fire. Hey, I was on vacation! And on vacations you take photographs and post them on Facebook, where anyone can find them.

"Good Morning America" also did a segment about me ditching my baby. They actually sent a television crew to my house in Toronto to interview me. I told them "a happy mother makes a happy child!" and similar, boring, clichés. After they ran the interview with me, "Good Morning America" arranged a panel of experts to discuss what I had done. They were asked how old a baby should be before its mother can leave it with others. The panel included Jill Zarin, who had appeared on the reality TV show "Real Housewives of New York," who backed me up. She pointed out, accurately, that most American women have to go back to work six weeks after giving birth. Depending on your point of view, having a pseudo-celebrity read your blog post, comment on it, and stick up for you in front of millions of viewers is either a good or a bad thing. Personally, I like celebrities, so I appreciated her sticking up for me. I also appreciate the millions of other mothers who have no choice but to go back to work after six weeks. Are they bad mothers?

Mostly, I thought, it was fabulous that I was newsworthy enough to follow a prince showing his butt in Vegas. Who wouldn't be flattered? It's the closest I'll get to a prince! The comments, however, kept coming in for weeks and weeks after the blog was originally posted. One charmer wrote on Mommyish.com, "I think she should take the little fucker down to Mexico with her, and feed the damn thing to an alligator." And that was a *nice* comment, but obviously from someone with a repulsive mind! More typical was the poster who wrote, "This Eckler is almost too much of a cunt to be real." Again, I ask, why do mothers feel the need to use the word *cunt* when they don't agree with someone else's way of parenting? And it's not okay for me to leave my baby in loving hands, but it's okay for you to call a ten-week-old baby a "little fucker" and "feed it to an alligator"? Well, both those comments are sweet … and truly egregious.

Another Mob Mom wrote, "You realize this baby is only ten weeks old, right? Infants that age need their mothers, need to bond with them, and even more so, need breast milk. She was just selfish. Her husband runs the charity golf tournament. Guess what? There will be another one. She could have waited. Instead she chose to pawn off her child, and use grandmother's love as a perfect excuse to do so. Bullshit. She is not a mom who puts her infant's needs before her own." First, Mob Mom, I wasn't using a grandmother's love as an excuse. I wanted to go. It just so happens that my son has a super-awesome grandmother who is more than happy to take care of him. Sometimes, I think she wants to adopt him. She wanted me to go, so she would get the chance to spend quality time with him!

Another Mob Mom wrote, "Puppies shouldn't be separated at ten weeks from their mom, but a human who needs the *emotional*, not only physical care should just suck it up? Quit being such a baby. Why only a one-week vacation? How about two? Or a month? I get that parents can be overindulgent, which is the other extreme. But ten weeks? For at least the first six months a baby needs mommy. That's just the way it is. No amount of rationalizing will change that, or convince any human with half a brain of anything different. If you can't sacrifice that for a child, don't have one." That's just the way it is? Why? Because *you* say so? Are you trying to say that if you're not sleep-deprived, stressed, lonely, have Cheerios in your hair, and are still attached by the umbilical cord to your baby, you're a selfish mother who should be hit by a bus? Basic hygiene, vacations, career, alone time, and autonomous hobbies, obviously, in Mob Mom mentality, are for neglectful, absent, privileged women, who don't care about their babies. And what about mothers who have no choice but to go back to work? Or fathers, who more and more these days, are staying home to raise the children. What would you say to them?

"This baby is only ten weeks old. That's vastly different from leaving a toddler. Ten-week-olds have not developed the concept of object permanence yet, so when Mom is gone, they don't understand that she will be back soon," wrote another Mob Mom. And yet another judgmental mom chimed in with, "I just don't get how she so desperately needs a break after only ten weeks. I don't dream of a kid-free vacation. I dream of an upcoming trip to Europe *with* my kids." Right, because children can really appreciate the architecture, food, culture, and the *Mona Lisa*, right? I know I'm not the only mother who needs a vacation after vacationing with kids, because, whenever my friends come back from a holiday with their kids, they say to me, "I need a fucking vacation after that vacation."

Some Mob Moms' thought processes can be seriously insane. "Want to know how your baby feels when you suddenly disappear? Reverse the scenario. Say your baby is abducted. A baby doesn't know that you're only going to be gone for ten days. It only knows that you're missing," wrote a commenter. Dear God! Did someone really just compare my leaving my baby in loving, capable hands for six days to child abduction? That's horrible. But it's up to other posters—and me—to sort out sensible opinions from crazy ones. It's best, I've learned, to just to ignore the crazies (or coconuts, as I like to call them).

And, again, I just love when Mob Moms play therapist. "If she's not willing to be there to give her child what's needed now, the least she can do is save up extra money for the years of therapy her child will need to overcome his lifelong feelings of worthlessness and abandonment that he can't understand why he has," wrote one. R-I-G-H-T! Because I left my baby in safe and loving hands, with Nana, to go on a six-day vacation, my kid *surely* will grow up to be a serial killer.

One of the best pieces of advice I ever heard about parenting is that every decision you make as a parent is right, and every decision you make as a parent is wrong. Once you accept that, you'll be just fine. And that holds true for trolls on the Internet.

There were so many haters after I was featured on "Inside Edition" that I became paranoid. I didn't leave my house without wearing sunglasses for a week. There were just too many Mob Moms after me about that post. "So what, you left your baby with someone you knew would take good care of him. That doesn't make you a good mom, any more than the drug addict who goes on a six-day binge, and leaves her baby with someone who took care of the baby. Moms who truly want to be moms don't take vacations, nor feel the *need* for a vacation from their babies. They grow and develop so quickly during this stage, a *real* mother wouldn't want to miss a minute, let alone volunteer to miss six days. I mean, being a mom literally means *no vacations* from your kids. That's pretty much the point of being a parent. Duh!" wrote an anonymous Mob Mom on Mommyish.com. Duh?

While I haven't read a ton of parenting books, I have read a handful of pamphlets while waiting at doctor's offices. Nowhere have I ever read, "Being a mom literally means *no vacations*." And here we go *again* with the Mob Mom conviction that only they know what it takes to be a Real Mom. I took a six-day vacation, and so, of course, I'm just a Fake Mom. I really wanted to respond to some of these posters, but then I thought, what's the point? It would be exhausting. And I had just come back from vacation all relaxed!

I actually made some mothers cry, which did make me feel bad. I don't like making people cry, even if I don't agree with them. "I have tears in my eyes. I can't believe someone could ditch their baby for even a day," wrote one poster. Well, I'm your living proof! Believe it! Not only did I ditch my baby for a day, I ditched him for *six* days.

Many others followed in this vein. "If you need a weekend away after only ten weeks," wrote one, "you weren't ready to become a parent. A breastfeeding mom could never do this. I'm glad your life works for you, but I'm also glad you're not raising my kid." Frankly, I'm glad, too, because I'm already raising two of my own children, two stepdaughters, and a yappy dog. My household is pretty full already, so you lucked out!

The fact is, by the time "Inside Edition" caught onto the story, along with every other mommy blog and newspaper, I had already been back from my controversial vacation for days. And guess what? My son was still the same blob he was when I left him. He didn't even look any different. He didn't scream when I held him. He smiled at me, and now, at fifteen months, he's constantly laughing and giving me hugs and kisses. Yeah, that six-day vacation really screwed him up big time.

I remain unapologetic for taking that vacation. I refuse to martyr myself to appease the Mommy Mob, with their self-righteous belief in the absolute necessity of maternal sacrifice and guilt. Happily, many mothers stuck up for me. (Thank you!) "I left my eight-week-old and my two-year-old to go to Bali and Thailand for ten days," wrote one supporter, who beat me by leaving her newborn even earlier than I did. Hurray! You are apparently a worse mom than I am. Kidding. "The trip of a lifetime was planned before we were pregnant, and my husband insisted we still go. I wanted to be sure he knew he was still a priority in my life, so I went. Was it hard? Yes! But I have absolutely no regrets. My children were well cared-for by my parents, nanny, and aunt, and uncle. I love how close my kids are with their grandparents. I have friends who have never left their school-age children even for a night. I try not to judge them, and I appreciate not being judged for my choices. Bravo to Rebecca Eckler for making her choice."

And, thankfully, not all mommy bloggers seem to be shackled to their babies. As one succinctly put it, "I can't believe the uproar over this! What in the heck is wrong with leaving your baby in capable hands? After reading many of the comments, I've come to the conclusion that those freaking out are jealous of the moms that leave their babies for a vacation for some reason or another. They either don't have anyone to leave their children with, or they don't have a husband that wants to travel anywhere with them, because they aren't any fun to be around, because all they do is judge everyone around them ... Worry about your own family and let everyone else worry about their family," argued one on Mommyish.com.

I don't feel guilty, or in the wrong, for leaving my baby behind. I ate some pretty fantastic guacamole and spent some quality time with my fiancé. And besides, how many mothers find the story of their vacation featured on two major television shows and in mainstream newspapers? Exactly! My son won't remember that I left him for six days, but I can't wait to tell him about the part he played in the drama that led to us both being talked about on a celebrity news program right after a feature focusing on Prince Harry's bare ass.

Outsourcing Bike-Riding Lessons: Genius or Missed Milestone?

*It took your kid five days to learn
how to ride a bike? Forget singing lessons;
shell out for developmental disability testing.*

I f there has previously been a culture of silence surrounding the reality of parenting, then blogs bring with them a startling cacophony of confessions. As a blogger, you want to be honest, sometimes almost uncomfortably honest, which may be both my strength and my weakness. It's a double-edge sword. But why lie?

Mob Moms definitely don't like it when you don't do everything with or for your children. They take great offense. It's as if you've just told them their child has a face only a mother could love. My daughter, finally, at age eight, learned to ride a bike. It took a long time because I was not confident enough to teach her myself. The thought of seeing her get hurt was just too much for me to bear. Same with her father. Both her father and I know when we are good at something; we also admit when we don't think we're up for the task. Just because I got pregnant and gave birth doesn't mean I also turned into a skilled bike-riding instructor, or even became skilled at stroller-folding.

So, of course, we were thrilled when I found a business that offers to teach your child to ride a bike. I think this is a genius business idea. I remember my dad trying to teach me to drive a car when I was sixteen. Along with seeing my nephew's baby penis for the first time, and going through labor, it was possibly the most traumatic experience of my life. There was a lot of yelling on his end (and he's pretty patient), and a lot of crying on my end, which is what happens when you stall the car in the middle of a major intersection, your father is yelling at you, cars are honking, and all you want to do is jump out and check yourself into an insane asylum, and take public transportation for the rest of your life.

So, thanks to this business that offers bike-riding lessons, my daughter learned to ride a bike in five days. Was I being too honest when I wrote that she was taught by a perfect stranger to ride a bike, a stranger who also enjoys and gets paid to teach kids to ride? I get that learning to ride a bike is a rite of passage for children. But is it a rite of passage for parents to have to teach them? I've taught my daughter a lot of things, such as how to brush her teeth, how to pee in a toilet, and how to fucking walk. Would it really affect my life, or hers, to outsource the bike-riding part of parenting? To Mob Moms, the answer is, hell, yes! To them, I am a hopeless, crappy parent. I have, apparently, ruined my daughter's childhood forever because I wasn't the one to teach her how to ride a bike.

"Congrats on being a half-assed parent," wrote one commenter on Mommyish.com, where the blog post first appeared. Another wrote, "As usual, I'm left wondering why the author had kids. She is just too materialistic and lazy to really appreciate what being a parent is all about. Perhaps a nice cat would have suited her lifestyle a bit better." Not really. I don't like cats all that much, but thanks for the suggestion.

And I wasn't lazy or materialistic! I never said I was. I am just not good at seeing children, especially mine, hurt themselves.

"What a shock," wrote another. "Eckler is again shuffling off her parenting onto someone else." Yes, I did. And that person was a much more patient person than I am and actually enjoys teaching children to ride bikes, along with proper rules of bike-riding. And, again, how can you adequately judge my parenting skills, based on my admission that I didn't teach my daughter how to ride a bike?

Another poster suggested, "Perhaps you would surprise yourself if you actually didn't give yourself another choice than to teach your kid how to ride a bike or drive a car. Don't underestimate yourself. You're probably not really that crappy of a mother, and care a whole lot, but balk at every opportunity of being hands-on." Thanks. I think. This comment was wrapped up in a whole lot of backhanded compliments, so I'm not sure if she was being supportive or nasty. As for hands-on, I'm the mother whose daughter would only poop on the toilet while toilet-training if I hugged her, which I did for months, each and every time she had to poop. So, yes, I believe I'm a pretty fucking hands-on mother, teaching my kid to bike ride aside.

But Mob Moms don't save their judgment only for other mothers, or me. They also feel it's perfectly acceptable to come down on innocent children. "It took your kid five days to learn how to ride a bike? Forget singing lessons; shell out for developmental disability testing," wrote one Mob Mom poster, whom I wanted to wallop. Was that necessary? For Mob Moms, it is horrifying and unacceptable for a parent to pay someone else to teach their children how to ride a bike, but it is within their moral compass, and perfectly acceptable, to bash a nine-year-old's mental capacity to her mother. Does anyone else find this appalling? And, frankly, my daughter is way more mature and classy than you are. Even at her age, she knows that words can hurt a person's feelings.

"My father taught me to ride my bike. It's a fond memory, despite the scraped knees! And my (now ex-) husband and I taught our kids ... What a fond memory for her, as she learned not only from her mother, but with the support of all of her friends and her sister, too! And when she finally got it, she was so very happy and proud of herself! You can't put a price tag on those kinds of memories." Well, actually, I can. I think the bike course was around $300, and my daughter was just as proud and happy as yours, once she could ride on her own.

Other Mob Moms, under the guise of being helpful, were way too concerned about the safety of my daughter. One wrote a series of questions for me, so many, in fact, that I truly felt like I had maybe murdered someone in my sleep, and was under police interrogation, with a bright light shining in my face. "What about her safety, Rebecca?" she asked, on Mommyish. com. "If you're too busy to teach her to ride, are you also too busy to go ride with her? Or do you let her ride alone? What supervision are you offering your daughter while she's on her bike? Has it occurred to you that she might have been happier to have her mother or father teach her, instead of someone else? I could go on, but I'll stop there." Thank God! I actually started sweating under this line of questioning. I don't feel the need, here or anywhere, to challenge "helpful" mothers who seem to worry way too much about my daughter's safety. All I will say is, She's alive! She can ride a bike! She didn't care who taught her, and she loves bike-riding now, with me.

Other Mob Moms completely lost track of the post and, instead of sharing their thoughts on outsourcing bike lessons, chose instead to just insult me. "Rebecca Eckler is a nasty, arrogant, passive-aggressive, mean girl. She's the girl you went to school with who everyone hated, but was so intimidating that no one questioned her self-proclaimed Most Popular Girl in School title," wrote one. Since I'm forty, and haven't thought of high school in a long while, not to mention I was quite shy, I'm not sure where all this antagonism is coming from. I'm talking about a happy moment! My child learned to ride a bike! It had nothing to do with whether I was popular or a passive-aggressive, mean girl. Talk about making assumptions, and what the heck does this have to do with bike riding?

The Mob Moms have no problem paying for swimming lessons or piano lessons, even if they know how to do both. But when it comes to paying for bike-riding lessons, while I didn't expect to get hugs from readers, I didn't expect to be stoned either. "You could be in real trouble if you can't handle seeing your children get hurt," wrote one. "It's a part of the maturation process, and it would be a good idea to learn how to cope with it in little ways, like teaching your child to roller-skate or ride a bike. Parents need to be able to help their children through the painful parts of life." Well, sure. I can swim, but does that mean I want to be the one to teach my daughter to swim? I can read and write, but I also send my daughter to school for that. I can play the piano, but do I want to teach her how? But according to Mob Moms, I'm not fit to be a mother, simply because I didn't teach her to ride a bike. And, yes, I've seen both my children in pain. My daughter once ran into a concrete post, knocking out a tooth, and I had to take my son to the hospital for stitches after he dived into the coffee table. I have seen them in pain. "I wouldn't even give her a live creature," one offended poster wrote. "Perhaps a rock?"

The thing with rocks is that I can't teach a rock anything, especially how to ride a bike. Even a hired professional probably couldn't do that. Any other suggestions? And I will tell you this now. I will be hiring someone to teach my daughter to drive a car, which is also a rite of passage for teenagers. Because there's no way I can handle being stuck in the middle of an intersection, in a stalled car, with enraged drivers honking and swearing at my daughter and me. I guess that, too, makes me unfit to be a parent.

Don't Hate Me Because I Help My Daughter with Homework

I love how you said you only do the
"fun homework." You are even showing her
it's ok to only do fun things and skip those that
are hard. I would be ashamed if I were you.

One of the biggest issues these days, among the trials and tribulations of parenting, is homework. There's just so damn much of it. Some schools are even considering banning it. I once cut out pictures of elephants for my daughter's school project. I cut them out for her because I can use scissors better than she can. I also find her homework kind of fun. So fun that I sometimes cross the line between *helping* and actually *doing* her homework. When I wrote a piece for Mommyish.com about this, I was glad the posters were behind their computers, in different cities, and different countries. They would have spanked me if they had been in the room with me, all because I helped, or more than helped her to cut out pictures of elephants to make her poster look presentable. Judging by the malicious responses to my post, you'd have thought I had actually *killed* an elephant. My daughter did the research for the project, but that wasn't good enough. Mob Moms think that any sort of homework help by parents is a crime against humanity. It's as if Mob Moms can't grasp that there is too much homework these days. One of my friends told me, after I complained that I was up until after 10 P.M. making sure my daughter did all her homework, that they don't give out homework at her daughter's school. I seriously considered switching my daughter's school, this no-homework school sounded so divine.

When she was in grade three, my daughter used to come home with word scrambles. I love word scrambles because I'm super-awesome at them. One of the words I had to unscramble, when I took over that portion of her homework, was the word *communities*. I recognized the word immediately, because she had been learning about communities for months. So when I saw the two *m*'s and a *c*, I easily figured it out. I did a little jig to celebrate, like a football player who just scored a touchdown. My daughter was super-impressed. There will come a time when she's not super-impressed with me, but at that moment, she thought I was supremely clever, and I felt supremely clever.

I know plenty of parents who help their children with their homework, because: (a) more often than not, there is just too much of it; and (b) their kids have other activities after school, and by the time they come home, have eaten and showered, they are just too tired to do it all by themselves. The one thing I've told my daughter, from the time she could understand, was that I'd never be able to help her with math. She was super-happy for me when I unscrambled the word *communities*, and helped cut out photos of elephants, but later, when she asked me what 8 × 7 was, it took me a while to figure it out because I was counting on my fingers. She was less impressed then, and just thought I was a fucking idiot and no longer so clever. But she was also swollen with pride, because she thought she was smarter than Mommy. After all, she figured out the answer before I did. It's nice to make kids feel good about themselves! Isn't that a part of parenting?

The Mob Moms did not like that I help my daughter with her homework, which I am especially likely to do if there is no time to get it done, because she just finished a two-hour ballet class, it's already 8 o'clock, and she still needs to shower and get through twenty minutes of reading, along with the required, nightly online math tests, plus French and science homework. Apparently, the offspring of Mob Moms do nothing but go to school and do homework.

A decade ago, before I started mommy blogging, I'd have shared with a friend over a glass of wine this little anecdote about cutting out elephants for a school project. With that limited audience of friends whom I could see, I would get a laugh ("Did you use those child-proof scissors?") and sympathy ("Oh, I know. The amount of homework is ridiculous! I was up until midnight making a fake volcano, because my son told me it was due tomorrow after dinner yesterday!"). But when you open up on the Internet, you discover that every mother has a contrary opinion, and an overpowering urge to post it.

"You are showing a huge lack of respect for yourself, your daughter's teacher, and your daughter," wrote one poster. "For yourself, because you think the only way you will be valued as a mother is if your daughter is highly successful in everything she does. For your daughter's teacher, because you are discounting their years of school, training, and experience. But mostly for your daughter. You are showing her you don't think she's capable of doing difficult work," wrote one Mob Mom, before adding the zinger: "And you are teaching her to lie!" Trust me, cutting out photographs of elephants does not show that I expect my daughter to excel at everything. And, really, is the scissor part of her homework assignment *that* difficult? Has any kid ever failed because they can't use scissors?

I think that standard is pretty low. I know she's capable, and she does too, of cutting out pictures. We both agreed that I could do it faster, after she pretty much fell asleep with her face planted in her bowl of chicken soup, with the pictures spread out in front of her on the kitchen table.

Another Mob Mom commented sarcastically, "What an amazing mom you are! Give yourself a pat on the back!" After I saw the finished elephant poster, I did give myself a pat on the back. It looked fabulous! It's hard work, as an adult, to make it look like your nine-year-old daughter actually cut out the pictures. (Just as it is hard work to come up with interesting content each week for a blog post.) In the same vein, one man I know, when it comes to Christmas, actually tells the salesperson to wrap the gift for his wife sort of messily, so it would look as if he had wrapped it himself. And my advice to parents helping with homework, especially if an artwork poster is needed to go along with the research, is to work hard to make it look as if your nine-year-old, six-year-old, or fifteen-year-old did it all by herself. You don't want to be caught. Another commenter wrote, "I love how you said you only do the 'fun homework.' You are even showing her it's ok to only do fun things and skip those that are hard. I would be ashamed if I were you." Well, Mob Moms who think you know my daughter better than I do, her favorite subject just happens to be math. To me, that is *so* not fun. It's fun for her, though. And when did childhood suddenly turn into something that shouldn't be fun? I have friends who help their children in college edit their essays. There are even professionals to help put together college applications to better their chances of getting in! So, really, what's the biggie about me cutting out pictures?

I like doing or helping my daughter with her homework because, for us, it's bonding time (when she's not asleep in her soup). Some readers understood this concept. "Good Lord, people! Get a grip! This mother is spending time with her kid, showing an interest in her schoolwork, taking time out of her own busy schedule to support her kid, and spend time with her," wrote one mom. Amen, sister! Couldn't have said it better myself. Cutting out pictures of elephants, or unscrambling words, is much more fun than, let's say, um, laundry, or asking your child to brush her teeth for the tenth time. But then—and how could I not see this coming, since I've been mommy blogging for a decade?—some judgmental, possibly insane, Mob Mom just had to compare me to the grandmother of a murdered child! For helping my daughter with her homework! "One wonders if Casey Anthony's mom had the same philosophy on childrearing. Just a thought," this commenter wrote. Oh, yes! Because I cut out pictures of elephants for my daughter's class project, my daughter will turn out *exactly* like Casey Anthony. Get a grip!

According to Mob Moms, I'm setting a horrible example for my daughter. "That's how spoiled, entitled, lazy children are made," added another poster on Mommyish.com. Again, helping with, or, in some instances, whipping off a silly piece of homework (and, yes, some homework is just plain silly) will not make my child spoiled, lazy, or entitled. She never has asked me to do her homework. And, as she gets older, I'm finding her less than interested when I ask her if she needs help. I have to tell you, it hurts. I enjoyed cutting out pictures with her and that bonding time. How often do we, as adults, get to do art projects?

Some thought I was just spineless. "This is cowardly. If you really believe that homework is not something your daughter needs to be bothered with, then tell the teacher that she will not be doing homework. Your daughter's lower grades will be an accurate reflection of her performance. Or, if you don't have the guts to let your child see a poor grade on their report card, then back off! Remove the damned distractions (sorry, 'activities') from her schedule, set her at the table for forty minutes a day, and let her be responsible for her own work," wrote another on Mommyish.com. Well, her singing, dance, and acting lessons are far from being distractions. She's very focused on them—she wants to be an actor. And I never said that all homework was pointless. I think a well-rounded child is something parents should aspire to. Mob Moms need to stop the lecturing.

I also abhor Mob Moms who feel the need to insult my daughter because of something I wrote. One mom commented, "Maybe her daughter is one of those girls who will be too pretty to do algebra? Later, when the daughter is a cheerleader, mom will be the 'popular' one who drives her around, does her homework, and gets the girls beer." Well, first, I'm not sure we have cheerleaders here in Canada, and, secondly, you're making a huge leap from cutting out pictures of elephants to buying beer. I mean, she's a little too young to drink anything other than fruit punch and milk, and if I'm ever going to buy her alcohol, it won't be beer. It will be Champagne, because that's how we roll. I kid.

My daughter is attractive, but the suggestion—talk about gender stereotyping!—that she will be "too pretty to do algebra" when her favorite subject is *math* ... again, I'm constantly in awe of Mob Moms who make such a huge leaps and assumptions, as if I had said to my daughter, "I've done most of your school project. Break time? I'll crack open the six-pack. You order the wings!"

Are there no parents in the blogosphere who see that helping kids with their homework is sometimes hard, and no trip to the ice-cream store? Sometimes helping is much more exasperating than actually doing it yourself. It can be like watching a class of four-year-olds trying to tie their shoelaces. How can these hypercritical mothers not see that a lot of homework seems unnecessary, or that there's just not enough time to finish it all without some help? Because, I guarantee, if I said I was getting her a tutor to help her, I'd just be called a slacker parent who thoughtlessly spread her legs, and should be raising a rock instead of a child. (A Mob Mom actually did suggest this.) As it happens, a tutor did join the conversation, which also means that some mothers, not just me, are hiring others to help their children. "I'm a tutor. Every day, I have at least one kid come to me and either ask outright what the answers are, or even worse, try to con me into giving them in the guise of explaining. ('Can you do the first one as an example? Hmm, I'm still not sure I get it. And you do the next one too, so I can understand, please? I think if you do just one more, I'll get it.' Or, 'I don't get this reading; can you summarize it for me and explain the main points?') Thanks to your silly and poorly edited article, I now know exactly whom to blame for this behavior. So, yeah, I'm gonna hate you, because you and parents like you make my job ten times harder. I have to be the asshole that you're too weak to be. You do your daughter no favors by letting her teacher think she's mastered skills that she hasn't, or letting her think she's accomplished something besides having more willpower than her mother." But why would you hate me? I don't send my child to you for tutoring. I shouldn't be blamed for other mothers sending their kids to you for help. And, frankly, these are children. Most children can be skilled manipulators, like pint-size lawyers. Of course they are going to try to get you to really, really help them. Is that such a shocker to you, as a tutor, that a child would try to trick you into doing his or her homework?

Truthfully, I don't think my daughter is going to be affected in the long run because she had help cutting out pictures of elephants. I would go to her teacher and say, "There's too much homework," but every parent in her class already complains about the amount of homework they get, and, also, her teacher scares me.

My daughter has about two hours of homework a night. And the school already has her for seven hours a day! So why can't I bond with her over homework? What's so wrong with steering our children to the right conclusion when sometimes it takes them so damn long to figure it out? There have been times when I felt like stabbing myself in the eye with a pencil crayon and eating her eraser, because it would be less painful than watching her try to make sense of her science assignment.

I love it when Mob Moms also happen to be teachers, because I'm always fascinated by what teachers say, behind mothers' backs, or to other teachers in the lunchroom, about us parents. And now they, too, are reading mommy blogs! In many cases, on mommy blogs, one can learn a lot about the thought processes of teachers. One commented, "As a teacher, I will never understand parents like this. Seriously, I know if the kid did their work themselves, or if their parents did it." Well, I certainly hope so! Even I can tell when a kid has had help with her school project, which is why, when I help, I at least make it look like the work was done by a nine-year-old. I'm not a teacher, but I'm smart enough for that!

When my daughter had to make a family tree last year, I helped with the presentation, but I did not help her conduct the interviews with family members she was also required to do, the most important part of the assignment. Parents were invited in to see all the family trees in her classroom when they were finished, and my heart sank when I saw them. I mean, really! I'm looking at these posters of family trees and I'm thinking: This child is in grade five. She is not a professional graphic designer, so there's no way I believe that she made this PowerPoint presentation of her family tree on her own. In fact, I think her parents probably hired a professional graphic designer, it was *that* good. It was clear to me that other parents had helped out greatly. I understand, because I also helped out, although not to the extent of doing a PowerPoint deck, but that's just because I don't know how to do one. If you don't want to help your child with their homework, that's fine with me. Kudos! Pat yourself on the back for raising a kid who does all her homework herself! You're obviously a Real Mom, because Real Moms, according to Mob Moms, do not help at all with homework and let their kids struggle through it.

Another commenter added, "I don't think it's a good idea to teach your daughter that the things she wants to do should always take precedence over the things she has to do. That won't serve her very well as she goes through life." Yes, she has to do homework, and I make her do it every day, but isn't there a bit of wiggle room for a child to do things she wants to do while not in school? You're only a child once. There will be plenty of time in her life when she will be faced with things she has to do, such as get a job, pay bills, and take care of me when I'm old, frail, in a wheelchair, and need adult diapers. Hopefully, at that point, she'll remember that it was her mother (me) who helped out with her school project on elephants, and will gladly pay me back by wheeling me around. Our children need us to help them with so many things when they're young, including homework. And we may need them to help us when we're old, and are recovering from a hip replacement. Just sayin'.

Ditch Days

Ms. Eckler, are you feeling insecure
about your relationship with your daughter,
or how you think people view your daughter
and/or aforementioned relationship?

A lot of Mob Moms do this thing called *projection*. Never before in my life, that is, before I started mommy blogging, have I seen so many people project their issues onto a perfect stranger. I could write, for example, that I love watermelon, and somehow some Mob Mom will project her miserable day, or bad life, onto me, by responding, "It's great that you love watermelon. At least you can afford that. And with electricity, too, you bitch!"

I wrote a piece for Mommyish.com in which I mentioned that I often take my daughter out of school to go on a Mommy-and-daughter vacation, when I feel that we need some extra bonding. Over one Mother's Day, for example, I took my daughter to Atlantis in the Bahamas, so she could enjoy the waterslides. She missed three days of school. They are, indeed, badass water slides. Since she's started school up until now (she's in grade five) I have never really worried about her studies getting in the way of enjoying life, as long as she keeps up her grades. There are many ways to teach children things outside the classroom. Doesn't parasailing, after all, have something to do with gravity? Isn't it more interesting to learn about dolphins than about the classroom's pet hamster?

I don't worry about her missing school. I always let the teacher know that we're taking the time off. (Of course, I don't say, "Because we're going to Atlantis. Yippee!") And I always ask what we should do while we're away so my daughter doesn't fall behind. No teacher yet has come out and said, "I think it's a bad idea to take her out for three days in a row." And so I will continue to do so until she no longer wants to go away with Mommy, or her teachers tell me she's missed sixty-eight days of school this year, and perhaps she should attend more often.

When I wrote about all this on Mommyish.com, half the commenters agreed that bonding time is important, just as important as school, and the other half, well, they were left … *projecting*. "It's a great idea, just sad for the 99.9 percent who could not possibly afford to do such a thing. A nice addition to this article would have been maybe giving some tips on how to do this on any budget, rather than an unlimited one. Not everyone can afford to leave the country for a week. Sometimes it's nice to offer help to others, rather than just speaking from a place of blind privilege," wrote one poster, adding, "I hope your daughter knows how incredibly special it is that she gets to do this." I hope so, too, since I've told her like a million times how special it is that she gets to go away. But I'm not a travel or money blogging expert. I'm a mommy blogger. There are many blogs dedicated to traveling on the cheap.

That was only the start of the projection. Check out this commenter who wrote, "I also have a nine-year-old daughter and baby son, and I'm sure my daughter would love to have a week away with just me, but we don't have the money to afford a vacation, or anyone to watch the baby while my husband's at work. Also, most people could not afford to take a week off of work. I guess I am a shit mom because I have to squeeze in my mother–daughter time when the baby is sleeping instead of swimming with the dolphins in Atlantis." Yes, you are a shit mom for not taking your daughter to Atlantis. That's exactly what I wrote. *Not.* Guess what, Mob Mom? I don't know what's going on in your life, but I certainly wasn't writing my post on ditching school and going to Atlantis *directly to you.* I never wrote that anyone who couldn't or doesn't go on vacation with their children was a shit mom. I didn't even insinuate that. I didn't even think that! I certainly don't believe that. That's you, my dear, projecting. Is it my fault that you can't go on vacation or don't have help? I wish, honestly, you did. But I can't write my posts to please everyone, obviously, and I do feel for people who don't have help or enough money to go on vacation. But taking it out on me, you realize, isn't going to get you to the Bahamas or swimming with dolphins either.

All the Mob Moms want and need to know, as one poster put it, "that hopefully Eckler's daughter recognizes how blessed she is and how grateful she should be." Well, let me raise my child. Please: it's no one's place to worry about her, except mine. She knows she's blessed, and she is grateful. You'll just have to trust me on this.

I also mentioned in my post that I like Ditch Days, when I'll pick up my daughter early from school, and we'll go grab a bite or see a movie, telling the teacher she has an appointment. Usually this happens towards the middle-to-end of the school year, when my daughter is tired and stressed out, and I'm somewhat jealous that the school has her for seven hours a day, and is still sending her home with two hours of homework, which leaves us with no fun or relaxing time together. It's as if we need to leave town just so we can bond, without me having to drag her out of bed and remind her ten times to clean her room. It's good for both of us.

"I was okay with this, a rare holiday during school time is fine, until I read that you encourage ditch days. Some schools in Australia are charging parents $60 a day whenever they keep their kids home for frivolous reasons," wrote one. This is interesting. I like learning how other schools "handle" mothers like me. But how can schools tell if it's a frivolous reason? I swear, once on a Sunday night, my daughter was complaining about a really bad earache. Seemed a little too convenient, the night before a big test at school. My daughter kept saying, "It feels like there's something flying in my ear." I didn't believe my own daughter, even though she was twitching really weirdly! But I took her to a walk-in clinic, because that's what Real Moms do. And guess what? My daughter really did have a fucking ant in her ear. Even the doctor was like, "I haven't seen this in fifteen years!" If I called a school in Australia and said, "My daughter has an ant in her ear. She's feeling a bit dizzy, so she won't be coming to school today," the teachers for sure would think I was making it up. It's like a child saying, "My dog ate my homework," but guess what? Sometimes a dog really does eat homework. I've seen it! Still, it's always nice to know what schools on the other side of the world are doing.

Others posted adamant comments about when a parent should bond with their child, as if there's only one right answer (theirs). "There is time to bond with your kids, and it's during school holidays. You're teaching her that she can bunk off whenever she feels like it. If you want more time with her, start limiting extracurricular activities. They should be put on the back-burner, not school," wrote one mom. Actually, I'm not teaching my daughter to bunk off whenever *she* wants.

I'm teaching her that *I* can bunk off whenever *I* want, and she's welcome to come along for the ride! Plus, not every mother can take off from work for school holidays. Many mothers I know have to make play dates at other children's houses because they still have to work during school breaks.

Posters were also overly, in my humble opinion, concerned about my daughter missing homework, as if it were their own kid who failed a major test. "How is your daughter going to do homework on material that she hasn't learned yet?" asked one concerned mother. "Homework typically reinforces what was learned in class that day, but you said that she's going to get her homework before you leave and do it on the plane ... I'm not trying to be snarky, I'm genuinely curious. If she's doing her homework on the way to a vacation that will cause her to miss lessons, meaning that she won't be there for the lessons that the homework is covering, how is that going to work? Unless the school isn't covering any new material ... in which case I would have serious questions about the quality and academic standards of her school." Well, it's a good thing you don't have to worry about that! I don't mean to be snarky either, but I hope you didn't stay up all night worrying about the academic standards of my daughter's school. Again, why don't Mob Moms think that another mother already knows about the academic standards of their own child's school? If I'm not questioning it, why should they? Do they think I never looked into the school she attends before I sent her there? But moms posting on blogs wrap up their judgments in a package labeled "Caring." And maybe, to give them the benefit of the doubt, they really do care. They sometimes show this, of course, by playing therapist. "Ms. Eckler, are you feeling insecure about your relationship with your daughter, or how you think people view your daughter and/or afore-mentioned relationship?" asked one, adding, "That was my general impression." No, I'm not feeling insecure about my relationship with my daughter, and never have, but thanks for trying to find a nonexistent issue for me to ponder over while we're waiting for our room service on our mother–daughter vacation while she's missing school.

Again, I love it when teachers chime in. I really admire teachers. "I am a school teacher and I see it a lot, one week a year is no big deal, but when it is 4 days for a holiday, 3 days for an ear infection, 5 days for gastro, 1 day for their birthday, 2 days before a long weekend to get a head start on weekend away, the last day of each term, because 'it's not an important day,' 2 because gram is here from interstate, it adds up, that's 21 days there … Yes, bonding is important, but it needs to work hand-in-hand with education, not be at the expense of," wrote one teacher/Mob Mom. Well, that's *great*. Because it proves my point that other mothers also take their kids out of school—I'm not the only one. I may be, however, the only one to admit it. And, yes, she always gets her homework done while we're away.

And then there are times I really feel that I'm being reprimanded, as if I were a student who put a piece of chalk into the teacher's coffee mug, got caught, and was sent to the principal's office, instead of being a grown-up who can make her own decisions when it comes to her daughter. Like this one: "As a teacher, [I can say] *every* day is important. Please don't send your child if he or she is ill, but otherwise? Send them every day, rested, fed, and ready to learn …"And: "If the kid was my student, they'd be sent on vacation with nothing, and have to make it all up when they got back … because I don't *have* work planned out two weeks in advance to give them," wrote another, with this added zinger to try and make me feel guilty: "In my experience, the majority of the time, the student never completely catches up after a week off, their grade slips at least a little bit, and the parents want to whine to me. Just another reason the hardest part of teaching is the parents." This made me laugh. This, too, should be on a t-shirt: "The hardest part of teaching is the parents." And here I thought it was the kid who bullied other kids.

Others just thought I was a jerk because I took my daughter on vacation, which to Mob Moms doesn't mean that I was there bonding with my daughter, but that I could afford it, which was enough to send them over the edge. "This article just comes off a bit … crass. I mean, it's great that you're Donald Trump or whatever … Try and put yourselves in our public-school-going, Walmart-shopping shoes: Imagine someone *complained* to you about how DARN EXPENSIVE her designer clothes are, and how TERRIBLY LOUD her new Ferrari is, and how she misses cooking because her and her husband go out to eat EVERY NIGHT? Wouldn't you think she's a total ass for obviously trying to rub her lifestyle in your face? Exactly," chimed in one Mob Mom. Um, I'm not Donald Trump—I don't have a comb-over. And I like Walmart. And WHY ARE YOU YELLING AT ME? I didn't intend to rub anything in and I don't eat out every night. Did I mention anything about designer clothes? Or what kind of car I drive? (Projecting, ahem, projecting.) I just mentioned that I take my daughter out of school sometimes to take a vacation or go to a movie to spend quality time together. Why is this so offensive? It's not as if I'm taking *your* daughter out of school.

"Most kids will get far more even out of the Atlantis resort, with a parent who spends quality time with them, than they will from yet another week at yet another factory-style school," wrote one supporter, to which another responded, "Those arithmetic or spelling rules? Not so much. No wonder so many devalue education." To which my supporter responded, "If your kids attend a school that actually teaches arithmetic and spelling, do share. My kids' teachers scarcely grasp these subjects. This is one area where I'm strongly pro-Eckler." Read that? *Strongly* pro-Eckler. It's music to my ears! However, I'm not going to lie. I don't think my daughter learned anything at Atlantis, except that they have some terrifying waterslides, and that dolphins are cute. But I learned something, which is that Atlantis is a total rip-off. I mean, really, charging me $48 for one photo of my daughter with a dolphin? Now that's offensive!

I Hate Parent–Teacher Interviews

How about meeting the person who spends countless hours with your child ... That doesn't matter to you? Don't you want to get to know the person that will influence your child for ten months ... Many of us take our jobs seriously!!!

wish there were a book called *Parent–Teacher Interviews for Dummies*. There are many, many reasons I don't enjoy parent–teacher interviews. First, it's a day off for my daughter, because at her private school, whenever there are parent–teacher interviews, it's an entire day off school. Secondly, I'm kind of scared of teachers, so I'm always the last to sign up for a slot, which means that I always get stuck with an interview first thing in the morning. Thirdly, and possibly most importantly, parent–teacher interviews don't come with a dress code.

I wrote a piece on Mommyish.com about why I used to skip parent–teacher interviews. Back when my daughter was in junior kindergarten through to grade two, before she moved schools, parent–teacher interviews were a total waste of my time.

I remember when my parents went to parent–teacher interviews, in the old days, they ran around the house with so much nervous energy and excitement, it was as if they had just met and had awesome sex. (Please, mind, do not go there! *Do not go there!*) I don't get nervous or excited. I get anxious, sweaty, and start stuttering in front of teachers. I also hate walking into a classroom and having to sit on one of those tiny child-size chairs that make me feel like an overgrown elf. I worry that when I get up it will be stuck to my ass, and that's pretty much what I think about during the interview: Will the chair be stuck to my ass when I get up? Will anyone notice me walking out of the school with a chair stuck to my ass? How will I drive home with a chair stuck to my bottom?

I don't understand the language teachers use anymore, either, especially at her new school. They may as well be speaking Russian or Sanskrit when they say, "While in investigative research your daughter is ..." Or, "During design technology class ..." Or, "In health sciences, she's ..." I'm left thinking, not whether she's doing well in those classes, but, What the hell are investigative research, design technology, or health sciences? What happened to, um, geography, math, and science? Or teachers will say something like, "She's reading at grade level according to the standards of blah, blah, blah in this district according to the statistics of blah, blah, blah," and I have no idea what standards or statistics they are using. I just want to ask, "She can read, right?"

So, when she was younger, I would just skip most of them. I figured if there were a problem, then I would get a phone call. I never got a phone call, and my daughter got great marks. As they say, no news is good news!

I've learned that many Mob Moms don't like it when you mention you have a child in private school. They automatically assume you are a privileged, entitled asshole in the same way they do if you mention that you have a trainer or a designer bag. Just reading those words makes them dislike you. "You are lucky to be an upper-class woman with children in private school, where you are afforded the contact you need and want with your child's teachers. You are also lucky to have the time to connect with your child after school, when you are not working three jobs just to keep your family fed, clothed, and housed. Not to mention with heat, lights, and water running. Your blog is arrogant and ill-informed … Congratulations for being an entitled, ignorant parent, who has no concept of what 99 percent of the world goes through every day," wrote one poster on Mommyish.com.

I know how lucky we are, but what can I say? Except that obviously you have a computer *and* electricity, because you are writing a comment on a blog post, and obviously you do have some free time, since, again, you are reading and commenting on mommy blogs. So you too should consider yourself lucky, because a lot of people in the world don't have electricity, or the time to read and comment online. Plus, if you're working three jobs, what the hell are you doing reading and commenting on a mommy blog? Maybe you should squeeze in the time to take a shower: I find showering quite calming. Plus, I do work, believe it or not, very hard.

And, as I said at the outset, I worry about what to wear to parent–teacher interviews. I know this sounds super-silly and superficial, and it is, but I do think about it. I lay out my outfits for parent–teacher interviews the night before, as if I were a teenager laying out clothes for the prom. I care what I look like because, no matter what anyone says, people do judge a book by its cover. (By the way, do you like this one?) I realize that all I really need is for the teacher to see me dressed as my true self. But I can't go dressed as myself! Because I work out of my home, and rarely get out of my pajamas, this option is pretty much ruled out. They'd be, like, "Um, Ms. Eckler? You do know that it's daytime? Why are you wearing that ratty robe and UGG slippers?" So I pull out my best Boho-chic clothes. I figure it's a nice compromise. I can still be the kind of cool mother, who doesn't really care what she wears, even though I do, while still being comfortable, while also not showing up in my pajamas.

Since my daughter started at her new school, the parent–teacher interviews aren't really parent–teacher interviews anymore. They are parent–student–teacher interviews. My daughter and I are supposed to attend together, so I can't get out of going. But I also can't say to the teacher anymore, "Just tell me what she sucks at and we will work on it," because my daughter is in the room telling us her goals for the year, while I'm wondering if the teacher likes my earrings and, still, if my ass is going to be stuck in the chair.

These days, I barely see my friends. They just text or email me. I email my daughter's teachers when there's a problem, and, yes, because it is a private school, the teachers will let me know if my child is having trouble with something. I also see my daughter's tests. I see her report cards. I really have nothing to say to teachers except, "All good? Just say yes, and I'll be on my merry way. Or say no, and tell me why, and we will work on it." But, unfortunately, my daughter is above average in all of her subjects, which means, why the hell should I get out of bed? Yeah, sure, it's nice to hear a teacher compliment your child, but sleeping in is nice, too.

But parent–teacher interviews are as important as having toilet paper for Mob Moms. "I hate to be the bearer of bad news, but parent–teacher interviews are really, really important. Even if all you do is show up and talk about shoes or the weather, your daughter will know that you and her teacher are working together and that you both care about how she is doing." But if this is the case, and I'm only going to talk to the teacher about shoes and the weather, I might as well be talking to a friend or, for that matter, the barista at Starbucks.

"Now, I know you are going to say that your daughter knows you care, but our kids need to know that we support and respect their teacher and vice versa. Kids are not born with intrinsic motivation. It is learned and developed. The first things that motivate kids are that we are proud of them and take an interest in their education. And showing up to an interview is the easiest, most effective way of doing that. You (and others) may think this is hooey, but I can tell you from experience that during parent–teacher interview time, traditionally, the parent I don't feel I need to see is the one who makes an appointment, and the parent who I really feel I do need to see does not show up, even after a request is made. So take fifteen minutes and go," wrote in one teacher to Mommyish.com. Well, obviously I take an interest in her education. Who do you think chose her school, drives her there, and picks her up every day? Who do you think reminds her to pack her knapsack? Who do you think asks her to show me her test results, and asks what homework she needs to get done? Me, that's who.

So, now I do go, even though I tell my daughter a million times a day how proud of her I am. I really just go to show the teacher that I take an interest in my daughter's education, and also maybe to show off a new dress, and to try to get over my fear of teachers. But I still think parent–teacher interviews can be pointless.

At my stepdaughter's public school, her parent–teacher interviews allowed five minutes for each subject. What the hell can be said or gleaned from five fucking minutes? In fact, it took longer to get to each classroom than the actual interview lasted. I went to her parent–teacher interviews with her father. By the time the introductions were made, and we had settled down in our chairs, there was just enough time to ask,

"All good?" The teacher gave us her marks, and then we were running to the next classroom. It was a complete waste of a perfectly good Thursday night, especially since she already knew her marks, because the teacher had revealed them to the class earlier that day. At least in my daughter's school we get twenty-minute slots!

"Sigh. I'm a parent. And a teacher. Seems like you've had pretty useless conferences, and they shouldn't be. The teacher should be giving you a lot of inside info about your kid. If they're not, feel free to take the reins and ask about learning styles, strengths and weaknesses, friendships, what your kid does during down time. Believe me, a good teacher will have a lot of valuable information about your child, things you're probably not aware of," another wrote. Do I really want to know information I'm not aware of? Sometimes ignorance is bliss, and unless my daughter starts croaking like a frog in class, or is crawling around like a dog, or is bullying someone, or refuses to listen to her teachers, or is swearing like a sailor, do I really want to know? Can't there be some mystery in life? And, to be crystal clear, even though teachers scare me, I have never met any of my daughter's teachers that I didn't love. I like teachers; I just don't like parent–teacher interviews. Or parent–teacher–student interviews.

But I never said that teachers don't take their jobs seriously. Honestly, I don't know how teachers do it. There's no way I could teach a class. I bow down to teachers. But because I don't like this aspect of schooling, I got scolded as if I were still in school, and forgot my homework for the twentieth time. "This article really disappointed me. I don't know how I happened to come upon it, but I did. I am an elementary school teacher. I have lots to say in response to this article, but I would rather not waste my time," this teacher wrote. So it's okay for you to admit you don't want to waste your time contributing to something that has to do with education, and also something that I wrote, which is my job, and you're a teacher, but I'm a bad person for not wanting to waste my time, even though you won't put in the time to, as you say, share all you have to say, because it's a waste of time? This teacher continued, "How about meeting the person who spends countless hours with your child (I spend more hours in a day with my students than most parents do). That doesn't matter to you? Don't you want to get to know the person that will influence your child for ten months ... Many of us take our jobs seriously!!!" I don't doubt you take your job seriously (especially since you used three exclamation marks after your last sentence!!!). But I ask, aside from seeing how you dress, your hairstyle, or how you decorated the classroom, how can spending five minutes with you mean getting to know you? We're not speed-dating.

I don't feel the need to really get to know my children's teachers, and I'm sure most teachers don't feel the need to get to know me. I don't mean to be snarky, but what are we? Six-years-olds who need to be besties? Or thirty-five-year-olds hoping to find our soul mates? If you want me to get to know you, let me take you out for a cocktail or two, or three, and then you'll open up, and I'll open up, and that's when I'd get to know the real you, and you'd get to know the real me.

Another teacher wrote, "Ahhh bliss!!! After coming home from a dreaded four-hour parent–teacher interview night, I can honestly say I'm enjoying my rum ... Oh ... And reflecting on how I (and the school) can better support our students ... There is no doubt a strong link between home and school that will provide a stable platform for students' learning, but it has to work *both* ways to be effective!! *Yes!!* I hear all us teachers say. Yes! It is *part* of our job to rear the next generation and *yes!* It is the parent's job to do the same ... *Thank you* to those parents that are doing the 'right' thing. To those that don't ... take some responsibility for your children."

See, even some teachers admit they dread parent–teacher interviews. This poster, a teacher, was driven to drink, for crying out loud, after a night of meeting parents. But I sure do hope you aren't drinking too much rum as you ponder how to support students. Drunk teachers are, well, who the hell wants one of those teaching or supporting our kids?

"I think they are *very* important for my child. I want to know how he is doing in school, what his strengths and weaknesses are, and what we can improve on, as well as how he is interacting with other kids and his behavior in the classroom," wrote one poster. I get all this. But with all the different ways we have to communicate now, I know that if my child is misbehaving, a teacher will call or email me. It's one beauty of technology when it comes to parenting! My daughter always tells me how she is getting on in school, and with her friends, and how she likes her teachers. At most, when I go to one of these interviews, I just want to fire off a few questions such as, "Is she hitting anyone? No? Does she swear at you? No? Is she disrespectful in any way? No? Is she failing anything? No? Okay, see you in three months then!" and breeze out of the room.

At least one other mother was supportive. "I happen to agree with the above article ... as a single parent it is hard enough to devote hours to homework each night, and then the demands of everything else. Teachers need to just do their job and teach, not dictate to parents, and take up more of their time, when they could be spending quality time with their kids." As a once-single mother myself, I understand this logic completely. You have my kid for seven hours a day! Also, while it may appear as if I'm insulting teachers or the education system, it's actually the exact *opposite*. I *trust* that the school has hired good teachers. I *trust* they have a system in place, so they know if my child needs extra help. Nevertheless, even though I don't enjoy parent–teacher interviews, I continue to go to them. Not to show my daughter that I'm taking an interest in her schooling. (Isn't hearing Mommy say, "Did you do all your homework?" every single night for ten months showing interest?) I go because it gives me a chance to get out of my pajamas and take a shower. And, for the next parent–teacher interview, I'm most definitely going to talk about shoes and the weather. Because I probably won't have anything else to say except, perhaps, "Can you help me get my ass out of this chair?"

part two

Icky! Too Much
Information?

It's Just a
Massage Stick!

Are you single? Because if you have a husband,
he should leave you. You're pathetic. I wonder how
your husband feels about your having toys to pleasure
yourself when he's away. You disgusting whore!

This post, because it touched on such a private issue, brought out the full range of responses from the Mommy Mob. I was attacked for opening up the discussion in the first place. Some moms called me a whore and denounced the other moms who left supportive comments. There was a lot of, "Way to go!" followed by insults against posters who defended me. In other words, just another day in the life of a mommy blogger.

When I wrote a post for Mommyish.com about my daughter finding my vibrator, the reaction was over the top—both pro and con. How the hell does one explain an orgasm to a child, who probably doesn't know the word *organic*? On the one hand, I was raked over the coals for *owning* a vibrator, as if I owned explosives and planned to make a bomb in my backyard. On the other hand, I had a great laugh when I read stories from other moms whose children had also found their adult toys.

Sometimes, in the mommy blogosphere, mothers actually share hilarious stories. There are Mob Moms for sure, but there are also normal women. And by *normal women*, I mean mothers who like and have sex, and who also own sex toys that their children have found.

So what's a mother to do, or say, when her daughter finds her vibrator and is singing into it like a microphone, as I did? She lies, of course, because the other option is explaining a vibrator, and I took the lesser of two evils. "Yes, you can use that as a microphone," I told my daughter chirpily when I found her dancing around in my bedroom with the vibrator in her hand. "It's really a massage stick. But feel free to sing in it!" My face may have turned the color of someone who has just blown up three hundred balloons, but my daughter thanked me and skipped away with her newfound massage stick/vibrator, pretending to be Selena Gomez. Just Selena Gomez who sings into a vibrator.

I admit my first impulse had been to scream, "Put that down now! That's Mommy's and you can't touch it!" There *is* something intensely personal about a vibrator, which is what one queasy Mob Mom must have been thinking. "Throw it away," she told me on Mommyish.com. "I have several toys, but the thought of using one after my child plays with it grosses me out. Seriously, I could never use it again without thinking about my daughter playing with it." Well, it's a good thing I have the worst memory. I barely remember what I ate for breakfast twenty minutes ago, let alone that my daughter found and used my vibrator as a microphone months ago.

Maybe this commenter was thinking what a lot of moms—not just Mob Moms—might have been thinking. Well, before we go there, I want everyone to know that I am neurotic about cleaning my vibrators after using them. So there! As for not screaming, I learned early on, the less you make a big deal about your children's minor crises, such as when they fall and hit their head, the less likely they are to cry. So, with this theory in mind, I allowed my daughter to sing into my vibrator. "La-di-da." Later, when she put it down, I raced to pick it up and hide it. And that was that. She hasn't asked for the vibrator/microphone ever again.

Another mom, responding to the mom who wanted me to throw my vibrator away, urged me to keep it. "Why would you have to get rid of it? Why would you have to get rid of your vibrator because your child found it? Why deny yourself something that is *good* for you just because it can make for awkward conversation? Who cares if you bought the vibrator for yourself? Who cares if you're a freak in bed? Who cares if you go to sex shops? You're an adult for crying out loud!" I am an adult. You're so right!

It occurred to me when I wrote the blog that if my child found my vibrator, other mothers must have gone through the same experience, and could commiserate. Most aspects of parenting are universal. Can we not all admit that the stigma attached to being a mother, who also is sexually active, needs to die already? I'm a mother. You're a mother. I'm not dead. Neither are you.

"My son found my fifteen-inch bouncy dick under my bed," wrote one poster on Mommyish.com. "As well as my rocking-horse dick, too." Oh, I just have *so* many questions after reading this! Such as, "My God! How do you fit that in?" And, "What the heck is a rocking-horse dick?" (I will Google that later!)

Another poster admitted, "My son found our vibrating cock ring. I don't exactly have a vibrator, but a massager that can get the job done if I need it, but the cock ring was in one of my hub's drawers, and my son was being nosy. We pretty much just told him it was Dad's and he needs to stay out of Dad's stuff. I don't believe we actually gave an explanation of what it was. He's never brought it up again though." Vibrating cock rings? Yeah, you just can't explain these things to children. You just have to lie, lie, lie, or pretend that someone is calling you from downstairs, and hightail it out of the room ASAP.

"In the same week, not only did my daughter find my vibrator, and was using it as a microphone while watching a movie in my room, but later that week she found my adult movies," wrote another sympathetic commenter. Like me, this mother lied to her child, and said the vibrator was for "Mommy's back, and to make sure it didn't get lost I was going to give her something else to play with," she wrote. Sometimes I actually think I can be friends with some of these women. Who doesn't love talking about sex? I especially appreciated the commenter who wrote, "All I am willing to say is anal beads and my four-year-old's birthday party. Let's just say I'm still trying to crawl into a hole." Um, hello? Why do you feel the need to crawl into a hole? That was probably the best and most entertaining children's birthday party anyone has ever attended in the history of children's birthday parties. Please don't crawl into a hole! I want to know more! And I want you to invite me to your child's next birthday party! I'll clear my schedule for that!

Of course, this being the blogosphere, not everyone was sympathetic. In fact, anonymous Mob Moms seriously want to ruin my life, or for me to suffer a painful death. One Mob Mom suggested that my partner leave me. "Are you single?" this poster wrote. "Because if you have a husband, he should leave you. You're pathetic. I wonder how your husband feels about your having toys to pleasure yourself when he's away. You disgusting whore!" Who's with me when I say, "I think this commenter should definitely get her own vibrator, so maybe she won't be such an uptight, judgmental bitch!" In fact, if she weren't anonymous, I would probably send her one myself. This post is a perfect example of how mommy blogging has changed motherhood. This generation of mothers is sharing their parenting years out on the Internet, like me, but they have a breaking point, especially when it comes to sex. And with or without the Internet, I can't believe how conservative some moms remain. Then again, maybe these posters just had a bad day ... or really need to get laid.

There were more of the same from the Mommy Mob. "Substitutions for the real deal with the love of your life don't cut it. They're cheap, like a cheap date, or a sleazy movie and pizza." Um, hello? I love sleazy movies and pizza! Generally, my fiancé and I use our sex toys together. When he's away, he actually wants to know if I've pleasured myself, not to mention the Skype sex we have. I love Skype.

Another Mob Mom took me to task on what she took to be a matter of security. "In your nightstand? What happened to privacy? When I was a kid, I didn't go into my parents' bedroom unless one of them was in there or I had explicit permission," this poster wrote. Others said I should be locking up my vibrator as if it were a loaded gun without a safety lock lying in my son's crib. "Find a secondhand, lockable makeup case with a number lock, and shove it under your bed or way up high in a closet," one poster suggested. Really? Has it come to this? Do I really have to buy a number lock, like the kind I had in high school for my locker, which would mean I would have to *remember* the combination? My brain is just too full to remember another numerical code for anything else other than my bank card and my email password.

And talk about taking the fun and spontaneity out of sex, and ruining the moment! "Yes, honey, I'm trying to find the cock ring for us. I think I hid it somewhere between my purses and shoes, or it could be under the bed, or maybe I left it under the washroom sink. Once I find it, I just have to remember the combination to open the lock on the box I hid it in. Was it 12–56–32 or 32–12–56? I think I wrote it down on a piece of paper somewhere. Maybe with our tax files?" By the time I got all that figured out, my fiancé could have pleasured himself, or driven to a sex shop to buy a new toy, or gone to the garage, brought out the chainsaw, and cut the damn lock open.

This post also led to talk of slut-shaming and rape culture after a poster called me a disgusting whore for owning a vibrator. So another poster was upset on my behalf that someone called me a whore. (For the record, I do somewhat believe that all bloggers and posters are indeed whores, but *attention* whores, not *sex* whores.) She wrote, "Who the hell are you to determine who is and is not a *whore? This* is exactly what's wrong with slut-shaming. You have determined yourself to be arbiter of female sexuality, and anyone who goes outside the limits of what you consider acceptable behavior is labeled as bad. This is the *exact same thing* the Taliban does. You may not be as *extreme* in what you consider wrong behavior, but you still think that after a woman crosses an imaginary line, that only exists in your and your ilk's sick, twisted little minds, she deserves shame, derision, and ostracism. That makes *you* a disgusting person." I am only too happy to get backup from posters. At the same time, I can't help wondering how the word *vibrator*, or the admission that I own one, led to mention of the Taliban. Then another Mob Mom asked, amazingly, what was wrong with slut-shaming. "Isn't being a slut a bad thing? Is that where we are today, a place where calling someone out for shameful behavior is something shameful in itself?" Um, what? What is your definition of a slut? Sex is not shameful. If it were, you wouldn't have children. You wouldn't be reading mommy blogs, and you wouldn't be commenting on them. Another stood by me, writing, "I found this piece to be one of your most mature, relatable, and funniest. For the record, since my daughter became mobile, I keep all my fun stuff in a pretty hatbox on a shelf in the closet. It also works wonders for keeping in-laws at bay." I so get this. When my fiancé and I go away, his mother stays at our house, and cleans like she's a professional, the type who actually vacuums under the bed, and cleans the shower tiles with a toothbrush. I know, though, the one thing she hasn't touched is the big, pink penis toy, which is under our bed. There's no dust under the bed after she stays over, but that damn big pink penis stays in the exact location it was left in. Yeah, maybe I need a pretty hatbox, too.

I have yet to write the post about my daughter finding my vaporizer, which is much different than a vibrator. A vaporizer is what I sometimes use to smoke weed. I told her it was for potpourri. If the Mob Moms can't handle my owning a vibrator, then I have the feeling they wouldn't be too impressed with my owning a vaporizer for the purpose of smoking weed. PS, I don't inhale (ahem). But, come on! No matter how mature you are, sex toys are still funny. Penis-type things will always get a giggle out of me. And what beleaguered mother doesn't need a giggle once in a while? What sane mother wouldn't want to attend a child's birthday party where anal beads come out just to see the expression on the host's face? Talk about a memorable party! So, now I'm off to get a pretty hat-box for my toys and vaporizer. Not to keep them hidden from my daughter, but from my mother-in-law, which I find way more embarrassing than my daughter using them as pretend microphone and me having to lie about potpourri.

Tampon Talk

*This woman is seriously mentally ill,
and doing damage to her children … She needs
help … I'd be seriously concerned about
having my kids in her orbit.*

was so mean-girled by Mob Moms after this post appeared. When my daughter was a toddler, one of her favorite pastimes was to play with my O.B. Tampons. She liked to hold them, roll them around, and line them up. It kept her busy for hours. Because the price point for tampons isn't that bad, I thought it was a fun toy for her to play with. Also, more importantly, tampons are quiet, small toys: they don't make any noise, or take up your entire living room, which as a parent, I'm sure you can appreciate. One day, my parents dropped by and my daughter held out a tampon to show my dad what she was playing with. He took it and stared at it with such a perplexed and mortified expression, it was as if he had just gotten *his* first period. I loved it!

When I wrote a post about buying sports bras for kids on Mommyish.com, in passing, I mentioned that my daughter watches me change my tampons. I think, at the time, I was trying to show how open we are with each other. She's open enough with me to ask for a bra (even though she is as flat as the table I'm writing on). And she's also comfortable watching me change tampons. To be clear, she doesn't go out of her way to watch me, and I don't go out of my way to show her, but if we happen to be talking and I need to change a tampon, often she'll trail behind me to continue our conversation in the washroom. But that little sentence, and mention of my daughter watching me change tampons, turned the Mob Moms into, well, an angry mob of moms who thought it (or I) was downright repulsive.

In fact, I think I could have said, "Yeah, I let her smoke crack cocaine last night," and the Mob Moms would have been more sympathetic. I have no problem with tampon talk (obviously). I am a woman. I get a period. My daughter is female. One day she'll be getting her period. Blame that on Mother Fucking Nature, not me. Mob Moms are so reserved, sometimes I can't help but laugh. I don't think they mean to be witty with their modesty, but they sure can be.

"I feel awkward changing my tampon in front of the cat. I can't imagine doing it in front of another human," wrote one poster on Mommyish.com. The disgust dripped from her comment like syrup. My eyes just grew big in utter wonderment— that a woman would feel awkward changing a tampon in front of a cat—realizing how ridiculous this was. I'm pretty damn positive you will not traumatize your *cat* by changing a tampon in front of him/her. And why should you feel awkward about your cat seeing you change a tampon? Every cat I know goes to the washroom in a litter box. Cats should feel awkward and embarrassed, not us women.

"I would have been scarred for the rest of my life if I had seen my mother change her tampon. Jesus H. Christ. This is so full of WTF that I can't even …" wrote another Mob Mom. Can't even what? Say the word *tampon* out loud? When did the word *tampon* become so appalling? Of course, the Mom Mobs, yet again, felt the need, as always, to play therapist. "This woman is seriously mentally ill, and doing damage to her children ... she needs help, serious extensive help. I'd be seriously concerned about having my kids in her orbit," wrote another. I highly doubt that I have damaged my daughter. And seriously! It's my daughter. I don't change tampons in front of her play dates or the mailman, or invite my neighbors to watch. If anything, she will be open with me when she gets her period. And, unlike me, whose mother never explained what a tampon is, at least my daughter already knows how to use one, and that it is perfectly natural.

I can't remember anything that happened in my life before the age of five. But Mob Moms seem to remember everything from the day they were born, as if they all have photographic memories. "As someone who vividly remembers being in the doctor's room while my mom got a Pap smear—I was two at the time—and was very confused and uncomfortable about it for a long time, mostly because I had no idea WTF was going on, I have to say letting anyone, let alone your child, watch you change a tampon is so full of ick," commented one. Maybe it is icky ... to you. But getting your period is also part of life and so is getting Pap smears for women. Maybe if your mother had explained to you what a Pap smear is, as I explained to my daughter what a tampon is, you wouldn't have been so icked out. One day, our daughters, too, will need Pap smears.

Mob Mom therapists love to judge how my child is going to turn out based on the flimsiest evidence. "You may think they are fine, they may never show any outward signs of discomfort or confusion, but you never know," wrote one. If this were the case, then my daughter would also stop busting in on me while I'm in the washroom. Or she would say, "That's gross mom." Another added, "Holy hell, was that TMI. Way, way, waaaaaayyy TMI." But aren't the TMI posts the ones that are the most honest and hilarious?

It really was TMI for some. I fear that I may have shocked some readers into having a stroke—although somehow they could still use their fingers to type. As this one did: "I'm not sure why she needs to see a used tampon ... I can't finish this comment. Some things are private. Pretty soon she will be privy to all of Rebecca's Vagina Activities, save (I hope) the Big One." Nowhere did I write that I show my daughter used tampons. Come on! She isn't looking in the toilet!

One of the problems with mommy blogging is that a lot of people can't handle TMI. As the mommy blogger platform becomes bigger and bigger, some writers do indeed feel pressured to keep upping the ante, revealing more and more about their private lives. I don't see myself as one of these writers. I've always written truthfully, and sometimes TMI is the result. I just write what happens in my life as a parent. Perhaps mommy bloggers need to set up boundaries, but this is hard to do when some Mob Moms are prudes, while others openly admit they are polygamists, or grew up in a "naked house." You simply can't please everyone. Someone is going to cringe at some aspect of your parenting, whether it's letting your daughter watch you change tampons, bribing her with chocolate, or letting her cry herself to sleep.

Posters are constantly worried about the effect my posts will have on my daughter sometime in the future. "What about her classmates, reading about how she watches you change your tampon and get your hoo-ha waxed?" Well, at least she'll be an expert and the go-to girl at school when others need help learning to use a tampon or waxing their legs, just as I needed a go-to girlfriend when I wanted to learn how to use a tampon and get my eyebrows waxed. There always needs to be that girl in school, because some girls don't have parents who are open with them, or even tell them about periods. Some parents don't even tell their daughters that they will get a period. How traumatizing would that be? My daughter will be the girl who shows them it's no biggie, and that every female goes through it!

And posters keep talking about me, wondering what goes on in my bathroom. One asked, "You don't do it *now*, do you?" I didn't even get a chance to respond, because another Mob Mom answered for me. "Well, the article says, 'She watches me change tampons,' so it does sound like it's an ongoing thing." Yeah, until I hit menopause, I will continue using tampons. Will my daughter continue to follow me into the washroom? I have no clue. I doubt it.

Surely, when you were a child, one of you readers must have barged into the washroom when your mother was using it? This one did: "I used to barge into my mom's bathroom all the time and saw plenty. And while I never saw her actually change a tampon, I saw something worse. Back in the early 2k, we had new eco-flush toilets that had a propensity to clog up on an almost daily basis. You haven't seen the worst of it until you see a backed-up toilet during someone's period. I turned out fine; no therapy needed!" I'm so glad you don't need therapy, but now with that image in my head, *I* may need therapy. I am so not ever going to buy an eco-flush toilet. So there *is* something more disgusting than having your own child in the washroom while you change a tampon. Thankfully, I've not yet written the post about how, when I was pregnant with my son, I did the pregnancy test in front of my daughter. (She wanted to be there.) I also, ahem, let her pee on a pregnancy test as well. (She wanted to see how it works.) Thank God, she wasn't pregnant. She was only eight at the time. Based on their comments, do you think Mom Mobs would understand how I allowed my daughter to do a pregnancy test for fun? I think we all know the answer to that. Even though it was a great moment. My pregnancy test came up positive. And my daughter was there to share that joyous moment with me.

My Horny-Whale Phase

*I think it's sad that you would not
be in the mood and tell your fiancé that
he can fuck you and do all the work.*

My sex life cracks my friends up. Not so much my anonymous readers or those with fake names. I wrote in a post on Mommyish.com that I had sex every day I was pregnant. I wrote how I mentioned this to a friend one day, and told her I didn't think I would be having sex with my fiancé that night because, as I explained, my vagina had gotten a little too much attention. I had had sex with my fiancé the previous night, had taken a spin class that a friend dragged me to that morning, and had a Brazilian bikini wax that afternoon. As I told my friend, and mentioned in my blog, "My vagina needs a time-out!"

My friends, as I wrote, were and still are amazed that we did it every single day during my pregnancy, up until, and including, the day our son was born! When I realized that I was six months pregnant, and that we had being having sex every day, I wanted to keep this thing going! It became sort of a competition—with myself. Also, it was enjoyable! Plus, it was easy, because I was so into it. I like to describe my time being pregnant as the Horny-Whale Phase of my life.

I also mentioned in my blog post that I had become slightly obsessed with asking friends, especially my married friends, how often they did it. The greatest reported frequency was twice a week, which I thought was pretty good after fifteen years of marriage. But I also heard from married friends, "Um, maybe once every three weeks." Even worse, I heard, "Only on vacations." (Well, goddamn. I mean, hopefully you go on vacations often, but even if you go on vacation three times a year, that's so not a lot of sex! Plus, wouldn't it be cheaper to have sex at home and put a mint on your pillow as if you were in a hotel and on vacation?)

I also admitted in the piece that I sometimes have sex with my fiancé *for the team*. Meaning, I'll do it even if I'm so tired that I'm not sure if I'm awake or asleep, or what my name is, because that's what motherhood and pregnancy do to one. Because I also know sex lasts only about fifteen minutes, I can certainly take one for the team. Sex makes my fiancé happy and feel close to me. I want him to be happy and feel close to me. (If you are reading this, fiancé, it's more like two hours, you rock star, not fifteen minutes like I said earlier.)

Some of my friends joke (or maybe not) that, as time goes on, I'll become less interested in having sex with my fiancé. "Talk to me in five years. You've only been together for three years," said one.

Well, it turns out that Mom Mobs were also horny moms when they were pregnant, which made me see them in another light, and made me fonder of them, knowing that I wasn't the only horny whale. "This made me laugh. My friends are the same. They can't believe it that I complain that being pregnant means our sex life has slowed down to only three or four times a week instead of every day. And I do sometimes consent when

I am not in the mood. I do it because I know my husband needs to feel close to me, and for him that means sex. And, yeah, it isn't that hard to lie back for ten minutes or so. Besides, my husband's idea of post-sex cuddling includes giving me a back rub, so I'm generally all for it," one commenter wrote on Mommyish.com. I'm all for your honesty, and I'll have to speak to my fiancé about back rubs, because usually I just get a towel thrown at me after (in a loving way!).

"Thanks for sharing your experience, Rebecca! I'm truly impressed by all the pregnancy sex, at the very least!" wrote another, as if she were cheering for me from behind her computer screen, or had placed a bet at a horse race!

But some didn't like that I had sex for the team. "I think it's sad that you would not be in the mood and tell your fiancé that he can fuck you and do all the work," wrote one. Well, yes. I do sometimes say to my fiancé, "I will have sex with you, but I'm just going to lie there, okay?" He seems fine with it. And, always, I end up getting into it.

"I can tell you right now that my husband would be turned off by that, because—gasp—he wants us both to have a wonderful time when we do it," a mom wrote back to the poster who also takes one for the team. To which someone else responded, "I think you are putting an unnecessarily negative spin on what I personally believe to be something a partner can do for another out of love (agreeing to sex when you aren't particularly in the mood). Sex, for me, doesn't always have to be about romance and the mood … My husband is neither turned off, nor does it mean he isn't interested in my pleasure, because he agrees to intimacy when he knows I wasn't particularly 'in the mood.' It can be quite a nice way to have sex, actually, as it usually starts with a bit of humor, and inevitably ends with both of us satisfied. So don't be sad for us, ok?" Exactly! We are happy, because we have a good relationship and can be honest with our partners, instead of lying, saying, "I have a migraine."

Mob Moms occasionally garner my sympathy. Really! Even though I sometimes feel as if I'm reading a schizophrenic's mind: Am I going to get nice comments, or not-nice ones? Is Mother Teresa coming out or Charles Manson? When they're nice, I want to magically jump through my computer, give them a hug, and offer them a cup of soothing green tea. I really wanted to embrace this poster: "I wouldn't have wanted to [have sex] every day, but I am a little jealous of pregnant women who say they have a great sex life, because my husband was turned off by the bump, and it made me feel so lonely and unattractive," she wrote on Mommyish.com. I don't want anyone, even a Mob Mom, to feel lonely and unattractive, especially when pregnant, especially as a result of her husband's attitude. Baby bumps are beautiful, so maybe her husband needs to have his eyes checked. I'd say this to his face if I knew who he was.

Others read the comments and formed their own opinion of others. "I see a lot of defensiveness and jealousy in these comments! Marriage and pregnancy don't have to mean near-celibacy. And, yes, it's okay to talk about it," added one commenter. Of course it is, isn't it? Sex is how babies are made, so obviously mothers have had sex! Well, not according to one Mob Mom. "Asking your friends about their sex lives isn't exactly classy. And making people who don't have the same sex drive that you do feel as if something is wrong with their relationship? Not exactly classy either ... We don't have to have sex every single day to prove that we love each other ... Sex is an expression of love, but it's not love, any more than kissing someone means that you'll pay for their dinner ... And most couples, not all, but most, go through dry spells. No shame in that."

If I can't even ask my own friends about their sex lives, whom can I ask? And my friends didn't mind answering at all. In fact, they continue to ask me how much sex I have to this day. I guess they are just as lacking in class as I am. And how do you know most couples go through dry spells unless you talk to your friends about sex? Are you, perhaps, basing your comment on the scientific survey of exactly one—you?

Of course, Mob Moms just dig and dig, as if it's their duty to tick you off. "Would you like a cookie or a gold star?" asked one about me having sex every day of my pregnancy. Even though the question was meant sarcastically, and probably rhetorically, I'm going to answer: "A cookie please and thank you. I'm starving after all that sex I just had."

But the comment I liked best was this one: "My favorite part of Rebecca's articles are the comments." See, we can agree on something. Even for me, the writer, often the best part is, indeed, reading the comments! There's nothing more entertaining. (Except, of course, sex while pregnant and trying to find a comfortable position, which is pretty entertaining when you're a horny whale.)

Vomiting-by-Proximity Disorder

I'm very much aware that I will be an "if you are sick go to Daddy" mother. I always expected backlash like, "you don't deserve to have children if you can't handle every aspect of their life." So it's nice to know there are others who are the same.

'm happy to announce that my daughter is ready for college parties! Thanks to the twenty-four-hour flu, she now knows all about having a garbage pail placed beside her bed, so she can just lean over in order to throw up. This is because I don't do vomit. I have a total aversion to the smell of vomit, the sound of someone vomiting, and even the word *vomit*. I'm the type of person who, when someone near me is retching, immediately feels the urge to retch, too.

This, unfortunately, even holds true when it comes to my daughter, the love of my life, for whom I really would do anything—except kneel next to her when she's throwing up. It's not an admirable affliction, to be a mother who has Vomiting-by-Proximity Disorder. You feel extremely bad for your child who is sick, and it makes it worse that you can't be there to hold her hair back, or at least rub her back while she's throwing up, as I wrote on Mommyish.com. Oh, the guilt! So I feel awful when she vomits, because I can't be in the same room, although sometimes I *am* in the same room. Unlike adults, who know when they are about to throw up, and make it to the washroom in time, children seem to puke out of nowhere. There's absolutely no warning. Or there is warning of a very limited kind, when, for example, they say, "I think I'm going to throw up," but before they even finish the sentence, they *are* throwing up, right on your pillow.

My daughter is well aware that I suffer from Vomiting-by-Proximity Disorder. The name makes it sound like I actually have a medical problem, when, in fact, I'm just a pathetic excuse for a mother who can't handle vomit. She now kind of gets the concept of throwing up, in the sense that she can sometimes tell if it's going to happen. She'll say, "I think I'm going to throw up," and then run to the washroom, covering her mouth. Sometimes she makes it to the toilet, sometimes not, but at least the vomit is in her hands, in the washroom. I am a good mother *after* the vomiting is finished. I rub her back. I clean her up. I change her clothes. I bring her ginger ale. I tell her it's going to be okay.

I was shocked, and pleasantly surprised, when the Mob Mommies didn't actually come down on me for this, not even the slightest little bit. I assumed I would get at least one, "Real Moms are in the washroom with their children when they are sick." Or "Real Moms can handle vomit." I did get one Mob Mom play doctor: she wrote, "It wasn't the flu. Stomach virus, twenty-four-hour bug, whatever, but that was not the flu." Okay. Whatever. She was puking, whatever the reason. Mostly, instead, what I got were wild, not-for-the-faint-of-heart stories from moms who also have a crisis when it comes to vomit.

"My daughter-in-law called and said her daughter puked all over the floor. She took her to the tub, washed her up, and noticed the dog went into the bedroom and began eating the puke. She said it was so bad she was almost puking the whole time she was giving her a bath, so she decided not to stop the dog," wrote a mom. Super-amusing? Yup! Do I feel like vomiting right now? Yup!

So many mothers out there just can't deal with it, which was a revelation. "Oh man, I can't do vomit either," one poster on Mommyish.com admitted. "I have always had stomach problems, and spent my childhood barfing first thing in the morning because not even medication could keep the stomach acid down." Another mother admitted she got mad when her kids puked, but would apologize to them over and over for getting mad. As she explained, she may have been meant to be a mother, but "I was not meant to be a cleaner of puke." What? You didn't sign the contract that said to be a mother you had to be a cleaner of puke? Me neither!

Moms may not like reading about designer bags but, my goodness! Do they like to share stories—about vomit of all things! "Once in my late teens I got too hot at work after eating Tabasco Cheez-its, went home, barfed without making it to the toilet, and the Tabasco Cheez-its puke smell was so terrible that there was a chain barf reaction down the hallway as my mom and aunt ducked in to see if I was okay, got a whiff, and turned tail!" Super-amusing? Yup! Do I now feel like vomiting again? Yup!

Posters who are not even mothers yet already know they aren't going to be Mother of the Year when they have to deal with their future offspring being sick: "I know that I will be the type of mommy who says, 'Go to your father with vomit.' I can handle everything else, from head lice, to asthma, diarrhea, cold, anything but vomit. If someone says they feel sick, I immediately feel like I'm going to throw up," wrote one. Do I feel like vomiting now? Yup!

Just as I'm almost dry-heaving while writing this essay, so were other moms when they read my post. "My husband is totally in charge of vomit-catching," wrote a fellow sufferer. "Not going to lie. Even my daughters know that momma cannot handle the vomit. In fact, I only scanned the first few lines of your post because I was feeling a bit woozy in antici-pation of you writing graphically about it." Ha! No worries! I mean, I would like you to read my entire blog, but you totally get a get-out-of-jail-free card for not reading this one. I don't want to make you sick or woozy.

Sometimes, as a mommy blogger, you learn some inter-esting facts from other moms, and that's when I find mommy blogging at its best. It's like losing and then finding your diamond earring in a swimming pool, it's such an enjoyable moment! After I posted this piece, I learned that there is an actual word for people who hate vomit. That word is *emeto-phobe*. Who knew? Thanks mommy blog reader! Not only did you teach me a new word, but also other posters really appreciated—seriously!—that someone in the mommy blogo-sphere knew the term for what they have to endure. "I have been wanting to know this word for years!" wrote a grateful mom. "My entire life, I've been more afraid of vomit than anything else in the world! Once a drunk 'friend' stumbled into my room during a party my roommates were having and threw up on my bed ... I couldn't stop crying and had to call into work the next day because I couldn't fall asleep ... Good to know I'm not alone. :)" Another mom chipped in with, "I, too, am a sympathy puker, and it sucks!" Yeah it does! In fact, I think I may need a barf bag right now.

Who knew that a post in which I actually admitted that I can't help my daughter very much (or at all) would get so much support? I was in complete shock that no one came down on me for this, because, when I help her with other things, like homework, or getting shampoo out of her hair, they can become like rabid dogs. The mommy blogosphere is just so confusing! "I babysat my godson once and he threw up," wrote another. "I was trying to take off his vomit-filled shirt with the tips of my fingers, holding my breath. He suddenly grew frustrated and took the shirt off himself and handed it to me. He was two, and he knew I just couldn't do it. I felt terrible, but I just can't do vomit."

I guess if you have a medical condition as I do—Vomiting-by-Proximity Disorder—then maybe moms are less judgmental and more compassionate. Perhaps I should start all my posts with a warning: "Just a reminder! I have Vomiting-by-Proximity Disorder. Be nice!" Maybe if they're aware of my admitted disability, they will acknowledge more often that there are some, or many, other instances in which we can't be Mother of the Year.

This poster on Mommish.com wrote exactly what I and many other mothers feel: "I'm very much aware that I will be an 'if you are sick go to Daddy' mother. I always expected backlash like, 'you don't deserve to have children if you can't handle every aspect of their life.' So it's nice to know there are others who are the same." It is nice, isn't it? Kind of like a Christmas miracle, a celebration at which, I hope, nobody drinks to the point of, you know, vomiting. (Please, oh please, someone hand me a barf bag?)

My Son's
Inverted Nipple

*If you had an inverted nipple, wouldn't
it make you self-conscious about taking off
your shirt in front of somebody?*

Mommy bloggers like me provide a narrative to go along with the long voyage of parenthood, a voyage that begins the second they post a picture of their newborn on Facebook two seconds after birth. So, of course, I wanted to write about my son's inverted nipple. How many times in a person's life, after all, do we get the chance, or have a reason, to Google *inverted nipple?* I had a first-rate reason, because my son was born with, and still has, an inverted nipple. I'm a firm believer that people's imperfections are what make them perfect, which is why I'm perfect, with my too-big nose, weird toes, and my propensity to be a cranky bitch before caffeine in the morning. See? My imperfections make me perfect!

I think my son's inverted nipple is kind of entertaining. When he was really young, I used to call out, "Come see a weird nipple!" and my daughter would race into the room to check out her brother's tiny torso. My daughter thinks he should go on one of those medical mystery shows, but what does she know? She's ten and doesn't realize that an inverted nipple is quite different from, let's say, Siamese twins, or the man with no limbs who gets around on a skateboard. But who knew there were so many others out there who know about inverted nipples? Only on a mommy blog could you find this out, thanks to posters who love to chime in about anything and everything. Even if they know nothing about inverted nipples, or have never heard of one, mother blog readers like to be parenting experts and join the conversation. Which, in this case, was fine by me. I wanted to know everything about inverted nipples! Not so much because I worried about my son, but because I was procrastinating by reading the comments following a version of this post on Mommyish.com. My fiancé, however, was initially worried that our nipper's nipple would blight his future, as if having an inverted nipple would ruin our boy's chances of getting into a good college, having a great career, or lead ultimately to his landing in jail after stealing cars. My son may end up in jail for stealing cars, but I'm pretty positive it won't be because of his inverted nipple.

I hadn't really paid attention to men's nipples before. And it still isn't a top priority for me. Other readers were similarly unworried. "He will almost certainly outgrow it. Or it will be essentially unnoticeable. Or it might be noticeable, like a small birthmark. Worst-case scenario, it is highly noticeable and bothers him, and it's fixed in a minor procedure when he's done growing," wrote one commenter.

Another wrote, "Two of my daughter's toes are webbed together. My ex was really freaked out about it, and, like, wanted to have it corrected as early as possible. But, it doesn't bother her. She's six, and goes to swimming lessons, and runs around barefoot. None of her friends cares. I don't think they even notice." That's because they probably don't!

Mommy bloggers are an interesting bunch. In this case, one poster on Mommyish.com went out of her way to do a bit of research. I like it when mommies in the blogosphere go that extra mile, even though I wonder where they find the time, or if they are procrastinating, as I was. In any case, you get an A for effort! "I just Googled *inverted nipples*, and, honestly, I agree with you. Most of the pictures I saw don't even look all that different from a normal nipple at first glance. It isn't until you really look at them that you notice there's something different. Your fiancé should really get a grip. It's not like the kid was born with an extra thumb or something noticeable," she wrote. The Mommy Mob, this time, didn't come down hard on me, but they were less generous with my fiancé, and because I love him, hurtful comments about him sting me. He's really the nicest person you'll ever not meet.

"Sure, he might get self-conscious about it when he's a bit older, in the locker room with the other boys, but only if he's raised with the idea that his nipple is weird and will cause people to pick on him. I highly suggest telling your fiancé to cut the nonsense in front of the kid, if he's still freaking out once the boy gets old enough to understand," wrote one. Well, poster, that day is a long way off. When you ask my son to point out his nose, he will stab himself in the eye. He also loves splashing his hands in the toilet. I have other issues to worry about before he understands what an inverted nipple is. Also, my main job as a mother is to keep the kid alive and happy. On that front, we're doing pretty well!

And then the day I posted about my son's nipple became even more exhilarating. People came out of the woodwork to share their stories about nipples. I had shivers all over, it was that thrilling.

"I have three nipples," wrote one poster. "The third is a tiny thing that is easily mistaken for a large mole, and hides under my left breast. I'm a DD. Once they found out what it was, past boyfriends found it intriguing, but they never noticed it until I mentioned it." Karma was most definitely on my side the day my inverted nipple post went live because another poster also had a third-nipple story. How could you not love nipple stories? "My husband has a third nipple. It's very noticeable when he has his shirt off. He has always had a sense of humor about it, and was in the habit of showing it off before we got together. He never had a problem with girls when he was younger, and it hasn't ever bothered or grossed me out," this woman wrote. I often wish my blog commenters weren't anonymous, especially the nice ones, especially the ones who either have, or know people who have three nipples, because I so want to see and meet them, and especially to examine their chests. That would make my day as exciting as the day I met Nicolas Cage (one of my favorite actors!) or the day my fiancé proposed. To my delight, stories of nipples kept coming! I was practically dancing, raising my hands to the roof, I was so excited. "My husband has three nipples," wrote another. "The extra one is inverted and tiny, so it actually just looks like a mole. It's not a big deal. I sometimes tease him about it, but all in good fun."

This was getting interesting, but because it is a mommy blog, and there are Mob Moms out there, of course there had to be some judgmental comments. "Well, place yourself in your son's position," wrote a Mob Mom. "If you had an inverted nipple, wouldn't it make you self-conscious about taking off your shirt in front of somebody?" Well, considering my son's still in diapers, and shits in the bath, I'm not sure he's all that self-conscious about a nipple. Perfect nipples were not high on the list of attributes I wished my son to have, anyway, and I certainly will raise him to know that an inverted nipple shouldn't matter to him, either. When he's old enough to know the difference between his ear and his belly button, I will most definitely stop any mention of his uniquely perfect nipple. Plus, I have a weird innie-outie belly button, and I'm still confident wearing a bikini. He'll have a good role model in me.

My fiancé doesn't even notice, or comment, on our son's inverted nipple anymore. But a commenter did chime in with, "My ex-girlfriend had one inverted nipple, too. It was actually kind of cute because when it was, erm, aroused, it went from an innie to an outie. Then she got her nipples pierced and it un-inverted all the time." This poster wanted me to tell my fiancé that if he doesn't like the inverted nipple our son has, then he can always just let him pierce it. I called my fiancé immediately at work to tell him this news, and he hung up on me, which I thought was pretty rude, considering I was just passing on a suggestion. It wasn't my idea.

But I have to say, I so wish I had a swimming pool so I could invite over all those men and women with third nipples on a really hot day, so they would be forced to take off their shirts. Talk about a fun afternoon! But maybe I will take my fifteen-month-old to get his nipple pierced. As most mothers know, even if they won't admit it, keeping your baby occupied for an entire day is like winning a gold medal at some Olympic sport, you're so proud you got through the day. Why not spend a day at a piercing-and-tattoo parlor? A change of scenery from the park, and endless walks and playgroups, would be nice. Who knows? Maybe Mommy will end up with a new tattoo?

part three

And the Mother of the Year Award Goes to…

Oh, the Horror of Letting Kids Watch Horror Movies!

*I'm sure if your daughter wasn't scaring
her kid with stories of demons, the other mom
wouldn't have taken the time to email you.
If your actions are affecting someone's child,
you should accept responsibility, instead
of complaining about it. Grow up!*

I feel like I'm being judged all the time, both as a mommy blogger and as a mom. If you're a mother, you probably feel this too, unless you are a totally judgmental Mob Mom, in which case you wouldn't think you were being judgmental or judged: you'd just think you were right, and everyone else was wrong. Posters who read mommy blogs often end up thinking, after reading a post, way too much about the author's home and family, instead of their own home and family, or so it seems.

I received a judgmental email from a mother at my daughter's school. The mother asked a question, which contained an implied but unspoken criticism. She asked, "Are you allowing your daughter to watch horror movies?" My initial reaction, as I wrote on Mommyish.com, was to ask a couple of questions of my own. "Does this mother really care?" And, "Why the hell is she asking me this?" But, because I quite like this mother, I answered her email, in one word: "Yes." I hoped the matter would end there. It didn't. It never—sigh—does.

She continued to email me. She wrote that my daughter was going around the schoolyard at recess talking about demons, and how they can take over your body and make your head spin. This mother's daughter overheard my daughter talking about this, and said her daughter was scared shitless. Yes, I told her, I "allowed" my then nine-year-old daughter to watch horror movies. She had, in fact, watched all four *Paranormal Activity* movies in one weekend. The mother wrote me again! "Doesn't she get nightmares?"

My reaction to her follow-up question was to ask myself more questions. "Is she asking because she cares?" And, also, "Why the hell would she think I'd continue to let my daughter watch horror movies if she was getting nightmares?" I mean, what kind of mother did this mother think I was? One who torments her daughter by forcing her to watch horror movies before bed?

When I picked up my daughter from school that day, I asked her if she had been talking about demons to her friends at recess. She said yes. Of course, I can't control what my daughter says during recess, and I definitely can't help it if another girl is scared of horror movies, but I did tell my daughter, "Girl, can you please keep the demons-taking-over-human-bodies and spinning heads to yourself when you are at school?" My daughter answered, "Sure." (I felt like a super-awesome mother for taking the initiative to stop my daughter from talking about demons, even though, inside, I was smiling at my brave offspring.) I also kept laughing at the email asking if I was allowing my daughter to watch horror movies. I mean, what next? Am I going to get an email asking if I'm allowing my daughter to stay up past nine? Or allowing my daughter to eat chips for a snack? But at least this mother came to me directly, I knew her real name, and we talk often. She wasn't hiding behind a blog handle, so I cut her some slack, and I still really like her.

Of course, the Mob Moms just had to jump in with their judgments and attitudes. "I work in advertising and have studied psychology," wrote one poster on Mommyish.com. "You are aware, I presume, that the media and the images used in advertising have a massive effect on adults. What makes you think that horror movies aren't affecting your daughter? Her personality is still being formed. Children are impressionable. You think nightmares are the only negative effect they could have? I don't think you are doing her any favors." Well, thank you for your insight. My daughter loves to be scared. And while you may have studied psychology, I took a law course in school. But I'm not a lawyer.

"Tell your kid to keep her mouth shut about it at school, because some kids, like mine, are a little more sensitive and easily freaked out," added another Mob Mom. Like many Mob Moms, they assume they know my daughter better than I do, as if they had been raising her for the last ten years. "I would worry about this. She is obviously having trouble differentiating between the fiction of the film and reality. If she knows it's pretend, then fine, but she clearly doesn't," wrote another commenter. Say what? Of course she knows a film is a film, and that no one is going to tie her down and do an exorcism on her (even though she would probably love that). It's the kids who are afraid of horror movies that don't know the difference, isn't it? And then I got a talking-to from a mother who thought I should have taken preventive action. "You probably should have had that conversation with her before she started going to school and talking about it to the other kids. I had a good three-month stint last year when my then six-year-old was absolutely terrified because some kid at school was going on about [the film] *Bloody Mary* in the bathroom, and "The Walking Dead" [television program] all the time." But then this poster added, "I don't give a hoot what other people let their kids watch at home, but when my sex life suffers because I have a terrified six-year-old in my bed all the time, it annoys me." So, really, and I don't mind, you are admitting that you're upset because your sex life was interrupted for a couple of months, and not because of your kid's nighttime terrors. Yeah, I guess I'd be grumpy, too. But, hey! There are other places to have sex, like on a couch, the kitchen table, or in the car, if your child is in your bed.

And, of course, there were many Mob Moms telling me I should grow up: "I'm sure if your daughter wasn't scaring her kid with stories of demons, the other mom wouldn't have taken the time to email you. If your actions are affecting someone's child, you should accept responsibility, instead of complaining about it. Grow up!" wrote one commenter. I wasn't complaining. I was stating the facts as they happened. And I did accept responsibility by telling my daughter to stop talking about horror movies. But what about the other mother, or the Mob Moms with "sensitive" children? Could they not have told their kids to tell my daughter to shut up if she was scaring them, or to tell the teacher to tell my daughter to shut up? I'm totally fine with that. Really! Tell my daughter, please, if she's scaring your child, to shut the hell up. Better yet, don't hang around her.

Mob Moms make me laugh, though. Take this comment: "I really don't think this mother was out of line asking you this question. I would be curious, too. My daughter used to be friends with a little girl, until I found out her mother lets her watch the movie *Dirty Dancing*. I don't let her over to her house anymore." Well, let me just say, you positively would never let your daughter come to my house. My daughter has watched both *Sex and the City* movies, along with the *Hangover* movies, about a dozen times, and can recite lines from them on demand.

I don't remember much about *Dirty Dancing*, except how hot Patrick Swayze was, and the line, "Nobody puts Baby in a corner!" I mean, personally, I found that line so inspirational that now I'm thinking I should *make* my daughter watch *Dirty Dancing*. I wouldn't mind seeing it again. But I truly have a hard time trying to imagine what would be so intolerable about *Dirty Dancing*, especially if you've turned on the television in the last, oh, decade … or hour. Have you watched any music videos in the last ten years? No, I'm assuming Mob Moms won't even let their children turn on the television or watch YouTube videos, and that they definitely don't know who Miley Cyrus is. Can they not, at least, comprehend the fact that it's kind of out of my control to police what kids are exposed to at school?

Mob Moms need to resign themselves to the fact that some jerk-off kid will debunk the Santa myth or brag about the latest sexy music video they've copied their dance moves from. That's just part of being a child going to school. Other posters came (somewhat) to my defense. "Who's to say horror movies are not reality? I'm bringing my son up with my beliefs that ghosts, spirits, poltergeists, and demons do exist," wrote one. Whatever. No judgment here. Just a warning though: Tell your kids to keep it to themselves, especially on the playground. Boo!

The Nine-Year-Old
Dropout

*Congrats on teaching your kid that
throwing a temper tantrum gets her out
of hard stuff. That's really going to
serve her well in the future.*

All mothers want their children to succeed. In fact, these days it seems they want their children to succeed at *everything*. The Mob Moms came out like critters to a roach motel when I wrote a post for Mommyish.com about my daughter dropping out of the school's track team. You'd think by their reaction that she had been training for four years for the Olympics, and was letting down an entire country. Obviously, she was not.

My daughter decided to sign up for track-and-field at her school, which was crazy from the start. First, she can't run long distance or even that fast. Second and more importantly, the practices were in the early morning, and if there is one thing I'm absolutely positive I know about my daughter—aside from the fact that she's my daughter—it's that she detests getting up early, as do I. But because I'm an awesome mother, I agreed to drive her to these ridiculously early practices three times a week. She was excited for the first practice, and not only because I got her there alive, which was an achievement, considering that I think I may have been asleep at the wheel. By the second practice, I was grabbing her leg and tugging her out of bed, saying things like, "You signed up, I'm up to take you, and at least your track outfit is super cute! You need to think about the positives, like your track outfit!" By the third practice, I knew it was game over. She started crying hysterically. "No one will notice if I'm there or not," she said through her sobs. "I'm not good at it. I hate it!" It was heart-breaking to see her cry like that, especially over something like grade four track-and-field. Save those sobs for your first heartbreak, I thought.

So I went back to bed and so did she, skipping the practice. My daughter was worried that the teacher would be mad at her for, essentially, dropping out. Actually, that's exactly what she did. I was 100 percent behind her decision, and not only because I no longer had to get up so early. I told her I'd write her teacher a note telling him that the track team just isn't working with our schedule. Which was not a complete lie. It was interrupting our sleep schedule.

I also told my daughter to never fucking sign up for any school team that has practices before 7 A.M. Ever. I think one valuable life lesson is that sometimes you are just not good at things, and if you can admit it, then you are brave and honest, which are good qualities. I don't like quitters in general, but I don't see any virtue in tormenting your child just to prove that because she signed up for a team, she has to stick with it, especially if she is on the verge of a mental breakdown. My daughter accepted that she was bad at track-and-field. I was proud of her! What adult excels at everything? I think her dropping out actually taught her another valuable lesson. And that lesson was not to sign up for anything that has practices when it's still pitch-black out.

Of course, the Mommy Mob did not see things this way. "You let her do whatever the hell she wants! She went to two practices, wasn't good enough, and that was it? Seriously? Do you know how to be good? YOU GO TO PRACTICE," wrote one poster in the comment section. I JUST LOVE IT when Mommy Mob posters use CAPITAL LETTERS to get their point across. It just adds that extra SOMETHING, like a secret spice in a salad dressing, which the chef refuses to share. For the record, I highly doubt my daughter would agree with this Mob Mom's assumption that I let her do whatever the hell she wants. If I did, she would still be sleeping with me every night, staying up late, never brushing her teeth, and never cleaning her room.

"Guess what? She's probably going to hit a point in everything, school, work, relationships, hobbies, plays, where she won't be good enough, and it's *your* job to teach her how to push through those points, and push herself to the point where she is good enough," wrote another Mob Mom. See, I disagree. I don't expect my daughter to always be good enough. Especially if it makes her so unhappy. Why push and push and push to make your child—and she is just a child!—only good enough, anyway? If I were going to push and push and push my daughter into doing something (which I don't and will never do), she better fucking well be a superstar at it. Anyway, your child will probably hate you if you are constantly pushing her to do something she detests. That's a risk you better think about before pushing your child to be "good enough."

"Congrats on teaching your kid that throwing a temper tantrum gets her out of hard stuff. That's really going to serve her well in the future." Can we get a grip for a second here? We're talking grade four track-and-field. She does hard stuff all the time, like school, math, ballet, living with me, and trying not to get hair in her food when she eats, just to name a few. "Yes, exactly," agreed another Mob Mom. "One of these days her daughter will have to go do something boring or stressful, out of her own initiative, and have to force herself to do it." It made me somewhat upset that other mothers seemed to want to flog my daughter for dropping out. I mean, they have children, too. But some posters took my blog as a personal insult. "I coach middle school track and you know what? If an athlete signs up to run and then bails on the team, she is never asked to run again. I don't care if she's Flo-Jo reincarnate, you have to show up and do the work. I have eighty other girls that are willing to fill any spot, so if an athlete has better things to do than come to practice, I will find someone who is dedicated to me and the team," wrote one. Okay, you do that. I understand completely. I also like how you have so many who want to join your team. Good luck with all your relays. I will be cheering on your team while I sleep.

The fact is, my daughter made a mistake by signing up in the first place. Have you never made a mistake? So why can't our children? If you don't make mistakes, how can you learn from them? If this happened on a regular basis, which it does not, I'd feel differently. But I don't think that a nine-year-old dropping out of the track team, after two appearances, ruined the team, or is such a big deal. If she were older, perhaps I'd make her stick it out. One poster wrote that she was happy that her mother, unlike me, made her stick with a commitment. "I remember having huge fights with my mom about this exact thing. I wanted to drop out of folk dance because it was boring, and she insisted that I go until the very end. Ultimately, I think she made the best choice for me, because it helped me realize that a commitment is a commitment … I am grateful that Mom would not let me quit, because that willpower became crucial during university, when I had to get my own ass to class." I'm sorry, but I have to ask: Did you folk dance your way to classes? That would be fun!

Now my daughter is on the swim team, and loves it (not a practice missed!). That's because practices are at lunchtime and right after school, and she actually loves being part of the swim team. See? She did learn a lesson. It may not be a lesson that Mob Moms can appreciate, but it is certainly an important one, and that was never to sign up for any team that starts practice when it's still pitch-black outside. Oh, and also, we all make mistakes and it's okay to admit it. Oh, wait. Mob Moms are perfect. I forgot. They *never* make mistakes.

Stealing from
Piggy Banks

*My dad used to "borrow" money from me to
buy beer. One of about a thousand reasons I don't
talk to him is because he never paid back a dime of
it. It's not borrowing if you don't ask first, and only
pay it back when your kid notices it's missing.*

Yes, I have stolen. Yes, I have stolen from my own
daughter. Yes, I hang my head in shame because I have
stolen from my own flesh and blood. This is all true,
except for the part about my hanging my head in shame.
What can I say? Sometimes my daughter has more cash than
I do, which is ironic, because she doesn't have a job, and yet
she seems to always have at least $100 in her wallet. I run
out of money at the worst possible times, such as the nights
my daughter loses a tooth. At ten, my daughter is still losing
her baby teeth and may or may not still believe in the tooth
fairy, but if I were her, I would definitely at least pretend to,
because the tooth fairy in my house set a very good prec-
edent by giving her $20 for her first lost tooth. Hey, it was an
exciting time! I was a first-time parent. And how the hell was
I supposed to know that children's baby teeth take years to
fall out, and that there are so many of them? The Mob—I'm
talking about the real Mob—doesn't have a problem with

stealing, or murdering for that matter. Mom Mobs, on the other hand, certainly had a problem with my stealing from my own flesh and blood.

One night, I ordered pizza and realized I had absolutely no money to pay for it, or to tip the delivery person, and they only take cash. I believe in tipping. So I went into my daughter's wallet (which means I also went into her room ... and her drawer), and was shocked to see she had more than $100 there. Now, I called this *stealing* above, but what I really mean is *borrowing*, because I had every intention of putting that money back into her wallet the next day. I have also borrowed money when she loses a tooth at night, and I need the tooth fairy to give her something! When my daughter told me that she looked in her wallet and was missing $20, oh, about eight months later, I told her I had borrowed it, and would give it back to her later that day. Which I did. But the Mob Moms did not see this as borrowing.

"You're teaching her that people in powerful positions can just take what they want, anytime they want, and are entitled to do so without consequence," wrote one poster on Mommyish.com. Considering it took my daughter eight fucking months to notice the money was even gone, I highly doubt she learned that as a lesson. She just shrugged and said, "Okay." You'd be lucky to have my daughter as a debt collector!

Other former children aren't as forgiving as my daughter. "My dad used to 'borrow' money from me to buy beer. One of about a thousand reasons I don't talk to him is because he never paid back a dime of it. It's not borrowing if you don't ask first, and only pay it back when your kid notices it's missing." I so agree with this in theory, but, um, I just wanted to tip the pizza deliveryman, and to make my daughter happy that the tooth fairy didn't forget her. I'm sorry your dad spent your money on beer. I feel for you. That's awful. The good news is that hopefully you won't repeat the same mistakes with your children.

"Dick move," wrote another. I appreciated the succinctness of this comment. As I did this one: "This is messed up."

"That is really sleazy," wrote another. "Really borrowing, replacing before the person notices, a small amount without telling is ok to do for the tooth fairy gig, but do all her teeth fall out on nights when you have no money?" Actually, yes! Yes, they do! I'm not sure why, but her teeth do all fall out on days I have no cash. Unlike the tooth fairy, who must make a million ATM visits a night, sometimes I just don't have the time. As for the cash, I usually use my debit card to make purchases.

I also love moms who make obvious suggestions like this one: "When she first starts talking about a loose tooth, check your bank to see if you can pay out, or if you need to get some cash." The tooth fairy that comes to my house isn't broke. She's just disorganized and can't always get it together in time for when the actual tooth falls out, which can take weeks. I can tell you, my first thought when my daughter mentions a wiggly tooth is not, "Oh, my God! I need to get to a bank machine," even though maybe it should be. My thought is more like, "This tooth fairy gig is costing me big time! And how many baby teeth do children have? When is this going to end? I should call my friend, a dentist, to find out."

Then there was this gem of a comment: "There's a big difference between borrowing and stealing. Do I borrow from my daughter? Yes. Do I steal from my daughter? Absolutely not. Why would I want her to think theft is okay?" Yes, I understand the *difference* between stealing and borrowing. But can we agree, poster, that at the end of the day we *both* are taking money from our children? And perhaps borrowing/stealing money is no worse than, let's say, stealing your child's Halloween candy, and what parent hasn't done that? And that's really stealing, because once you eat that mini Kit Kat, you have no intention of giving it back, because that would be … impossible. And I know many parents do this, because the day after Halloween, if I call any of my friends with kids, they answer with their mouths full, saying, "Sorry, just eating some of my kid's Coffee Crisps. I love Halloween."

It turns out a lot of mothers borrow or steal—you choose the word—from their children. "This made me laugh!" wrote one mom with a sense of humor and a super-smart kid to boot. "I used to borrow from my son's piggy bank from time to time. One day, after he had been saving for a while, he asked if I would take him shopping. He was six. He was so proud because he had saved $42. I went to get the money from the piggy bank and found it empty. Clearly I had borrowed and forgotten to replace it, so I went into my own wallet, and got out $42, and handed it to him. He lit up, reached into his own pocket, and said, 'Wow! Thanks! This with the $42 I took out of my bank this morning makes $84!'" I'm relieved to know that there are other mothers out there who steal/borrow from their children. But I'm super-impressed that this six-year-old could add 42 + 42! Who knows? One day your son may be a leading CEO or philanthropist!

I'm not sure why some moms were surprised by my admission, when so many others admitted to doing the same thing. "I do this. It's usually the mowers. I always forget to get cash for the mowers. I do ask first, but generally I run up a tab before I pay him back. Then again, my mom matches all his bank deposits, so mostly he just wants me to take it to the bank. If that makes me a terrible parent, so be it," wrote one mother thief/borrower on Mommyish.com. Another admitted that, "I've been known to borrow because I need it for the pizza delivery guy, or something the school is having [that] the kids need it like *that day*, but I always ask, and I always pay it back. They keep really good track of their money, so they would notice. Being the sons of a CPA mother, they are very good with their finances." It's always the pizza guy, isn't it?

Of course, it wouldn't be a modern mother blog without someone using the word *douche*, or some variation of it. "Seems kinda douche-y to take it and not pay it back. Even if you were the one that gave her that money, it was probably as her allowance, or a gift, or money from some chore, so it really was *her* money, not yours," wrote another poster on Mommyish.com. As I said, I did indeed pay it back. And the money she has (or had, depending on if her tooth fell out, or if I wanted to order a pizza) was not an allowance, or money for doing chores. Why? I don't believe in giving money for chores. I'm not paying my children to clean up after themselves, or to clean the rooms that they messed up! But that's another topic. One supporter wrote, "This is exactly the kind of article that makes me feel bad about objecting to anything else Rebecca Eckler writes. She's not stealing from her kid! She's not failing to pay her back. She's honest with her daughter, who clearly doesn't have a problem, or she would either say something or keep her money somewhere else. She hits a spot where she doesn't have cash, borrows it from the person who does, and pays it back. It's not great that she waits until her daughter notices, instead of remembering at some point on her own, but it works for them." The truth is, I'm totally forgetful, so there's no malice in my not paying her back immediately. And, of course, it wouldn't be an attention-grabbing blog if posters didn't go off on an entirely different topic, which, in this case, was "Why the heck does my daughter have more money than I do?" It's a damn good question, though.

"Am I the only one who was wondering why a six-to-nine-year-old would need/have a hundred dollars in their wallet in the first place?" asked one Mommyish.com poster. "When I was a kid, if I had money, it was from relatives for a birthday, or from picking up dog poop in the yard for a quarter per bag … not fun! My college allowance from my mom was $100 per month because I needed it for food … not sure what I would have needed that for in elementary school." Which is exactly why it is okay, sometimes, to borrow money from elementary school kids! What the hell do they need it for? In fact, I'm wondering that too! Where the heck did my daughter get all this money? "I don't know about 'need,' but my kids have been known to rack up pretty good savings. It comes from all kinds of things: birthday presents, the tooth fairy, earned money through doing chores … They are good at saving, too. My youngest saved up over two hundred bucks for a game system he wanted." Another added: "Was a bit stunned myself. My grandparents gave birthday gifts, and I had only one aunt, so it would have taken me four-to-five years to save the amount. Plus, my parents wouldn't have allowed me to have it in my possession if I just left it lying around, and didn't notice when it was gone. Of course, they wouldn't steal it, either." Well, times have changed. Ask any kid to pick up dog poop for a quarter, or even five dollars, and they'd look at you and say, "Eh, not worth my time." No longer is the rate for babysitting $3 an hour. It's more like $20 an hour. Kids are way savvier about making money these days. As for my daughter not noticing, it's not a surprise, especially if you know my daughter. This is a girl, after all, who once walked into a dog bowl full of water outside Starbucks because she didn't notice it. Still, with her soaking wet foot, we headed into Starbucks, where I paid for her hot chocolate. With my own money … from my own wallet. And I'll try my hardest from now on not to borrow/steal from my daughter's piggy bank, even if I pay it back. Now that I have another baby, the tooth fairy will visit again soon enough. I won't need my daughter's cash. I have a backup kid. Thank God for kids and their piggy banks!

Cranky Little...

Way to call your child a "cranky little fuck."
Yet another fine example of how you're such
an ignorant parasite on this planet.

once wrote that my daughter was being a "cranky little fuck." In a post on Mommyish.com about why I wasn't hosting a birthday party for my one-year-old son, I just happened to mention that we had held a big blowout party for my daughter's first birthday, and she pretty much cried the whole time. She had, indeed, been acting like a cranky little fuck. I want to be crystal clear: I didn't call her a "cranky little fuck." I said she was *being* or *acting* like a cranky little fuck. There is a difference, a huge difference. Just the same, my description didn't sit well with the commenters.

Angelina Jolie made headlines around the world for calling one of her children, when one of her posse was a baby, a "blob." Well, babies are kind of blobby in those first few weeks. They really don't do anything other than sleep, cry, and go to the washroom in their diapers. They are like blobs. Cute blobs, but blobs nonetheless. So, yes, I think it's perfectly acceptable to call a baby a blob. Plus, I just love that word *blob*, so there's that.

"Way to call your child a 'cranky little fuck.' Yet another fine example of how you're such an ignorant parasite on this planet," wrote one poster, predictably, I guess. I also used to call my son a "meatloaf" when he was a newborn, which was being generous, because at least a meatloaf you can eat. But some, or at least a handful of posters backed me up. "Well, I chuckled," wrote one in my defense on Mommyish.com. "My son is quite often a cranky little fuck, too. I love him to the point where I would tear the head off anything that tried to hurt him, but he is, quite often, a cranky little fuck." Oh, how wonderful to read such honest comments! What baby, toddler, child, or even adult, for that matter, hasn't acted like a cranky little fuck at some point?

Another responded to the first commenter, the one who called me an "ignorant parasite on this planet." "That seemed a bit uncalled-for," she wrote. Thank you! A lot of what is posted on mommy blogs is a bit uncalled-for, and that's an understatement.

"It left a bad taste in my mouth as well. But, you know, everyone that kisses her ass, thinks it's okay to talk about their children in such a horrible way. I'm wondering if they talk to them that way," wrote one commenter, who apparently needs a mint for the bad taste left in her mouth. Well, wonder no more: *Of course* I don't speak to my children that way! I do kiss them with my mouth! And who is kissing my ass? I would love to have people kissing my ass! Where are these people? Please, send them my way!

"So sad that u describe your daughter the way you do ... with the f-word," added another. No, it's not sad. I find it pretty f-word hilarious, but I won't profess to understand the thought processes of Mob Moms. Obviously they just don't have children who act like cranky little fucks. Ever. They have angelic children who always say please, never have tantrums, and always stay in their beds at night. Others were concerned that I refused to throw my son a first birthday party, as I mentioned in my blog on Mommyish.com, because of what had happened with my daughter and her first birthday party. My blog was titled, "I'm not doing squat for my one-year-old's birthday party." A lot of mothers completely understood this. As one wrote, "That's how I feel also. My daughter can have a party when she's old enough to ask for one."

"Glad to know that I am not the only one who thinks throwing big bashes for a one-year-old is stupid! To be honest, hubby and I used our daughter's first birthday as an excuse to bbq. We ate some good food and cake and our daughter went to bed. Now that she is older and will be six, bigger parties can be more appropriate, and the best part? She'll actually remember it!" Exactly. I learned my lesson. If I asked my daughter what she remembers from her first birthday party, in which I went all-out with magicians, caricatures, catered finger food, and even a bartender (for the adults, not the kids), she'll give me a blank stare and say, "I ate cake? Did I eat cake?"

I want Mob Moms to admit, if only to themselves, that a one-year-old's birthday party is just an excuse to dress them up in a sweet outfit, and take a picture of them with their hands in cake. The said one-year-old is completely unaware that it's his or her birthday, can we admit that? For me, it's also, "Hey! I kept you alive for a year! I'll have a cupcake with you to celebrate." Other mothers, thankfully, did even less than I did, which is pretty impressive. "On my daughter's first birthday, we sat her down in the dining room in front of her cake, surrounded by all her presents and cards, took her picture with her hand in the cake, and took some pictures of us with her. Then we all got cleaned up, I dropped her at daycare, and my husband and I went to work. We were out of the house by 9 A.M.," wrote one on Mommyish.com. Unfortunately, a

Mob Mom had to attack this woman by writing, "That is kinda just wrong. You rushed through *your* child's birthday to ditch her at daycare? Really? Next time, get a dog, not a kid." Right. Because if both parents need to work, obviously they shouldn't have kids. Or if your kid is in daycare, then obviously you shouldn't be parents. Or if you don't throw a huge party, you shouldn't be a parent. According to Mob Moms, that is.

I think this woman was genius. She finished her one-year-old's first birthday celebration by 9 A.M. I'm lucky if I can brush my teeth by that time. That's got to be some sort of record for a birthday celebration! But I was attacked for not having a big blow-out birthday party for my son, as I did for my daughter. "I think u should do something. How is that fair u celebrated ur other kid's one-year-old birthday, but ur son doesn't deserve to have his birth celebrated? U sound like maybe u resent him or something. Why is he or his birthday less important than ur daughter's?" Right. Obviously, I resent my son, because I didn't want a catered party with twenty other one-year-olds and their parents. As for my son, he doesn't care about presents: he just likes the wrapping paper. He'd be thrilled with an empty tissue box. He got a ton of presents, and he really enjoyed the boxes they came in. And he's not less important. I'm just less dense about birthdays for children who cannot yet hold a fork. One poster backed me up by writing, "Do you really think he will care? I am the second youngest in a family of five kids. By the time I arrived, one-year-old birthday parties were no longer a thing in our family. While turning one may be important, a birthday party is not ... In no way do I feel less loved or appreciated by my family because of that." Perhaps this person still felt loved because *no one remembers their first birthday!*

At least I learned that big, expensive, blow-out parties for one-year-olds are unnecessary. Some moms and dads continue to have trouble accepting this. "Couldn't agree more!" wrote one dad, and then continued: "Well, actually, I could agree more, as my wife and I sit here in bed trying to pick out invitations for our one-year-old's birthday. We really should know better, considering our six-year-old asked today, 'Did I have a first birthday party?' Hmm, guess he forgot the forty-plus people that were there for his pirate-themed party, where he hit Grampa in the balls with a plastic sword." I think it's sweet, though, that this couple actually put so much thought into their second child's first birthday, including picking out proper invitations, as if it were a wedding. And so your six-year-old hit Grandpa with a sword in his private parts at his pirate-themed birthday party? It sounded like your son—though maybe not Grandpa—had a great time, even if he didn't remember it. (Grandpa will!) And, at least your sword-wielding son wasn't acting like a cranky little fuck. Mob Moms do not like hearing that. It's probably just better to think it. Ironically, many moms commenting on mom blogs act like cranky little fucks, too, not that I'll ever say that, or that they realize it. I'll just think it.

Ten Stages of Hangover Parenting

It's not hangover parenting
when the nanny takes over, sorry.

1. **The Wake-Up:** Head pounding, room spinning,
   I wake up, groggily begin putting pieces together after
   the debauchery of last night's celebration in honor of
   my birthday. Naked in bed. My fiancé is beside me.
   Flashback of him picking me up from hallway floor last
   night, carrying me upstairs, undressing me like a baby.
   Oh, my God! I have a baby! Leap out of bed. Dear God,
   what kind of mother am I? The guilt sets in.
2. **The Other Flashbacks:** Baby still sleeping. Check
   clock. Nanny starts in five minutes. Still dizzy. Bed
   is where I want/need to be. Get back into bed, head
   pounding. Thank the karmic gods profusely that my
   baby has slept until almost 7 A.M. Did I really kiss a
   girl or two last night? Another flashback! I did! But
   kissing other women is not cheating. Shit! Speaking

A version of this article was first posted on Mommyish.com.

of other females, I also have a daughter. Where is my little girl?

3. **Remember Nobody Has to Go to School:** Jump up out of bed again to wake up my daughter, but then remember she has no school today, which is why I smartly picked last night to celebrate and get wasted. I thank the karmic gods again that my daughter loves to sleep in. I can buy myself a few more hours of rest. I was so smart to have planned to get drunk on a night before a morning when I didn't have to get my daughter off to school. Maybe *not* so smart to do all those tequila shots and kiss my girlfriends. Eh. I'm a good kisser. And sharp enough to plan on being hungover. Smart planning is what motherhood is all about, especially when it comes to getting wasted once in a while.

4. **The Discovery of Bruises:** Wake up again. Phone is beeping with texts from friends. "Are you okay?" And, "That was so much fun!" And, "Are you alive?" And, "How are you feeling this morning?" How am I *feeling*? I'm old, a mother, and hungover. I'm *feeling* fucking tired, as always, but now I also feel like a piano fell on my head. This is why I do not drink. Hangovers and motherhood do not mix. And, ouch, my leg! I ask my fiancé where I got the big bruise on my thigh. "Maybe when I accidentally dropped you trying to carry you upstairs last night," is his answer. Wonderful. Now I feel hungover *and* fat.

5. **There's Only Children's Advil in the House:** Speaking of feeling fat, must call trainer and cancel workout. I try to text him, but even this task is too difficult in the state I'm in. I need Advil. Super-fucking-annoyed when I can only find Advil for six-to-eleven-year-olds. I try to do the math. My daughter sucks on

two and a half of these Advil melt-aways when she has a headache. So I need ... what? Twelve? I pop one in my mouth and spit it out immediately. I don't care that it's fruit-flavored. It still tastes like shit. But it's that or Baby Tylenol. Actually consider downing the remainder of the Baby Tylenol before remembering that I put adult Advils in my red purse, the one I used when I went to see my daughter's school concert.

6. **Fast Food Run "for the Child":** I fall asleep again and then wake up to find daughter watching television. "Do you want to go to McDonald's?" I ask her. The only thing I think will make me feel better is a large fries and fountain soda (the best for hangovers!). "You're the best mommy in the world," my Golden Arches-loving daughter says. No need to tell her I'm the one who needs McDonald's, or why. "Yes, I am the best mother in the world," I respond.

7. **Mirror, Mirror:** Decide to brush my teeth. Big mistake! I catch a glimpse of myself in the mirror and see the mascara clumped under my eyes and on ... my chin? I look revolting. My hair looks like I've just been in a tornado. The bags under my eyes are as dark as the sky turns when a storm is about to hit. I look old and haggard. Maybe I am dead. Big mistake to look in mirror. *Huge.* Sink into depression. This, too, is why I don't drink anymore. (Or so I tell myself over and over.)

8. **The Swearing-Off of Shots:** I tell my fiancé, who is also hungover and at home, that I can't talk. Literally. I can't form a sentence, except to say, "I'm too old to do shots. *I'm too old!*" Head back to bed.

9. **The "Do You Remember?" Game:** "Don't you remember saying to that guy to take his pants off?" my fiancé asks, laughing. "No," I manage to get out. "You

are so funny when you're drunk," my fiancé continues. "You don't remember feeling that woman's breasts to check out her boob job?" "No," I say. He keeps pressing, and I'm getting annoyed. I just want silence. "Come on! You don't remember anything at all?" he asks. So I spit back, "Do you remember how you said you'd put up the baby gates three weeks ago? Or the fact you promised to build a tree house for the kids two years ago?" Yeah, didn't think so. That shut him up.

10. **Put off Drinking until Next Birthday:** Eventually decide that I am indeed a hilarious drunk. Also decide that I'm terrible at drinking, especially after becoming a mother. Two days later, I still feel and look like crap. I'm still taking Advil regularly. The thought of any alcoholic beverage makes my stomach churn as much as the thought of flavored, chewable Tylenol for children. Wonder how I did this almost nightly in my twenties. Is it age, motherhood, or both? Decide I will be wondering *forever*, or at least another 364 days, because this mother is not drinking again … until, maybe, my next birthday.

Posters on Mommyish.com thought this post was as comical as I found my hurting head comical. Not very. I've also learned that many blog readers detest you if you have a nanny. You could be the nicest, sweetest, most generous person in the world, but if you dare admit that you have a nanny, it's game over, because obviously you are not parenting if you have help. Nannies, by the way, are wonderful. Everyone I know who has a nanny, pretty much, if they had to make a choice between keeping their husband and keeping their nanny, would keep their nanny without even thinking about it. Nannies are not just for privileged people.

When I learned how much my brother spent to send his child to daycare when my nephew was a baby, I was, like, "For a couple of bucks more, you can get a nanny! A nanny who will not only take great care of your child, but also remind you when you are nearly out of toilet paper, and always find your keys and wallet for you! Sometimes, she'll even make your dinner!" Alas, it doesn't matter. If, God forbid, you have a nanny, then blog posters assume you are a half-assed parent, as opposed to perhaps being a parent who has a career.

"You lost me at my nanny starts in five," wrote one on Mommyish.com. Another followed suit: "It's not hangover parenting when the nanny takes over, sorry. How about being woken up by a crying child, or one crawling into your bed demanding attention and breakfast? Instead you get to roll over and go back to sleep. Boo fucking hoo!" And, "It's not parenting if you have a nanny." And, "I do think it's an issue that the article is called 'Ten Stages of Hangover Parenting' when the nanny was there. Rebecca didn't really have to actively *parent* the baby. It would be a much different hangover experience for someone with children the same age as hers if they had no nanny."

Well, duh. Of course it would be a different experience. I'm so grateful that I didn't have that different experience, considering the next morning I could still barely walk in a straight line, and having a child demand I make her breakfast while I was hungover (or maybe still drunk) sounds absolutely horrid. In fact, if I knew I didn't have help, I probably would never have enjoyed myself … that much.

Even though the post was about hangovers, another mom on the anti-nanny bandwagon wrote: "Life is so hard when you have a nanny and a trainer! Give me a break, Rebecca. I thought this was actually going to be something that I could relate to. Nope. Also, saying kissing girls doesn't count as cheating further stigmatizes lesbians, as liking girls is just silly, and fun, and not real affection, and also only for the benefit of guys! Good Grief!" Yes, readers did not exactly appreciate that I have a nanny, nor were they pleased that I kissed my female friends. I'm not sure what they thought was more appalling. Well, all I have to say is you definitely don't want to go out and get drunk with me, because I always end up kissing girls when I'm plastered. It's just my thing. Silly? Yes! True affection? Who's to say? I was plastered. "When I read that part about kissing, I was insanely annoyed," wrote one poster, whom I guess doesn't appreciate Katy Perry's song, "I Kissed a Girl." "Sorry to say, girls: Having that sort of intimate moment with either a man or a woman is considered cheating, in the same way oral sex is considered cheating."

The only person I really care about thinking that I'm a cheater is my fiancé. And I always tell him when I kiss my girlfriends, if he's not at the table across from us watching. He doesn't seem to have a problem with it, so why should anyone else? In fact, I think you're never too old to get drunk and make out with your girlfriends, as long as your children aren't left at home alone playing with matches, a pile of newspapers, and firewood. Moms need to get their party on once in a while, too. And, really, the kissing part wasn't that intimate. It was just silly fun. We were in a bar full of people, everyone laughing and drinking, and the music blaring. We were not at some fancy restaurant where couples sit next to each other over a candlelit dinner, whispering sweet nothings into each other's ear.

And then there are the commenters who always like to add that they don't "normally" like my posts. They say this time and time again. "I don't normally like your posts but ..." Which means they still read them, even though they don't like them, and my byline is right there. That's like me hating ketchup-flavored chips and eating a bagful. Why would I do that? So, of course, I wonder why these readers who don't "normally" like them, read them. Are these moms being held hostage, and forced at gunpoint to read my posts? One wrote: "I don't normally like your posts all that much, but I got a great laugh out of this one. Right now, I sip my tea, and vaguely recall yelling at my game with Russian profanities after honey whiskey last night." Hey, I'd like to know some Russian profanities and also what game you were yelling at! Was it Candy Crush? Solitaire? Or were you drunk when you commented? Please share (if you're not lying in bed hungover).

Mob Moms always somehow make me laugh, even if they don't mean to be amusing. I loved the poster who chimed in with this observation: "So that's why you haven't posted any atrocious articles in the last couple of weeks." Well, at least you noticed. And sometimes Mob Moms are completely right and will get no argument from me, even if their comments are mean-spirited. I wouldn't say that being hungover was the reason I hadn't posted an "atrocious" mommy blog for a couple of weeks. But being hungover *was* the reason I didn't post any articles for a couple of weeks. You got me there! As your prize, the next drink is on me! And a big, juicy kiss!

Do You Have
to Pay?

You're pathetic! Of course you have to pay.
The bottle was defective? Come on! I know your
type. I can tell by the way you blog. You think you're
something special because you're a single mom.

started my own blog soon after my daughter was born. It was
called Ninepounddictator because that's what she was. She
weighed nine pounds, and when she bawled, I ran. When
she was hungry, I ran. When she made any sound at all, I ran.
She was a nine-pound dictator, for sure.

I wrote a post when she was a toddler about how she accidentally dropped and broke a bottle of apple juice in a store. I thought then, and still think now, that the bottle, which was plastic, was flawed, because no plastic bottle should break the way it did, especially this type of plastic bottle, where you need strong teeth to rip open the lid. (I know. I know. It's bad for your teeth, but Real Moms open things with their teeth, because everything is so damned baby-proofed these days.) Even though I was buying, oh, about a dozen other items that I had dumped on the checkout counter, the store clerk was pissed. He said I had to pay $1.39 for the broken bottle of apple juice. So, after that incident, I asked readers of my blog,

"Do you have to pay?" I thought I was just starting a conversation, which is mostly what a blog is supposed to accomplish.

But this was when I discovered that I wasn't immune to trolls, and that I was going to need a thick skin to carry on mommy blogging. Let's just say, after ten years of mommy blogging, my skin is as tough as an ultimate cage fighter's.

"It was $1.39. Why wouldn't you pay for it? I'm assuming that if it hadn't been dropped, you would've been able to drink it, right?" commented one. Most thought that I should at least show a willingness to pay, just as, years ago, women used to show a willingness to pay on a date, by pretending to reach for her wallet. Ha! "I think you should offer to pay for it. But this has happened to me, and I've never had to pay if I've offered. For instance, we were on vacation, and went to a Ben and Jerry's, and I bought my son a huge ice-cream cone, and he dropped it when I handed it to him. They immediately said to leave it on the ground and got him a new one, and then someone came and cleaned it. Oddly, another person in line tried to pick it up and eat a 'free ice cream that was perfectly fine,'" wrote in one. Which also proves that there are peculiar people in real life, and not just in the blogosphere. Who would want an ice-cream cone that has been dropped onto a dirty floor? Unless, of course, it was cookie dough, and then maybe, just maybe, I could see the appeal of licking ice cream off the ground.

"I would offer to pay, out of courtesy. Out of courtesy, I would expect the storeowner to not accept payment, especially if I were making other purchases. I mean this with kindness, but it actually *is* your daughter's fault that the bottle broke, not the fault of the apple juice manufacturer. Regardless of whether or not the bottle was defective, the fact is (accidentally or not) she dropped the bottle. One of the issues with our society today is that I feel we do not accept as much responsibility for our actions as we should. We tend to look for someone to blame. A small thing, breaking something, but something that can be extrapolated into a larger issue down the road," added another. What road is that exactly? Is it on a map? And, then, out of nowhere a compliment and a free offer!

"I *love your books!* Adore them! We bought your book *Knocked Up* and in one week, six people read it. I just finished the baby one *[Wiped!]* and adored it as well! Just to let you know, I am an absolute fanatic about scrapbooking, so if you ever need someone to scrapbook your daughter's life, feel free to ask me :)," wrote another, which put me in high spirits, not only because she loved my books, but also because she offered to scrapbook my daughter's life for me, which I could use, since I have yet to put the hundreds of pictures of my daughter in any kind of album. I need to find this woman.

But back to, "Should you pay?"

Other mothers expressed themselves fervently: "Absolutely *don't pay!* Apologize, then that's the end of it." And, "Of course, you shouldn't have to pay. Stores have insurance for just those types of things. It hasn't happened with my own children, but I've been with my cousin, and had her drop an entire gallon of milk, and it was brushed off as, 'eh, it happens.'" That's right. This is why we don't take our children into china shops. This is why china shops have signs that say, "You break. You buy." But this was, basically, a convenience store, not an expensive glassware store.

"As someone with a master's degree in marketing, I would be shocked if the store asked you to pay for a $1.39-item broken accidentally by a little girl. It probably only cost twenty-five cents, and you were going to purchase other items. Smart stores understand that how you handle the customer matters *much* more than one small item … I'm also shocked by the people who said you should pay. This was not vandalism, a large-ticket item, or on purpose. I hope you folks don't work in customer service," added another, reading my mind.

Well, this small post also brought on the angry Mobsters who wondered obsessively why I didn't use a cart, and questioned the etiquette of letting a child consume something before actually paying for it. It's almost as if these mothers have never taken their kids grocery shopping (which, in fact, is intelligent, because nothing good ever comes from taking a toddler grocery shopping). "Yes, you should pay. And why not use a cart?" asked too many to count. Okay, flog me! I didn't use a cart! Is that really a character flaw? I'm the type who will try to carry all eighteen bags of groceries at once from my car to the house, in order to make only one trip, because I'm lazy. That might be a character flaw. "The only reason I don't let my kids eat anything before it is purchased is I am paranoid that I will not have my bank card with me. I have forgotten it before, and do not want to be accused of stealing," wrote another.

These comments were mild compared to one that followed. I think it was one of my first anonymous hate messages, which could be considered a milestone in all my years of blogging about parenting. "You're pathetic!" wrote this mom. "Of course you have to pay. The bottle was defective? Come on! I know your type. I can tell by the way you blog. You think you're something special because you're a single mom. You're not. Nothing unique here. Lots of people are single parents. Lots of people parent. It's hard at times and great at times. It's just life. No special breaks just 'cause your hands were full. I'd give extra sympathy to those parents whose children are disabled and have a real challenge on their hands. Get over yourself." Obviously, I don't think I was special for being a single mom, and, really, do children of parents who are together never drop things in stores? I've never seen any statistics that show children of single parents are more klutzy than those with parents who are together.

It left me thinking, "Wait—why are you getting so upset? Why are you so angry because I asked a question, and wanted honest answers from readers?"

I didn't tell readers of my original post how I responded to the intolerant store clerk. But I will now. I did, in fact, pay for the apple juice. Did I end up buying the twelve other things on the counter? Nope. Accidents happen. Even if it was my daughter's fault, I believe that customer service counts for a lot. The store clerk was obviously a child-hater, and I'm not buying anything from a child-hater. Well, perhaps not a child-hater, but one who is willing to lose a loyal customer over a $1.39 bottle of apple juice. You will never find me at that store again. But you may just find me licking cookie-dough ice cream off the floor of a Ben and Jerry's. Don't judge!

part four

Thanks, But I Already Have a Shrink

My Son's
Miniature Junk

*I think she might be special needs, and they
are forced to let her write, just like Walmart is
forced to allow special needs people to work as
greeters. Scratch that. That was really rude of me.
It's insulting to the special needs people to put
Rebecca Eckler on their level.*

Sometimes, when I think of mommy blogging and the responses I get from my blog posts, I think of those Facebook addicts who post the latest and greatest updates about their kids' potty training (complete with pictures!). I also wonder why there are so many women and mothers who can be so hypercritical, as if there was a memo I missed saying that, because you have children, you have the right to condemn other mothers. I admit I'm not a serious blogger, in the sense that I do not tackle, say, public policy or foreign tax issues. But when I sit down to write my mommy blogs, I am as serious as a heart attack. I believe that motherhood, and all its ups and downs, matters to people. But some things are foreign to me and therefore worth sharing. Such as baby penises. When I was pregnant with my son, I wrote a piece for Mommyish.com about how I was terrified of having an infant penis in my home.

I once caught a glimpse of my nephew's penis shortly after he was born, and I was shocked and shaken to the very core.

I may have even blacked out for a few seconds. My nephew's four-week-old penis was the weirdest-looking thing I had ever witnessed, aside from a see-through frog that my daughter showed me in one of her Fun Facts books. His penis was all balls. Attached to my nephew was a teeny-weenie penis, about half the size of my pinky finger, if even. I may be being generous. Or that's what I thought after I glimpsed it, before I ran out of the room as fast as if I had just walked in on my parents having sex with another couple, while screaming, "What was that? Oh, my God! What was that?"

When my sister-in-law came out of the room after changing her son's diaper, she found me, still feeling faint, lying on her couch with a cool compress on my forehead, and she said, jokingly, that, luckily, her son had a big penis. I was, like, "Are you kidding me? I'm not sure what the hell that was, or if that is considered a big penis for a baby, but I'm highly disturbed. Can you call my shrink? He's on my speed dial." And then I passed out again.

Needless to say, I never went in to watch my nephew get a diaper change again. Seven years later, I was expecting my son, and, to tell you the truth, I was still traumatized by the sight of my nephew's junk. "They just look so weird," I said to one of my friends, who has three sons, when I was still pregnant. "I know, I know," she responded. "They are so weird looking!" I think I was afraid of taking care of a baby penis, not only because baby penises look like something a three-year-old would make out of Play-Doh, but also because I don't have a penis, so I am completely at a loss about how to take care of one. It's not like a plant you just have to water. Even adult penises are weird looking. Sorry! But they are. They serve a purpose—a good one for women and men sometimes—but I thank my lucky stars almost every day that I don't have to walk around with one attached to me. I'd rather walk around with a furry tail.

When I think of adult penises, I can't help wondering, "How do you stride around with that thing all day?" And, "Why do men rest their hands on their penises when they are relaxing?" I can tell you, as a woman, I don't rest my hand on my vagina when I watch television.

I've asked men (usually friends, not strangers) about their penises, questions such as, "What happens when you play soccer? Does it just flip around?" And, "Can you sleep on your stomach comfortably with that thing?" And, "Do you ever just want to sit down to pee?"

I've spoken to mothers who have only boys, and, when they find out they are going to have a girl, are worried about taking care of a baby vagina. I'm like, "But you have had a vagina your whole life!"

The Mom Mob came out in full force when I blogged about how much this worried me. Unlike my friends in the real world, who understood and agreed completely that baby penises are odd, they just had to tell me what a terribly dreadful mother I was. I wrote that it wasn't only the prospect of early morning hockey practices when he got older that had me scared of having a boy, it also was his miniature junk. From the comments I got, you would have thought that no other mother in the world ever had a possibly irrational fear about something to do with their unborn or newborn baby. I had a friend who was so worried that her newborn had a pimple on his cheek that she took him to the doctor. Did I judge? No.

I never thought so many mothers on Mommyish.com would call me out on this, even though, as a fun fact, if you Google, "Why are mothers so judgmental?" more than 5,800,000 answers pop up instantly.

"She's pushing forty, but has the maturity of a twelve-year-old. And that's being generous," wrote one Mob Mom on Mommyish.com. Another Mob Mom agreed, writing, "Her brain just halted development at twelve." And then others jumped on the bandwagon, denigrating my intelligence and supposed immaturity. All my life I was raised to think that no question is a dumb question, and I still believe this. "Grow up," wrote another mom. "One half of humanity has penises, the other, vaginas. Get over it." (Actually, I think there are more vaginas out there than penises. Just saying!)

"I think she might be special needs, and they are forced to let her write, just like Walmart is forced to allow special needs people to work as greeters. Scratch that. That was really rude of me. It's insulting to the special needs people to put Rebecca Eckler on their level," wrote another anonymous poster. Well, I am insulted as well, but mostly disgusted. In the first place, I have a special needs family member, so I am acutely offended when people make fun. Secondly, what do you Mob Moms have against the greeters at Walmart? The greeters are one of my favorite things about going to Walmart. In fact, they are one of the only things I enjoy about Walmart. It's like going to a sushi restaurant where the entire staff says goodbye to you. It makes you feel good.

"You shouldn't be a mother, period," wrote another. And, "Seriously? What the fuck is wrong with you? Get some therapy woman." Now, why would I waste $200 an hour on a shrink to talk about my fear of baby penises? (Well, if Freud were still alive, perhaps I'd give it a go. I'd love to hear what he had to say). I have friends in the real world to discuss my fear of baby penises with, and they don't charge me anything to hang with them.

But this commenter was not the only one who thought I needed a shrink, or more. "I think she's a danger to her baby. She needs psychiatric evaluation, because she does not sound normal." No, what is not normal (at least, in the way they look) are baby penises, and I was simply pointing that out. And why, exactly, would I be a danger to my baby? Just because I admitted I was petrified of my son's baby penis doesn't mean I planned to chop it off.

Mob Moms also don't like gender stereotypes. One commenter wrote, "Are we on "Candid Camera"? Was this really an article? Weird how it's seemingly socially acceptable for women to sit around giggling about baby penises, pointing them out in ultrasounds, laughing at how silly they look, their erections, etc. ... Imagine if it were dads going on about their daughters' privates like that." Why would a dad do that? Men are a totally different species from women. There's so much they don't understand, such as yeast infections and PMS. And you just proved my point. Many women giggle about baby penises. Plus, vaginas are nicely tucked away. Penises? Not so much. Vaginas aren't funny. Penises are funny, and, as far as I can tell, a nuisance to live with, which makes them more amusing. My fiancé is constantly tucking his penis in some new position or other. Mob Moms need to get a sense of humor. They also need to be more supportive of women like me, because, after all, we have in common the difficult job of being mothers. How can we *not* laugh (or at least giggle) at penises? Mob Moms don't agree with having a little laugh. Nor, apparently, do they care about mothers with phobias. Wrote one, "Baby penises are cute. And frankly I *love* the adult ones! I could play with my lover's penis for hours!" After reading that, I wondered if I was the one on "Candid Camera." I also thought, "I think it's great that you have a hobby!"

Many mothers refuse to admit or even acknowledge that baby penises are alien looking. Another poster chipped in with, "Wow, you are an idiot. I have more of a problem with how fascinated you are with baby penises. That's what's disturbing ... Grow up and stop thinking about baby penises. It seems you think about them way too much." But I didn't actually think about them way too much. I thought about baby penises the perfect amount of time for a pregnant woman with a first-time penis growing inside her. And I was not spellbound by them—I was terrified. How can mothers, even Mob Moms, not see that something is out of whack with baby boys' junk? Can they not see that there is a scale issue going on? That little penis and those colossal balls? Do Mob Moms need glasses?

As for the Mob Moms who think I'm going to traumatize my son by making fun of his junk, again, I think he's just a little too young to be "scarred for life," as one commenter suggested. I admit she has given me something to think about. What will this mean, years from now, for the kids who are the subject of all this blogging, even if mommy bloggers are sharing natural, but often seldom discussed, parenting issues? But I'm writing about my experience as a parent, not about his experience as a baby. How much you want to share is an individual choice. But most mommy bloggers, including myself, do think quite consciously about what they, or I, want to share online. Of course, what commenters post online is another matter entirely, because of their anonymity and fake names.

Because I mentioned penises, Mob Moms, as they always do, started calling me, for lack of a better word, a slut. That's not very considerate or helpful, obviously. I don't understand why women on the blogosphere need to be anonymous. If they really believe what they write, then why wouldn't they admit who they are? The answer, of course, is that if their identity were known after the horrific things they post, they would probably be fired from their jobs, or their friends would think they were crazy.

"I merely pointed out that Rebecca Eckler is not exactly new to penises, as she has written about her sexual dalliances quite openly. The fact that she slept with her current boyfriend on the first date, and felt the need to share this fact with the world, suggests that she's better acquainted with the penis than this article would have you believe," wrote one Mommyish.com commenter. Yes, I did sleep with the man who is now my fiancé, and the father of our son, on our first date. I am a grown woman, I was single and, in my defense, I only slept with him on the first date to get over someone else, which is a perfectly rational reason for sleeping with someone on a first date, especially if he's damn good-looking. I never claimed not to have seen an adult penis before. But adult penises do not look like baby penises.

Just the same, according to Mob Moms, because I have this fear of baby penises, I am dumb, need psychiatric evaluation, therapy, am a danger to my baby, and, to top it off, I'm also a whore for sleeping with someone on a first date, which really had nothing to do with my baby penis phobia. One commenter even suggested a drinking game. "New drinking game: Take a swig every time the word *penis* appears in this article!" Well, if that's what tickles you, go ahead. But, by line two, you'd probably be wasted, so it's not a very good idea, especially if it's your turn to carpool. Being drunk in front of your children is just so not cool. (As a side note, Mob Moms seem to love to invent drinking games inspired by my blogs. They write things such as, "Take a shot every time Eckler mentions ..." Alcoholics Anonymous can thank me later for making potential recruits out of so many blog-reading mothers.)

My all-time favorite Mob Mom comment in response to my baby penis post, because it was so absurd, was this one: "This is why the government needs to start testing people prior to approving them for reproduction. Otherwise, people like Rebecca Eckler will continue to reproduce, creating more Rebecca Ecklers. Dumb breeds dumb." This one left me speechless. Wait! I do have something to say. If you think the government needs to interview or test people before they have babies, then I think you are more insane than you think I am. And if dumb breeds dumb, doesn't that make your children dumb, or, for that matter, you dumb? (Which is quite obvious from your oh-so-normal comment. Not!)

Flash forward to my baby son's birth when, of course, I fell in love with him immediately. But I still think his penis is strange looking. Does that make me a bad mother? Mob Moms think so. But I also have an irrational fear of gas stations. When I pull in to fill my car's gas tank, I'm positive I'm going to blow myself up. So I guess I'm not fit to drive either.

But I'm sure Mob Moms who have sons think their baby boys' penises are works of art, like a Picasso. Guess what? Baby penises, as well as adult penises for that matter, are not works of art. I'm no longer scared of my son's miniature junk, but I still think there's a dimension issue going on. Why? *Because there is!* And don't even get me started on his new miniature erections. After being called stupid, promiscuous, and mentally ill, among other things, just for writing about penises, you'll understand why I'm afraid to write about his miniature erections. The Mob Moms would go batshit crazy, because, of course, miniature erections of the sons of Mob Moms are enthralling, a milestone that should be celebrated, and probably scrapbooked. In the real world, however, women do discuss and laugh at baby penises. Plus, it's not as if I show it off to everyone, saying, "Weird, right?" But in Mob Mom world, everything, including baby penises, is perfectly normal looking. And, maybe this is a female thing. My fiancé, when asked what he thought about our baby's penis, was like, "I don't think anything really." Or, "He has an erection." But he's a man. Erections are what he thinks about for 80 percent of his day. Which is another reason I'm happy not to have a penis attached to me.

Labeling My Food

*Labeling food was a way of life [when I was]
growing up with two brothers. Today, with a
twenty-three-year-old son, we continue to label
anything special, both in the fridge and on a shelf.
Otherwise, it's fair game, and you can be sure
it will be eaten before morning!*

finally found a great use for Post-It notes. I wrote a piece for
Mommyish.com about how I started to use them to label
my food, as if I were living with obnoxious roommates, or
stashing my lunch at the back of a shared office fridge. Yes,
that's right: "my food." I started using Post-It notes because
I was getting beyond annoyed. I always seemed to be last to
get any food in my house, as if I lived in some poverty-stricken
orphanage, where it was first come, first served, survival of
the fittest, and if you were small, you had to fend for yourself,
like poor Oliver in the play *Oliver.* I am fending for myself by
using Post-It notes. If only Oliver had some. It *seemed* that
way, because it happened to *be* that way. Listen! I'm an easy
eater and not picky at all. All I need is orange juice in the
morning, a Diet Coke in the day, and my trusted M&Ms for a
snack. When I really, really want any of the above, that means
I really, really want them, as desperate as if I were a vampire
out for blood. In addition to these items, well, yogurt drinks

and bananas would be nice, too, but that's about it. You see, I am really easy to please when it comes to groceries.

If you have a large family, you know what I'm talking about. Actually, even if you have a small family, I'm sure you get annoyed, too, if you wake up with a craving for a big glass of orange juice, you open the fridge, pick up the carton, and realize there is only one fucking sip left. First, what idiot (I say this with love) in my household puts a teaspoonful of orange juice back in the fridge? (Okay, sometimes I'm the idiot. But usually not.) When it's someone else who leaves a virtually empty carton in the fridge, it can really get your day off on the wrong foot. Especially if it's 6:45 in the morning and you need orange juice to wake you up.

I'm sure as hell not laughing when there's one sip of orange juice left. I'm pissed. I'm not laughing when I get home to find all the Diet Cokes are gone, when I bought a case two days ago. I'm definitely not laughing when the family-size bag of M&Ms has been devoured before I have the chance to eat even one, even a blue one, and I hate blue M&Ms.

Because my fiancé's two children live with us 50 percent of the time, our household is often full, and the fridge empties quickly. Living in my house are my daughter, my fiancé, our son, my fiancé's two daughters, our live-in nanny, and me. That's a heck of a lot of mouths to feed. Don't even ask about my midnight runs to get milk from the gas station, or how long our grocery bill is. If I go on a full-on grocery-shopping expedition, the bill is like one of those handkerchiefs that clowns pull out of their coat pocket. The bill just keeps rolling out of the cash register. Running up the tab takes so long I could practically get my car washed and detailed while I wait for the bill to stop printing. As it is with a clown and his never-ending handkerchief, it's kind of funny at first. Then it just gets annoying, for me, and for the people behind me in line, who are probably wondering if I'm running a restaurant instead of a household.

Now, if I see there's only one can of Diet Coke left in the fridge, even though there were twelve there the previous day, I write my name on a Post-It note and stick it on that can, kind of like an amulet, as if warding off vampires by wearing garlic around my neck. People know it's *mine, mine, mine,* because the can of Diet Coke has my *name, name, name* on it! Everyone in my house, except the dog and baby, can read, and the dog and baby don't drink soda. And I don't have to worry about getting stopped for speeding when I'm racing home, obsessed about getting the last remaining Diet Coke. Post-It notes are a hell of a lot cheaper than speeding tickets. I don't think the excuse would fly: "Sorry, officer. There's only one Diet Coke in my fridge, and I need to get home before the kids so I can enjoy it!"

"I have four kids and a husband so I understand your dilemma … to a point. The first thing you must do is to *let it go*," wrote one poster on Mommyish.com. "Don't take it as a personal affront when the kids (especially the step kids) finish the orange juice. They aren't doing it out of spite. Buy a second fridge, put it in the far reaches of the basement, and buy your must-haves in bulk. If the reinforcements are not convenient (i.e., in the kitchen fridge), the kids are less likely to finish them. If this doesn't work, find an alternative that is appealing to you but not them. Switch to pineapple juice if no one else likes it. Buy liquid egg whites or vanilla Diet Coke, if it means the kids won't touch it." This commenter meant well, and I appreciated it, to an extent. I know the children aren't doing it out of spite. But, really? Really? I can't just let it go!

First, this poster is assuming that I have a good memory, which I don't. If I have to hide my food somewhere that is not convenient for the kiddies, then I will most likely forget where I hid my stash in the first place. Secondly, I'm terrified of going down to the basement, so there's that. Finally, why should I have to shell out for a new fridge and change what I eat and drink just because the kids wake up before I do, or get home earlier? It's fine, in theory, to switch regular Diet Coke for Vanilla Coke, except I *hate* fucking Vanilla Coke. Also, while I like pineapple juice, I would have to ask each member of my family, individually, if they do, too. Can you imagine? "Hey guys, do you like pineapple juice? Oh, two out of five do? Ix-nay on the pineapple juice." Then I would have to ask, "How about cranberry juice? Anyone here like cranberry juice?" Doh! Three in my family like cranberry juice. I guess I could say, "Maybe this will be easier if you tell me what juice you absolutely detest, and that's the juice I'll most definitely buy!" My point is, buying a new fridge, hiding my stash (with my awful memory), and then trying to find something that no one in my family likes except me, seems like a heck of a lot of work. Post-It notes are just so much easier! In fact, they were invented to make our lives easier, weren't they?

Mob Moms also thought I would be screwing up my family relationships by using these oh-so-offensive Post-It notes with my name written on them. "Have you thought about how a Post-It system is going to affect your relationship with your future stepdaughters?" wrote one on Mommyish.com. "Try to see this from their point of view. Their parents are split up, which isn't easy on any kid. Then their dad moves in with this lady with a kid of her own, and has a baby with her. (Don't forget the insecurity and jealousy that comes along with a half-sibling.) Also (again, from a preteen girl's p.o.v.), new lady is *crazy*, and thinks all the orange juice in the fridge belongs to her. So crazy new lady goes on a Post-It frenzy, like the world's most vindictive and OCD-stricken college roomie." I got a huge chuckle from this. I am labeling, like, maybe three items in my entire kitchen. I am not going on some maniacal Post-It frenzy, like someone having a mental breakdown, going to the hairdresser and having my hair shaved off, à la Britney, and being taken to the hospital strapped down with cuffs. I'm not seriously mentally ill!

"Keep calm," I want to tell this poster, "and just Post-It." Another poster wrote back to this concerned mother: "I think you are clueless as to the reality of a blended family. I come from one, we are as close as can be, but my mom never had a say in anything my brothers from my dad's first marriage did … If I were in the author's shoes, I would have a talk with the hubs and tell him what's been going on, then have a small discussion about it with all of the kids, so it's not accusatory. Just say, 'I am an adult contributing to this household, and from now on, I am going to label things so you all know they're mine, and I expect you will all respect that …'"

I'm glad this poster is on my side, and offers somewhat sound advice. Like her blended family, we, too, are super-close. However, I could not, personally, say to my family, "I am an adult contributing to this household, and from now on I am going to label things so you all know they're mine, and I expect you will all respect that," without laughing uncontrollably. It would come out like, "I am an adult (giggle) contributing to this household (giggle, giggle). From now on I am going to (giggle, giggle) label everything, so you all know they're mine, and I expect you will all (howling laughter, with tears streaming down cheeks) respect that!" Forget the Post-It notes. This little speech would definitely make them think I had gone nuts, it is so not me.

It would be a very mature way to go about things. But it's really so uncharacteristic of me to say something so serious like that, even though it reads well on paper. That's because I'm not that fucking mature (obviously, or I wouldn't be so stuck on my Post-It note idea), and, anyway, making that statement turns my Post-It note system into a bigger issue than it already is. They are old enough, after all, to understand that if they see my name on something, then they really shouldn't touch it. End of story. No biggie! Putting Post-It notes on a few grocery items isn't all that radical. I'm not making a political statement, walking across my lawn with posters saying, "My Diet Coke. My Diet Coke!"

Another poster liked the idea that what I need is a private cache. "I agree with the other posters [who say] that your kids may feel unwelcome if they open the fridge and all the food has Post-Its," she wrote. "Can you just buy a mini-fridge and keep it in the garage/storage room or something for your food? It would be easier for them to remember [not to] take food from that fridge without permission, because they are just used to taking food from the regular fridge." It's as if all the posters imagine that the inside of my fridge is plastered with Post-It notes, like a lamppost covered with flyers. Again, there are only three items I have to have. I really don't give a damn about the rest. And even if I did have room in my garage or storage space for a new fridge, do I want to go all the way there every time I want an M&M? No. I just want to go to my kitchen, like normal people. Mob Moms often say, or almost always say, our modern culture bows down too much to our children, and that we have to be parents to them, not friends. So, why then should I bow down to my children, by having to buy my own fridge and hide food, as if I were going into hibernation for the next six months? It's my house. I'm not sharing a dorm room.

"Get yourself a six-pack of Diet Coke and a couple packs of M&Ms and hide them underneath your bed for an emergency stash. Get a can of frozen OJ and leave it in the freezer for other such emergencies ... teens will never take it upon themselves to make the OJ from frozen. If your kids eat the last of something, send them down to the local store to get it for you when you need [it] (as our parents did whenever we brought the car home on empty). Or, put on your big-girl panties and either deal or get into the car and make a special trip. Either way, stop acting like you're twelve," commented another. So, again, according to a Mob Mom, I'm supposed to change my eating—and underwear—habits for the kids? When did children start running the house? I'm the one paying for the food and going to get the food, so why should I be stuck with some sloppy-second frozen orange juice, and let my kids have the fresh stuff? Also, I don't love the idea of hiding food under my bed. First, I'm not a hoarder! Secondly, I'm scared of attracting mice or some other sort of bugs, not to mention the dog, which can and will sniff out the chocolate, eat it, and then quite possibly die. Do you want my dog to die? Do you want me to drink warm Diet Coke?

Many posters felt that I shared too much information, as if they were overhearing my fiancé and I fight about why he doesn't buy the food I like, which I did mention in the post. But it is kind of true. When he buys groceries, he does so more with his children than with me in mind. I know this because I don't remember the last time I ate a foot-long Fruit Roll-Up (who the hell came up with the foot-long Fruit Roll-Up, anyway?) or ham. But even if you felt like you were listening in on a private conversation, I only mentioned how we argue over groceries. It's quite boring. Trust me, we have way more exciting arguments. Still, it's not the job of my blog readers to play referee or judge, even though they most likely will.

"It actually looks more like a teenager's Facebook post, what with all the words in caps, and so much *me*, *me*, *me* going on. Honestly, curious here … Rebecca, does your fiancé read your articles? And, if so, how does he feel about you airing all this dirty laundry?" asked another commenter. Well, I have written about our sex life, and, truthfully, I can't tell you if he reads my articles. You'd have to ask him. I don't think he does, because he rarely, if ever, mentions them, which actually kind of hurts my feelings, considering that he's supposed to be my number one fan and all. At least the Mob Moms read them, so I should be grateful that others are.

"Hi, Rebecca! I like the Post-Its. I come from a blended family, too. I get the frustration of not being able to eat the things you want to eat (it's such a simple, visceral pleasure!) and that sharing matters. Maybe, just buy two of everything and split the fridge. One shelf is just for you. The others (which have all the foods they like!) with OJ and eggs and everything are shared. Consequences for eating the forbidden food include extra chores. Maybe even extend it a little. Everyone gets a little something that no one else gets to take. Just a thought!" wrote one commenter, who, again, obviously meant well. But wouldn't taking over an entire shelf from our fridge and calling it mine be way more psychotic and insulting than just putting a Post-It note on a few items? And, really, I'm so not going to punish children for eating by making them do extra chores. "You took my Diet Coke from my shelf! Now you have to mop the floors! And you're grounded until you're twenty-five!" Yeah, then my stepchildren would really like me.

It's not my nature to act that way. They are still children, and children do stupid things, such as leave an empty carton of orange juice in the fridge. But I am allowed to get mad, or feel frustrated, and then write about it, when my beloved food is eaten sometimes before I've even seen it.

"My mother used to divide up the leftover mashed potatoes into two separate containers, with my name on one and my brother's on the other, after that one time we physically wrestled over the last bit left in the fridge ... I would say maybe you should just be more proactive in your grocery shopping? Don't wait until your precious orange juice is completely out, but instead buy another jug when you see it's running low?" contributed another. See, that's my point. Exactly! I have no clue when we're running low because, with so many people living in the house, I don't even get a chance sometimes to taste my orange juice before it's gone, or there's one sad sip left. It's really hard to be proactive, when the people are eating at a rate that outpaces trips to the grocery store. I don't even get the chance to see if we're running low. There's no light that goes on in my fridge, like the warning light in my car that indicates when my gas tank is almost empty. (Hey! Some genius should invent this! A talking fridge that says, "You are running low on orange juice. Alert! Alert! Alert!" Like in a spaceship.) But, as it is, there is no gray area: either the food is in the fridge, or the food is gone.

"Labeling food was a way of life [when I was] growing up with two brothers," wrote a sympathetic Mommyish.com reader. "Today, with a twenty-three-year-old son, we continue to label anything special, both in the fridge and on a shelf. Otherwise, it's fair game, and you can be sure it will be eaten before morning!" Amen, sister! We food-labelers may be in the minority, although obviously we are out there, so we have to stick together, kind of like a pack of Post-It notes. Maybe we could start a club exchanging different colors of Post-It notes like a coupon club?

Some of you may be wondering how putting Post-It notes on my food affected my stepchildren. Well, guess what? I came home a few days after writing the piece, and opened the fridge to see a solitary Diet Coke with my name on it. I didn't write it. My stepdaughter did (such a sweetie!). And, yes, it turns out that with a large family, the fridge is fair game, and something I will need to get used to. Perhaps, by labeling my food, I'm just giving myself a little head start. Plus, with all the technology these days, Post-It notes are not really necessary. But I have found a use for them. Really, the company should be thanking me. I may just be one of the few people keeping them in business.

Hospital-Room Hosting

Do not make the nurses the bad guys.
They are paid to take care of you and your
little one, not correct your issues with your
families. If the nurses wanted to be bouncers,
they could have avoided all of their
schooling and student loans.

Sometimes I think readers have this idea that once they become mothers and find themselves devoting substantial time, effort, and energy to their children, their opinions become less valid, which is what can happen when you are constantly talking baby-talk all day long. Then they discover they can read and post their views on a mommy blog and feel significant again. I get this. Your voice is heard, or read, on a mommy blog, while your friends have ditched you, assuming you are too tired or busy to go out because you now are a mother. And your husband suddenly has started staying late at the office, not because he's having an affair, but because he hates putting the kids to bed. But just because a person can comment, it doesn't mean she has to be rude. And just because she CAPS HER ENTIRE COMMENT doesn't make her points ANY MORE VALID. As in an argument, just because you are screaming doesn't mean you're right.

One of the best things about my son's birth was that he arrived early! Just a week early, but I went into labor quite quickly, which meant I only had time to get into the car, while screaming at my fiancé to speed the fuck up. What I actually screamed, I think, was, "You get, like, five speeding tickets a week, and *now* is the time you decide to drive like a senior citizen in a snowstorm?"

My son was born shortly before midnight, which for many reasons was an awesome time to give birth. For one thing, it was too late to call my friends or family. For another, it all happened so fast that neither my fiancé nor I had a chance to charge our phones before we went to the hospital, which meant that, really, we couldn't call, text, or email them even if we wanted to—which we didn't. (Oh, I'm not talking about *you!* Of course we wanted to call you! But our batteries were dead.) It was quite divine to have the night alone with just my fiancé and our brand-new baby.

When I had my daughter, I had a semi-private room, which would have been fine if the woman next to me wasn't Amish, and had eighteen people in her room at all times. Her guests were very nice and polite. As they walked past me, the men would take off their hats and bow. I liked that. They have good manners. Before my Amish roommate and her relatives visited, no one had ever bowed to me before.

But I also had my in-laws in the room, my first fiancé, my mother, and numerous others, whom I can't remember. I'm the type of gal who doesn't like hosting. I find it stressful. I would much rather attend a party than host one. I'm also a much better guest than host. That goes double when it comes to hosting a party in a hospital room. I had just had a C-section. I had a catheter hanging over the side of my bed. I was wearing a hospital gown with mesh underwear, and a pad so big I felt as if someone had stuffed a snowsuit into my mesh underwear. It's not exactly the outfit I wanted people to see me in, not to mention the fact that I was exhausted and in fucking pain. Plus, I couldn't even offer visitors something to eat, except my placenta, which is becoming quite popular, and ice chips! What a party!

I told people I didn't want visitors when I had my son, and that they could come to see me at home, but word got out, as quickly as gossip spreads in high school. It was as if I was the first person in the entire world to have a baby, people were so adamant that they had to visit. Because I was drugged-up and tired, I wasn't up to arguing, so I let in anyone who wanted to come, although I often pretended to be asleep, which was easier and kinder than saying, "Can you get the fuck out?"

But since my son arrived early, no one even knew I had gone into labor except my fiancé, whose chest hair eventually did grow back, after I pulled chunks of it out with each contraction. It was the best blessing-in-disguise that my meatloaf came early. We're a pretty close-knit family, and I knew the moment my family, and my fiancé's family, found out I had had the baby, they would be in my room quicker than it would take to piss off Gordon Ramsey. And they did.

I wrote a post mentioning that I found it impossible to tell my friends and family, whom I love, that I didn't want them in my room for hours and hours, because I knew it would hurt their feelings. It wasn't as if I was on my deathbed. I even contemplated telling people the incorrect date of my C-section, so they'd think that I was having my son a week later, but I reckoned they'd never forgive me. That's how timid I am with people I love, because I know they only want the best for me. I don't think this makes me a spineless person. I think it makes me a nice person.

Readers had some interesting comments in response to this post. It actually became pretty entertaining, because it turned into an argument about the duties of nurses. How did that happen? But, in the mommy blogosphere, every blog post is an opportunity for people to stick their noses in your business and judge away about anything, even if it has nothing to do with the original topic.

"Nurses *can* and actually have a *duty* to protect patients recovering from *major abdominal surgery*. When you check in, make sure you are a No Information Patient," wrote one. I wish I had known about that option, but even if I did, I had other things on my mind—that I was having an emergency C-section, for one thing, and that I hadn't packed an overnight bag, or even diapers. My parents and friends would have found me anyway. Trust me. They're like drug-sniffing dogs at airports.

Another wrote, "I also like the suggestion of changing the C-section date and telling nobody." Yeah, live and learn. Live and learn. I should have done that, and then dealt with the fallout after. But parenting is a lifelong learning lesson, which starts, basically, when you hear that first baby wail.

Readers have been in my situation, but even worse. "I have been there ... twice. Second time around I requested privacy from my partner's family after my caesarean, and they ignored this and were there anyway. They held both of my babies before me, either without my knowledge or knowingly *against* my wishes," wrote one. She's still pissed off. I understand. She continued, "My second daughter is now eighteen months old and I am still angry about it. In fact, I hate them for it. They totally ruined the experience for me ... with both babies because of their self-importance and disregard for my *obvious* need for privacy." I feel for you. See, even if you *do* say something, people often refuse to listen to you. It's like when you get an invitation for a no-gift party, people still arrive with gifts. Mind you, it's difficult to stay mad at someone whose intentions are good ... especially if they bring gifts.

Others blamed my fiancé and me for the crowd in my hospital room. "You and your husband are responsible for this mess, not the nurses. This is all a result of *you* being a spineless doormat, so *you* are the one that has to figure out how to fix it. I do suggest that you and your husband do a Google search for a group called Dealing with In-laws and Family of Origin for tips and rules for you both to learn and follow, in order to limit the drama you're creating in your lives," wrote one. Thanks for the recommendation, but let's just say I'm about to guess, presumptuously, that you did not grow up with Jewish parents, the type that practically force-feed you if you dare to have only two helpings, call you three times a day, and if you don't call them back, they think maybe they should just drop by and see if everything is okay. And, frankly, my fiancé and I are kind people, not gutless doormats. We love our families.

"All of this *fail* hurts my eyes," wrote another. Fail at what? Letting people into my hospital room? Not liking people in my hospital room after I had surgery? I didn't fail at one thing, which a number of commenters seem to have overlooked, which was the most important thing: I had a baby!

Others assumed, for some reason, that I blamed the nurses for allowing people to visit. I don't. I didn't. The thought didn't even cross my mind. Just the same, one poster wrote, "Do *not* make the nurses the bad guys. They are paid to take care of you and your little one, not correct your issues with your families. If the nurses wanted to be bouncers, they could have avoided all of their schooling and student loans. You are an adult and are therefore responsible for your actions as well as your inactions." Okay. I'll remember that for next time, especially as there won't be a next time. Also, I don't remember asking any of the nurses to act as bouncers or, for that matter, as family therapists, although, clearly, by day three in the hospital, with relatives in and out, I could have used some family therapy or a bouncer. I only remember asking the nurses for, "Drugs! More drugs!" and maybe some help getting to the washroom. Nothing else.

My best friend came to visit at 10 o'clock at night the day after my son was born. She lied and said she was my sister. I so appreciate that she made the effort, though I don't remember her visit. "Where did he"—meaning my newborn son—"get that hat?" I asked my fiancé. "From your best friend last night!" he responded. "She was here for more than an hour!" Well, excuse me! I just had major abdominal surgery, hadn't really slept in forty-eight hours, and was still high on drugs (thankfully). Was I supposed to remember? But it was a damn cute hat my best friend bought.

Some moms were shocked, as one poster wrote, "by (a) people who comment here and blame *you* for not wanting to start fights with a large family, when you are very pregnant and will later have major abdominal surgery; (b) the rudeness of your family and friends to just invite themselves to something so private. It is *not your fault* that they are being insensitive; and (c) people who think it is not a nurse's job to protect their patients when they are drugged to the gills, vulnerable, overwhelmed." See, now this is the type of woman I would really have liked to have on hand during my hospital stay. She sounds as if she'd be a fabulous bouncer. And if I ever have another baby, I'm going to have a wristband-only policy. You don't have one? Sorry! No wristband? No entry.

Mother's Day: The Biggest Letdown of the Year?

*You are the most selfish woman
I've ever "met."*

One of my friends refers to Mother's Day as The Biggest Letdown of the Year. I see her point. What mother, on at least one Mother's Day, hasn't wanted a redo or rewind? This is why, as I wrote on Mommyish.com, I'm very proactive when it comes to Mother's Day. I think Mother's Day, my birthday, and anniversaries are important because I like to celebrate. I also like presents.

I have said things to my daughter's father such as, "I think Rowan wants to buy me a Prada purse for Mother's Day." Now that she can speak, I'll get her to call him herself and say, "It's Mother's Day in one week. And I can't go shopping with mommy, because I want it to be a surprise, but I want to buy her a purse." Trust me, her father has numerous degrees and is no chump. He knows I'm the one plotting my daughter's phone calls to him. It doesn't take a genius to figure *that* out. Unlike Mob Moms, my daughter's father just laughs it off, like, "Here we go again." We have a very amicable relationship.

I have to be proactive because my daughter doesn't know if it's Wednesday or Friday. She's constantly asking what day of the week it is. Why would she know when Mother's Day is? So, just to be sure, even though her father has never forgotten to acknowledge me on Mother's Day (in the form of a phone call and present), I'll also go out and buy myself something, because, fuck, it's Mother's Day, and Mommy *deserves* a new purse for being a chauffeur/cook/housekeeper 364 days a year!

Now I have stepchildren who live in my house 50 percent of the time. This led me to wonder, just wonder, in my post on Mommyish.com what, if anything, they would do for me on Mother's Day. Although I'm not their mother, I am a female adult figure in their lives, one who regularly provides them with a roof over their head, makes sure there's food in the fridge, and lets them raid my closet to borrow my clothes. I also buy them Halloween costumes, let them borrow my brushes, and take care of their dog. I have watched them play soccer. I have even attended parent–teacher interviews with them. Unfortunately, there is no day called Adult Female Figure Day, or even Bonus Mom Day, so unless I start a new routine in our house once a year, called Bonus Mom Day, I won't be getting any Hallmark cards to honor my role as stepmom. And being a bonus mom is far from easy, as anyone who has stepchildren knows. (Hallmark, are you there? Create a card for us Bonus Moms! It's the least you can do.)

One of my best friends is a stepmother. Her stepchildren's biological mother actually sent my friend flowers one Mother's Day, with a card that read, "Thank you for being such a wonderful influence in my children's life." I found that so touching and so did my friend. What my friend didn't find so touching was the fact that her *husband* (with whom she also has a child) didn't acknowledge the day at all, not even with a damn homemade card or "Happy Mother's Day" scribbled on a napkin. My friend could only laugh (after she cried) over the insanity of having the father of her child and stepchildren do absolutely nothing, while her stepchildren's biological mother was thoughtful enough to acknowledge her on Mother's Day and even order flowers for her. Now that's class.

My stepchildren have their own phones and are old enough to know it's Mother's Day. So, as I wrote in Mommyish.com, I simply wondered if I'd get a call from them, or any sort of acknowledgment—even a macaroni picture frame (which would be surprising as they are twelve and fourteen). I also wrote that I think my fiancé would probably be the one to remind them that it might be a nice gesture to call or text me. I knew he would do something himself on Mother's Day, because I am also the mother of his son, and he knows how important the day is to me. I mentioned in my blog post that, since my stepchildren have entered my life, I have been super-proactive. I love them and, while I may not be their biological mother, I definitely treat them as if they were my own children. So instead of treating myself to a regular Mother's Day gift now, I wrote, I might treat myself to a really *expensive* gift. I don't want Mother's Day to be The Biggest Letdown of the Year, after all.

Of course, it turned out that many moms are so thrilled with all those macaroni picture frames their children make at school that nothing else matters. I also mentioned in my post that I think mothers who say they don't care about Mother's Day are either saints or liars. Big mistake. Apparently, no Mob Mom is either a saint or a liar, and while they are only too willing to call me names, they definitely don't like to be called out. The commenters on Mommyish.com went crazy.

"You are the most selfish woman I've ever 'met,'" wrote one. I'm so selfish because I buy myself a gift? But that was just the start. A lot of Mob Moms, as mentioned, took issue with my suggestion that mothers are either saints or liars. This is strange because all my friends, who are living and breathing *real* mothers, have never said to me, when I ask how their Mother's Day went, "It was the best Mother's Day ever!" Usually, I'll hear, "It was fine." Or, "I don't want to talk about it." Or, "It was exhausting. The kids made me breakfast but guess who had to clean it all up?"

Of course, Mother's Day is a Hallmark Holiday, which for many people means it's not real. I know that. Who the hell doesn't know that? But I don't care what label you put on it. Don't we mothers deserve one day a year to be honored, pampered, and maybe get a sleep-in? If it takes a Hallmark Holiday to get that, then why not take advantage of it?

"I'm just going to say this: My husband and I don't celebrate Valentine's Day, and don't put stock in Hallmark Holidays. I'm not a saint or a liar. It's just the truth. Mother's Day is completely a Hallmark Holiday to me, and I don't imagine that changing when I have a child," wrote one. I love it when non-mothers chip in because, if you're not a mother, then you haven't been through a Mother's Day, when, possibly, the father of your child, or teenage offspring, totally forgets it. When all your friends are being acknowledged, even in the slightest way, and you are not, trust me, you will feel the sting. Get back to me, I wanted to say to this poster, when you have kids and they forget Mother's Day. Or, if they don't forget, and your little one gives you that macaroni picture frame he worked so hard on at school, my guess is that you are suddenly going to love and appreciate Mother's Day.

"I hate commercial holidays with a passion, and I definitely don't consider myself a saint, and I'm not very happy about being called a liar either," wrote another. Well, I wasn't writing to *you* personally, but I still find it hard to believe—what with stores everywhere and nonstop commercials reminding people it's fucking Mother's Day—that you don't care the tiniest bit. But it turns out that a lot of Mob Mobs just don't like any kind of celebration. "We don't celebrate most holidays either. We don't do anything on our anniversary or Valentine's Day, and adult birthdays *might* inspire a card, but not usually. Mother's/Father's days are not real things. No sainthood or lying involved. I just think most holidays are stupid." Wow. Downer? And if Mother's and Father's Day are not real things, then why are they marked on every calendar I own? Frankly, why wouldn't you celebrate your spouse's birthday? Why wouldn't he celebrate yours? Celebrating is fun!

If I didn't receive even a card from my fiancé on my birthday, I'd fucking lose my shit. Are Mob Moms actually saying they'd be a-okay if their spouse, boyfriend, or children didn't do anything for their birthday? I find that as hard to believe as I do that Kim Kardashian doesn't leave her house without spending two hours putting on her makeup. But Mob Moms also lost their shit over the fact that I'm, apparently, not my stepchildren's even *bonus* mom because, at that time, my fiancé was still technically married to his ex-wife, even though he had long ago moved out, and had a separation agreement in place before we met. "If you are *not* married to these children's father, you are *not* their stepmother!!! You have no connection with them whatsoever ... other than being the unwed mother of their half-brother. I have been a stepmother for thirty-seven years, and I have never expected a thing from any of them ... for Mother's Day or otherwise. I don't even *expect* anything from my own children ... you are truly disgusting. You ought to wake up and get over yourself," wrote yet another angry poster on Mommyish.com.

I reread my post and I actually did write: "I don't really expect anything" from my stepchildren. My post was more about how Mother's Day can be a letdown, with a little pondering about what stepchildren these days do or don't do for their stepmothers on Mother's Day, since blended families are becoming the norm. I definitely have a connection with my fiancé's children; maybe not a blood connection, but we certainly like hanging out with each other, talking, and asking for and giving advice. Again and again, I was reminded that I was not their mother, which I know, because they didn't come out of me, and they live with their mother 50 percent of the time.

"Oh, and you're not their stepmother anyhow," wrote another. Sigh. "Last you mentioned your so-called fiancé [he] wasn't even divorced yet. You're not a stepmother until you're married to their father, in my humble opinion." She wasn't alone. "Do any of these children have jobs? Do they earn any money? Anything that you receive from *the children* would have been paid for by their father, right? Exactly *whom* do you expect to bestow gifts upon you on Mother's Day? Your ex and your boyfriend! For spreading your legs and popping out two kids? One for each? You didn't even carry and give birth to two of them. Kids that you don't exactly take very good care of, unless it's to your benefit. You're such a faker!" I just need to ask, isn't there more to mothering than the fact I spread my legs and popped out two kids? Because that is the easiest part! And, yes, I do take good care of them. But, again, with the whole "I spread my legs" thing! Jeez. Get over it!

I have no idea why Mob Moms need to mention that I'm not their real mother, or care so much that I'm not married, or that I'm "unwed," as they say, which just gives it that extra, intentionally negative spin. And why bring up my marital status, or non-status, when I'm just writing a post about Mother's Day? There are a lot of unmarried mothers and single mothers out there, as you will find when you crawl out from under that rock. Mob Moms apparently have never been divorced, never met anyone who has gone through a divorce, and never read anything about how common divorce is. So I guess they don't know that divorce can take years to get sorted. Mob Mom moral guardians who jump down my throat because I was with a separated-but-not-divorced man really piss me off. His marital status is not a problem for me, for him, for his children, or even for his ex, so why is it an issue for them? At least there was one supporter who wrote, "I don't see what the issue is with her boyfriend still being technically married. If he was still with the first wife, that's one thing, but they are clearly long separated. If the marriage is over, then it's over, and a piece of paper isn't going to make any significant difference. Divorces can take years to figure out. What are people supposed to do in the meantime— crawl under a rock somewhere?" Although this comment had nothing to do with Mother's Day, I appreciated her support, because, yes, although I'm sure Mob Moms would like me to crawl under a rock, I prefer to keep things moving forward in my life, and that included finding a nice man and life-mate.

I have also learned from my years of mommy blogging that you should never mention anything you own, or want, that comes with a designer label. It's just asking for backlash. I wish now that I had written that I just wanted a purse instead of saying exactly what kind of purse I had in mind. "Damn, lady, you have more issues than *Newsweek*. And your whole 'Mommy deserves a new Prada,' is beyond obnoxious," wrote one. I figure if I had just written mommy deserves a new washer and dryer, or toilet seat cover, people wouldn't be so, well, offended. Sorry, I like Prada. I love the design. "You expect your ex-husband to pay for a Prada purse for you? I have been married for seven years and will be thrilled if my children make me a sweet card or buy me flowers on Mother's Day. When did Mother's Day become a second Christmas? Do you need expensive gifts to feel valued as a mother?" questioned another Mob Mom on Mommyish.com. No, I didn't *need* a Prada purse to feel valued as a mother. That's plain ridiculous. I just wanted a new purse! And can you not see that by saying you'd be thrilled if your children made you a sweet card, that you do indeed care about Mother's Day?

Even though Mob Moms often proclaim that they are speechless—many posters say that's what they are after reading a post they don't agree with—they have no problem dishing out their opinions in comment threads. Like this poster: "Wow. I'm speechless. I mean, here I am, out-of-state for an Army school, and haven't seen my husband and ten-month-old son in over two weeks. I have yet another three weeks before I see them again. Do I bitch about getting any-thing for Mother's Day? No. But stop the presses! Rebecca freaking Eckler wants a Prada purse. Hell, all I want to do is see my family. How about trying to be a little less selfish and just enjoy the fact that you can actually be home for the holiday?" Sure, I feel for this mother who hasn't seen her husband and son in more than two weeks and won't for another three. But, I've also learned over the years that a lot of other mothers project their own issues onto mommy bloggers. Which is fine. We all need to vent. But it was your choice—one you should be proud of—to go to Army school. Am I calling you a selfish mom for leaving your children behind for five weeks? And, by the way, you definitely were not speechless. You seemed to have a lot to get off your chest.

It's true that the headline on my story was, "I'm Scared That My Stepchildren Will Let Me Down on Mother's Day." Internet editors need catchy headlines to attract clicks. That's just the way it works in the blogosphere, just as retailers lure customers into their stores by putting up sale signs. I do not write the headlines that appear over my blogs. Many readers don't know this—why would they? So I cut them a bit of slack. And, often, it's the headline that gets me into trouble, rather than what follows. But I'm not going to blame the editors, because they pay me, and the headlines are pretty fucking clever, in the sense that they are funny and draw readers to my blogs. I thank them for this.

"You're afraid that your stepchildren will 'let you down' on Mother's Day? Something is very wrong with the way you think. Please seek therapy before you damage your stepchildren," wrote another amateur psychologist. Thanks to the Mom Mobs who constantly urge me to get therapy, I can't help but wonder if I really do need help. But I don't wonder for long. I'd just like to say that if I listened to these moms, I wouldn't have a roof over my head, and I wouldn't be able to buy groceries, let alone a Prada purse. I'd be fucking broke if I went into therapy every time the Mom Mobs told me I need to seek help. Maybe these moms just want to post something—anything—and the idea of seeking therapy can be plopped into almost any discussion. They say, "Seek therapy!" just so they make a contribution. It's not helpful, but at least their voice is heard (or read), which may make them feel better.

Another Mob Mom was worried about the kids: "Let them celebrate with their mom and don't put so much pressure on them," she wrote. "I'm sure they feel enough as it is. Poor girls. It must be so hard on them. It must be hell to have two mothers to disappoint." See how my articles are taken out of context? Not once did I say anything about Mother's Day to my stepchildren. There was absolutely no pressure on them. But she was right about one thing. It would be awful to disappoint two mothers. At forty, I'm still trying to please mine! But remember, as so many blog posters have pointed out, I'm not their mother! (Actually, I consider myself to be their part-time, non-mom mother, which is a mouthful.)

In the mommy blogosphere, there is always at least one mother who can understand my plight, and sometimes I just want to kiss them full on the mouth, I'm so appreciative. "Not going to touch the stepchild thing since I don't have any. But I am also being proactive in trying to make Mother's Day not be a letdown," wrote a supportive mom. "I'll be sending my husband a very detailed email about what needs to be done, since I don't think my fifteen-month-old can handle it all. It's not about material things—I don't want presents—but, damn it, I work hard to make my own birthday enjoyable, the birthdays of others enjoyable, and I work hard to make Christmas and other holidays enjoyable, and I want to enjoy Mother's Day. If it were left up to my husband I might get a card. I'd rather be proactive and tell him exactly what I want than try to fake happiness over something. The whole 'It's the thought that counts' [concept] only matters when actual thought is put into something." I felt bad for this poster—because the Mob Moms started attacking *her!* Which is often what happens when someone admits to something another mother finds unacceptable. It's as if they consider themselves better than the mom commenting, so clearly being right exempts their nasty comments from being considered plain bitchy. "I can't agree with this," a poster wrote back to her. "If my husband presented me with a detailed list of what he needs me to get to make Father's Day or his birthday live up to his standards, I would laugh in his face, and very gleefully do zero of those things. Being a martyr and expecting everyone to jump to your demands is pretty ridiculous."

Isn't it ironic that when I mention that if we dare to ask for something, we're awful people, and yet a Mob Mom can say she'd laugh gleefully in her husband's face and do *zero* for him? Which, I ask you, is worse behavior? Even I want to divorce this woman.

But moms in the blogosphere are more than willing to fight back, which can make blogging kind of fun, especially when they're not attacking *me*.

The mother who was attacked for planning to make a detailed Mother's Day list for her husband fired back to her critic: "I'm glad you are not married to my husband then, since he is the one who asks for lists. And good for you for being so above it all that your feelings would not be hurt one iota by not having your husband say, 'Happy Mother's Day.' The fact that you would laugh in your husband's face, and do nothing that he asks for on Father's Day, makes me sad." Oh, snap! Commenter of the Day! I will never believe that so many mothers in the blogosphere think Mother's Day, or any Hallmark Holiday, is trivial. Do they really not give a damn if their husbands or partners don't wish them a "Happy Birthday," "Happy Mother's Day," or "Happy Valentine's Day"? In real life, where humans talk to each other instead of hiding behind a computer screen, I can tell you, every woman I know would all be pissed if their spouse totally ignored, or forgot, these occasions. And this is not a gender stereotype. I'm sure my fiancé, or my daughter's father, would be upset, too, if I didn't acknowledge either of them on their birthdays or Father's Day. Men also are sensitive about these days. I may ask for gifts and an acknowledgment, but I also give gifts and an acknowledgment, even on so-called Hallmark holidays.

I ask my fiancé what he wants for Father's Day. I'm also pro-active that way. Last time I asked, he wanted to sleep in and a new pair of soccer shoes. Did he get that? He sure as hell did. He also got breakfast in bed and that wasn't even on his wish list. I did this because, of course, I spread my legs and his penis just happened to fall into me. No, I did it because humans like to be acknowledged, particularly on special occasions. And it makes me happy to do things for others whom I love and appreciate, just as much as it makes me happy to receive a damn gift on The Biggest Letdown of the Year—Mother's Day. Which it won't be … if you're proactive. So, did I get my purse? I sure as hell did. And I walked out of the store feeling that life is great. As mothers, we are constantly doing things for our children. Every day is Children's Day. When you think about it that way, what mother doesn't deserve a new purse on Mother's Day, even if she has to buy it herself?

Stalk Much?

Surprise, surprise. Rebecca Eckler is having a scheduled C-section. Allow us to marvel in her amazing mother skills.

There is one argument that bores me to death when it comes to motherhood, or actually before motherhood. But at least we have Mob Moms and their ridiculous comments to make the argument a little more amusing. I'm talking about C-sections, a never-ending source of interest to mothers, soon-to-be mothers, and want-to-be mothers. I've had two, both planned. (The second one was because I had the first one.)

I had a C-section the first time because I was terrified to the point of both bawling my eyes out and having panic attacks at the thought of a vaginal birth. I was more scared than I would be if I were stuck in a cage with hundreds of tarantulas. Those who have had not-so-bad birthing experiences, or say they did, can't seem to grasp that many, many women are terrified of giving birth naturally. But I'm not going to go on with my reasons for having a C-section, mostly because I'm tired of it, and also because I believe it's a woman's choice to have a baby any damn way she wants. End of story. But, as I wrote in a piece for Mommyish.com, I'm not "too posh too push." Trust me, a C-section is anything but posh. It's truly disgusting. If you want to see what one looks like, just Google it. I did, and I had to turn off the video after about four seconds, which was four seconds too long for me.

I admit that I was a wimp. I'm not a martyr when it comes to pain. I'm so not one of those women, swollen with pride, who say, "I was in labor for seventy-two hours. It was nothing, like a walk in the park!" That's about seventy-one and a half hours more than I want to be in pain! Ten years after writing about my first C-section for another publication, I still get emails from people asking me who my doctor was. Because these women, like me, are having panic attacks just thinking about labor. The point I'm getting at is that Mob Moms attacked my mothering skills even before I was a mother, which is like me auditioning for a play without getting to say one line before the director says, "Thanks. We will be in touch."

"Surprise, surprise. Rebecca Eckler is having a scheduled C-section. Allow us to marvel in her amazing mother skills," wrote one, who went on to list all my shortcomings. This poster somehow found the time to compile this list, which means she either doesn't have children, she dumped her children in front of the television, has way too much time on her hands, or needs a new hobby, which shouldn't be me. Even I can think of something better to do than write out a top-ten list about someone I don't know, such as meeting a friend for a coffee or counting how many Cheerios come in a box. Eerily, too, this commenter seemed to know way too much about me, albeit she got her facts so wrong. But, one way or another, as if she were preparing to go to court, she presented the case against my status as a mother. This is the list. My comments are in square brackets.

1. She smokes, in an attempt to help increase her kid's likelihood of asthma and cancer. How sweet is that? [I smoked maybe two-and-a-half cigarettes during my pregnancy.]

2. She schedules a C-section because she knows the importance of having that baby out ASAP, so that (a) they won't get fat and gross looking, and (b) by getting a C-section, Rebecca can get that last-minute tummy tuck in, too. Because it's super-important that your kids have a hot, sexy mom. [Did not have a tummy tuck. Didn't even think about it.]

3. She has a nanny raise her kids because, like most people would do, when she figured out she couldn't really get the job done she hired someone who could. That takes a lot of courage to admit you can't raise your own children. [I raise my children. My nanny helps out a lot, especially when it comes to finding my car keys, but I make the decisions when it comes to parenting. And I never admitted, nor would I, that I can't raise my own children, because that's a lie. I have a career, so I do need help.]

4. She throws money and gifts at her kids. Sure, it may partially be to ease her guilt, but a lot of it is selflessness, a lot of it is because she knows the importance of making sure your children know the world revolves around them, and will always cater to them. This helps when they are grown and entering the workforce. [I don't spoil my children. I don't throw money at them. I don't throw gifts at them, either. Do I cater to them? Sure I do, as any mother does! I have no guilt. Talk to me when they actually enter the workforce, since I'm not running a child sweatshop out of my house, I promise you that.]

5. She doesn't attend school functions. This may sound horrible but think about it. She has diarrhea of the mouth, she knows if she goes to that school play she will endlessly spew bullshit out of her mouth, thus embarrassing her children. So when she stays home, it is out of love. [I attend a lot of school functions. Do I enjoy all of them? Nope! But I go! And I don't think my children are embarrassed by me. If they were, they wouldn't beg me to come to their functions.]

6. She talks like a middle school dropout. She does this so her children will be humble. [In your opinion, I may *write* like a middle school dropout, but I don't speak like one in real life. You wouldn't know this because I have never actually spoken to you. And how would this make my children humble, anyway?]

7. She puts off getting married indefinitely. She does this to witness to her children that you should never make commitments you can't keep. She knows (a) she cannot truly love anyone, she has no soul, therefore doesn't want to marry someone under false pretenses, and (b) that eventually her fiancé will either leave her for someone who's hot and has mild intellectual abilities, or will stab himself in the eardrums so he doesn't have to listen to her endless idiotic babble anymore. Either way, the marriage wouldn't work, and she doesn't want to put her children through that. [Are you fucking crazy? And which is it? Do I have no ability to love or is my fiancé going to leave me?]

8. She uses her vibrator and makes sure her daughter knows it! This way, when her daughter is of legal age, she will be good and ready for her mom to introduce her into the family business: whoring it up. [You *are* fucking crazy, and disgusting!]

9. She uses Botox. She does this not because she is truly vain, but she does it in an attempt to show her daughter the most important thing in life: looking like somebody you're not. [I tried Botox twice. My daughter doesn't know. Also, you're wrong again: I did Botox because I *am* vain, which is the reason almost everyone who does Botox does it.]

10. She feels when her child vomits. This may seem like a cop-out but that's the beauty of it. She does it because she knows her child would be more devastated to see puke on her mommy's Kate Spade shoes. She's simply humoring her daughter's wish for her mom to look stylish. [You make no sense. And I do not own any Kate Spade shoes.]

I admit, I feel kind of honored to have a top-ten list of my life being a mother, even though it is slanderous. For a minute, after reading this post, I felt as I would if David Letterman were writing about me, the only difference being Letterman is funny and this woman is just plain … creepy. If someone who obviously hated you remembered everything you ever wrote, over ten years, wouldn't you find that just a little disturbing?

All I said in my post was that I had a scheduled C-section because I was scared. All the information this mom referred to came from earlier posts, written over years in blogs, magazines, and my books. Which makes me think some commenters are serious stalkers because they know, or think they know, everything about me.

I actually had an amazing amount of support for this post, but I would rather share, at least at first, the hateful ones, because they are so astonishing. Sometimes truth really is stranger than fiction. This is definitely the case with the following comment on Mommyish.com. "Women are meant to give birth vaginally;

C-sections are for emergencies, not for whiny little brats who think they're too good to give birth. Using a mental disorder (panic attack) was frankly ridiculous and insulting, and then to insult your healthcare workers who helped your entitled ass by cutting you open and removing the baby you were too lazy/childish too push out was the cherry on the cake. Give thanks you live in a country where entitled whiners like yourself are accommodated by the healthcare system."

First of all, every single nurse and doctor got one of the best bottles of wine I could find after my first birth, as a thank you. I was an awesome patient the first time around. Not so much the second, when I had another scheduled C-section (because, once you have one, you are automatically allowed another, kind of like free refills at McDonalds). But still, how does one jump from me saying, "I'm scared!" to someone else referring to my "lazy entitled ass"? You're right! I'm too lazy and posh to push. During my C-section, I just lay there watching re-runs of "Friends" while getting a pedicure and my hair styled. Not! Also, panic attacks are a serious medical issue. Just ask anyone who has experienced one.

"I resent the comment, 'who think they're too good to give birth,'" wrote a supporter. "I most definitely gave birth to my daughter, but via C-section. Sorry, I feel like women who shame other mothers for having C-sections are just bitter, because their vaginas are destroyed and will never be the same. I'd be bitter, too. I saw a friend have to get an episiotomy, and I swore that very day that I would *never* deliver vaginally. My daughter is perfectly healthy, as am I, so I don't see the problem."

This poster was smart and funny—that line about being bitter because their vaginas were destroyed? I'm still laughing—but why she would choose to watch a friend get an episiotomy is beyond my comprehension. How did this poster find herself in this position? Why didn't she turn away or pretend to faint, as I would have done? No wonder this poster didn't want to give birth the natural way. And so the argument goes back and forth. "Giving birth hurts. The first time is scary, because you have never done it. Yeah, I get that. But to have an elective C-sec just because? Giving in to irrational fears, that is childish. Why bother having children if you are so frightened? I gave birth to four children vaginally, hurt like hell the first time. You were not allowed your epidural until five centimeters, so I spent some time crying and yelling. Thank God for the person who invented epidurals! I still went on to have three more children. Never once considered a C-section," wrote another. And that was your choice and I support it, as I think you should support mine and others. And, just as posters ask me if I want a cookie after reading some blog in which they feel I'm bragging, I feel like asking these mothers who think I'm childish for being scared if they want a cookie, because they went through labor for four days or had ten children naturally. They seem to expect a prize more than I ever do. I also think that many women who have vaginal births forget about the pain. That's why they go on to have more children.

Another poster asked, "How do you plan to teach your children to handle irrational fear?" Irrational fear? I'm fearful of many things that are irrational, like gas stations and sweet potato fries. But does that make me a bad mother? Just because I was afraid doesn't mean my daughter will be afraid when she may give birth. And, trust me, my children don't remember how the heck they came out of me, just as I don't remember how I came out of my mother. Do you remember how you came out of your mother?

I plan to teach my C-section-born daughter to conquer her fear of spiders by screaming when she sees one, as I do, until someone comes and kills it. That's rational. I had already gone into labor before my second C-section, so I *do know* what labor pains feel like, and I can tell you, they can't be described except to say it's the worst pain you will ever feel, and I know that I would not have lasted without killing myself or various members of the hospital staff. In fact, because it was an emergency C-section, I didn't even know the name of the doctor who performed the procedure on me, but I could tell he wanted to get me in fast, and get the baby out, when he started operating on me. (It was almost midnight and his shift was probably almost over. Which was fine by me.) I also, during my second C-section, learned a lot about the new restaurants in town, because that's what the doctor was talking about with the nurses. Others might find this rude. But hearing about the latest restaurants actually took my mind off the fact that I was being operated on, and was about to have another child in, oh, about fifteen minutes. And the doctor was right. That new oyster restaurant was fantastic, so thanks for the tip, Doctor whose-name-I-do-not-know.

And, again, C-sections are not posh at all! Suddenly, after my second baby came out, I heard a choir of screaming nurses going, "Oh, my God!" They jumped back from the operating table as if there were dozens of snakes in the room. I'm not sure what spurted out of my stomach after the baby came out, but they all leapt back as if they had never seen anything like it. Perhaps what spurted out of me, after the baby, were the grilled cheese sandwich, the bag of Cheezies, the tacos, the French fries, and the carton of ice cream that I ate three hours earlier.

In any case, posters love weighing in on C-sections, no matter how tired the argument is. "And, yes, I am too posh to push! I love when people use that as an insult. I have no qualms saying I'm too posh, and I find the process of natural childbirth animalistic and frankly disgusting. I hate gore and

I hate pain. Why would I put myself through that discomfort?" offered one. Who can argue that giving birth naturally isn't animalistic, unless you are a Scientologist? Have you heard the screams of women in labor who refuse medication, or even those that get medication? They sound as if they're being slaughtered.

Others on Mommyish.com had advice for, well, the entire world. "Message to the world: Stop scrutinizing my vagina and my choices. We are not living in the Dark Ages anymore, but still behave like we do. Witch hunts and high horses, oh my!" wrote another. How could you not love this comment? I pinky promise you that at least I will never scrutinize your vagina, or anyone else's for that matter, except maybe mine.

Sometimes, I feel that I'm doing good work, almost like a social worker, when I blog. "Thank you so much for this article. The last few weeks, I have been scrounging the Internet for someone who understood me and the way I felt, and I have finally found something. Every time I even think about the possibility that a doctor would deny me the ability to elect a C-section, I break down and sob to the point that it is difficult to breathe … If you know of any doctors who would be open to allowing me an elected caesarean, *please* let me know," pleaded one. Mommy blogs, as shown in this instance, can be a positive resource for a woman looking for like-minded and supportive people. And since Mob Moms are always experts on everything to do with parenting, from which stroller and diaper is the best, to whether or not a C-section is acceptable when you are terrified, a reader will find an answer somewhere on a mommy blog, eventually.

Sometimes as an author in the mother blogosphere you have to either laugh or cry, and, sometimes, if you're lucky, you'll get to do both! I wasn't sure what to do after reading the following comment: "I had a horrendous labor last time and swore that I was never going to do it again … I never want to feel that way again and want a C-section this time around. Also my pelvic floor is completely shot. I can't even get a cough without needing lady towels." I do, I really, really do feel for this woman, who obviously has been tormented by giving birth. She should get her C-section! And I hope that she doesn't catch a cough too often, especially if she's not stocked up on lady towels. My best friend tells me not to make jokes sometimes, because after four natural births, she pees (just a little) when she laughs. But, how can I *not* laugh at "needing lady towels"? Is that a polite way of saying *maxi pad?* Or *adult diaper?* In any case, I enjoy polite, old-fashioned talk.

But the reaction to my piece on C-sections, especially when it came to the Mob Mom who seemed to know every aspect of my life (but didn't, really), shook me to the core. Sometimes when I write a blog, I can't help but look over my shoulder, even if I'm completely alone in my house, to see if someone is watching and judging every sentence I type. It's not always fun and games being a mommy blogger. Sometimes, it's just damn scary, especially if you have a Mob Mom following every single thing you have ever written. More eerie, I think, than a vaginal birth. Then again, I'll never know either the posters or what it's like having a vaginal birth, will I?

part five

We're Not Living in the Dark Ages Anymore

Marriage Is So 2006

*She's a real piece of work. I think she's
just trying to justify her poor choices and make
herself feel better, by hating on the people that
actually have legitimate children with
their legal spouses.*

I didn't come up with the saying, "Marriage is *so* 2006," although I wish I had. My funny and intelligent friend came up with it after getting knocked up, accidentally, by a man whom she loved but was not engaged to. If I had come up with the same line, I would have phrased it differently, more along the lines of, "Marriage is *so* 2003," which is when I had my daughter, accidentally, and wasn't married. I wrote my friend to congratulate her on her pregnancy, and also added, "Baby daddies are the best!"

Mommy Mob posters on Mommyish.com were *enraged*—the married ones, anyway—because they assumed I was bashing marriage, which I was not. I love weddings! Once, at a wedding, the bride made a speech thanking her brother so profusely, for almost an hour, that you would have thought she was marrying him and not her fiancé. I honestly thought she'd pull an Angelina Jolie and start making out with her brother. So, of course, I find weddings fabulous, especially

Jewish ones, where everyone dancing looks as if they should be featured on "America's Funniest Home Videos," and the bride looks terrified being held up on that chair. I'm thrilled when friends tell me they are engaged. So I am not at all against marriage. It's just not for me, at least not now, or maybe never. Or maybe not never.

Mob Mommies also had issues with the term *baby daddy*. I may have gone a little too far, for the conservative readership of my posts, by writing on Mommyish.com that, "First comes love, then comes marriage, then comes pushing the baby carriage, is no longer the norm. What I see as the norm is, First comes love, then comes baby, then comes marriage, which admittedly doesn't have the same ring to it. But in my life, and many others, that's the way it goes now.

When I was pregnant with my son, with Baby Daddy #2, I met Baby Daddy #1 for brunch with my daughter (Baby Daddy #1's). When Baby Daddy #1 saw me walk into the restaurant with our daughter, he said, "Well, you are certainly pregnant!" To everyone else in the restaurant, we probably just looked like a blissful family out for greasy eggs on a Sunday morning, with a second baby on the way. As I mentioned in my post, there are numerous celebrities who are engaged but not yet married when they have their babies. There are numerous celebrities who have put off weddings to have their babies first. Some celebrities have babies and don't ever plan to get married, as far as we can tell. But Mob Moms don't believe me when I say marriage is not a priority for me. They seem to think I'm attacking married people. "Do you think you could *possibly* be more offensive???? Good grief, just stop bashing marriage already," wrote one poster in the comment section. Another added, "Why must you put down people that have children within marriage? What are you trying to prove? That your situation is so much better than everyone else's that did it the '2006' way?"

Mob Moms are so competitive. I'm not competing with you by comparing my situation to yours. I don't even know you! And I'm certainly not trying to prove anything. I'm just saying it's becoming quite normal to have a child and not be married first, or at all. Even my ninety-two-year-old grandfather, who was upset when women started to wear jeans—that's how old-fashioned he could be—understood this. Mob Moms, even in this modern day, were unable to agree. "Maybe this *isn't* the norm and maybe you're just trying to constantly reassure yourself of how wonderful you and your choices are, despite the fact that you seem to have constant doubts." But I don't have any doubts! If I eventually find myself wanting to get married, I will get married. And even if I had my doubts about marriage, how could you not understand why? Have you never come across the statistics on divorce? Do you not know how many people cheat in marriage? Do you know how hard it is to live with someone day in and day out?

"She's a real piece of work," wrote another Mob Mom. "I think she's just trying to justify her poor choices and make herself feel better, by hating on the people that actually have legitimate children with their legal spouses." I'm not sure exactly what poor choices I've made—except, in some people's eyes, not walking down the aisle in a dress I will wear once in my life—and I feel perfectly fine, thanks very much. As I will repeat, I'm not hating on married people. Most of my friends are married. And, dear God! Are you actually saying that my children are illegitimate? If so, the rotary phone is again ringing in your house.

"I know, right?" agreed another poster, who just can't get over the fact that I'm a mother who has never been married. "Call me old-fashioned. It's not that I couldn't get over the love–marriage–babies structure of events—it's what happened and it's what I wanted. I don't think that, as women, having multiple children by different fathers is something we should strive for." Okay, because obviously I'm now striving and on the lookout for Baby Daddy #3, and after I'm done with him, I'm obviously going to find Baby Daddy #4, and then Baby Daddy #5. I waited nine years, people, to have another child after falling in love again. Even Kate Winslet has three different children from three fathers, and does anyone judge her?

I have a friend who has three different children by three different men. People judge her, but never any of the fathers (who have other children with other women). So, it's okay for men to have multiple children by multiple women, but not women to have multiple children with multiple men? Plus, I only have two children from two different men, and their age difference is almost ten years. I could have had nine babies in that time, before finding a man whom I really wanted to have another child with. I was patient.

Mob Moms make so many assumptions about authors of mommy blogs. My favorite on this topic was the poster who wrote, "Is anyone else kinda surprised that Eckler would pass up an opportunity to wear a ridiculously expensive dress, be showered with gifts and attention, and have a bunch of people tell her how beautiful she looks?" Oh, how you don't know me at all! My perfect-wedding dream outfit would be a pair of jean shorts, a white tank top, and bare feet, on a beach, in front of my now built-in ring bearer (my son), and my maid-of-honor (my ten-year-old daughter) and my stepchildren (photographer and hair stylist).

I still stick by my opinion that baby daddies are great because, if they are already fathers, you can see how they treat their own children, just as I saw how my Baby Daddy #2 treated his two children before having another child with me. Having a baby with a man who is not your husband may not be the new norm, exactly, but it's certainly becoming more normal, and people should just accept it. It's like people who say you should only eat glutton-free food. I don't. But I don't judge people who do. As I say to my still-single women friends, those who are desperate to meet a man, Well, you can always wait for marriage. But you can't wait forever to push that baby carriage. My daughter doesn't care at all that I never married her father. Just the same, she plays at planning her dream wedding and I help her. And guess what? She wants to wear a red dress and have a red cake. Normal for a wedding? Nope. But perhaps, just as baby daddies are becoming the norm, red wedding dresses might become normal option, too.

Engaged to Be ... Nothing?

*You can't be engaged to someone
who's married. You're his mistress,
even if they are separated.*

I often get sucked into those inane, but entertaining, Yahoo lifestyle stories. You know the kind: "Ten Signs Your Man Is Losing Interest." Or, "Ten Easy Ways to Lose Weight While Eating Ice Cream on Your Couch." Or, "Signs You Are Procrastinating by Reading These Articles." A story I got sucked into reading recently was about celebrities who have long engagements.

As most people who follow my blog posts know, I have been engaged twice, but have never been married. (Are you sick of hearing this *yet again*?)

It seems that people are held to a different standard of behavior, depending on whether they're celebrities or not. (Kate Hudson has been engaged for years with her second baby daddy.) At least, that's the impression you get if you pay attention to the commenters sitting behind their computer screens. People seem to have a real problem with the fact that I haven't been married, and I have so-called illegitimate or bastard children, all because I didn't marry either of the children's fathers. Hello? Do you not read lifestyle stories about famous basketball players who have, like, thirteen children with five different baby mamas? Or a politician living two different lives? I was engaged to a man and had a daughter with him. The relationship did not work out. Flash forward seven years and I met another man, got engaged, and had another baby. The Mob Moms didn't like it when I mentioned in a post on Mommyish.com that I hate it when trolls call my children *bastard* or *illegitimate*, just because I didn't marry their fathers. Nor did they like the post I wrote about being engaged with no plans to get married.

There was a lot of arguing about the meaning of particular words. When people use phrases such as *out of wedlock*, *bastard baby*, or *illegitimate children*, it makes me wish that society could somehow catch up with the year I live in. And by *society* I mean the Mommy Mob. "Those words tend to be used these days mostly in reference to the offspring of adulterous relationships," wrote one in the comment section of Mommyish.com. "Which technically Ms. Eckler is in, given her fiancé is still married to another woman." Ouch. But more on that later. "Illegitimate: Born to an unmarried couple. Which is what your kids are, right? Not trying to be nasty, but hey, people judge you for your choices … unfortunately they judge your kids, too. I'd be way more upset about people calling my kids bastards, but that's just me," added another. Well, me too. And I appreciated that you took the time to look up the meaning of *illegitimate*. But tom-*ah*-to, tom-*eh*-to, right? *Illegitimate*, *bastard*, and *out-of-wedlock* are pretty much the same fucking thing, unless you are one of those women who ask which paint color you like best: the cloud white or the lush white? Dude, they are the fucking same color. They just have different names.

"As much as I criticize Rebecca," wrote another who backed me up, even if she just had to throw in that she often finds fault with my posts, "you're dead wrong. Using the term *illegitimate*, whether you recognize it as such or not, is essentially degrading to the children, just as much as *bastard* is. Can't we agree that regardless of how enraging Rebecca is at times, that calling the children offensive and degrading names is out of line and off limits?"

Well, these days, nothing is off limits, especially in the mommy blogosphere, where more and more mothers are showing their true feelings, as if they've all swallowed an honesty potion. Another picked up the argument about using the word *illegitimate:* "That's the definition. I'm not saying that makes it okay, but that is what it is. Facts are what they are. Author has two children with two different men that she was not wed to in any legal or religious way. And there are still people who feel very strongly about that." Obviously. I *can* read the comments.

Let it be recorded that when I wrote the post, it is true that my fiancé wasn't technically divorced, but he had moved out long before I met him and later had a child with him.

Readers also didn't understand why I would accept a proposal but have no plans to get married. Yes, it's true. I have been engaged twice and never walked down the aisle and, truthfully, I can understand why readers may find this puzzling. On the upside, I have never had to plan a wedding, figure out the seating arrangements, and lose that extra five pounds like every bride I've ever met seems to do. Like most, we would have to invite relatives who can sit nowhere near one another, because they haven't talked to one another in thirty years, because, oh, I don't know, someone forgot they made plans to play squash, and the other one sat there waiting, and they just can't seem to *get over it* three decades later.

I was at a party once with my fiancé and another of the guests was a divorce lawyer. I asked him what would happen if my fiancé and I got married, even though he hadn't had his divorce papers signed. It turns out he would be a polygamist and could be sentenced for as much as fifteen years in jail. I totally thought we should definitely get married after learning this, because how awesome a story would that be! "Sorry, my husband couldn't be here. He's in jail. He's a *polygamist!*" People at a party would actually want to talk to me.

But it's not my fiancé who likes this super-long engagement. I hate it when posters, or anyone, think it's always the woman in the relationship who is pushing for the wedding date. Never once have I said to either fiancé, "Set the date! Set the date already!" I'm not anti-marriage. I simply like being engaged. It's like one long honeymoon. Yes, it's as annoying as the person in front of you at Starbucks who puts in a highly specific order, such as, "I'll have a decaf latte with 1 percent milk, but make the temperature exactly 120 degrees, and can you add a pack of Sweet'n Low, but make sure you put the Sweet'n Low in first, and I'll also have the tiniest pump of vanilla flavoring," when I am asked, "So when are you getting married?" But all the people close to me in my life, who are not on mommy blogs and speak to me in person, have now given up asking. I think they're just waiting, like my family, for the Facebook post announcing my elopement. (Keep waiting.) Or they really don't care whether I'm married or not. Frankly, my friends and parents have lost interest in my marital status, unlike mommy blog readers, who care as much as if they were planning their own wedding.

But I still call my fiancé my husband when I introduce him to people I don't know that well, which bothered mommy commenters a lot. Why? Not sure. Not only do we live and act like a husband and wife, but also I feel and act married. And it's easier than saying, "This is Jordan. He's my fiancé and the father of my second child, the bonus father to my daughter, and I'm the bonus mom to his two children." I think our children may want us to get married, but only so they can dress up and be flower girls and photographers. They have never asked, even though they know we're engaged, when we are finally going to tie the knot. And if our own children don't care, then why do adult strangers on mommy blogs? How does my not being married, or my calling my fiancé my husband, really affect your life?

"LOL," wrote one commenter on Mommyish.com. "You can't be engaged to someone who's married. You're his mistress, even if they are separated." Dear God. Though I sometimes wish I *were* his mistress. That way I wouldn't have to listen to him snore every single night! And, hey, I could use the occasional night to myself. What tired mother couldn't? What is better than having the entire bed to yourself, so you can lie spread-eagled, luxuriating in the extra space? And I disagree with the sentiment that I can't be engaged, because I am, and I have a ring to prove it. I even saved the proposal, which my fiancé wrote out and read to me when he asked me to be his wife.

My fiancé proposed to me in the most romantic setting, a private table on a beach with rose petals, flowers, and candles everywhere. There was even a bottle of Champagne, but because I was pregnant at the time with our child (Oh, my God! she was pregnant even before the engagement! I think I'm going to faint!), I could only take a couple sips, which was unfortunate. I love champs!

I wear the diamond ring that came with the proposal on the fourth finger of my left hand. I accepted the proposal because it was a fucking beautiful ring. Kidding. I accepted because this is a man I love and want to spend the rest of my life with, even if it will be a five-year engagement or thirty-year engagement.

I often mention how I'm not married. (Did you notice?) And I write about it without any feeling of embarrassment. But once a professional mommy blogger (which means she gets paid to write about parenting), who I thought was a friend, wrote about me in her blog and threw in, "She has another daughter with another man," which had nothing to do with the story she was writing. The way her post read made it seem as if it was something that I should be ashamed of, as if no other woman out there has ever gotten divorced, met another man, started a new life with him, and had another baby. Ironically, her blog's title has the word *modern* in it. After reading this friend's post, I was, like, "I guess I really don't know this woman." Who knew she was so … *conservative?* And, hello? So *not* modern. I mentioned in my piece for Mommyish.com that I thought it was unnecessary for her to add that sentence. She eventually apologized. I accepted her apology and consider her a friend again.

"This man ain't her fiancé, let alone a husband, as she introduces him to people. Also, Eckler, what's so wrong about pointing out that you have two children by two different men you never married? You have no shame about that right? They are the facts. If it bothers you that she mentioned it, you need to explore why," wrote one Mob Mom, playing therapist yet again. "If he's still married, you're not engaged, sunshine. You can't be engaged to marry a man who's already married." Well, tell that to my fiancé who proposed to me, and talk to my left hand. (I'm talking about my ring finger, not my middle finger, *Sunshine*.)

I also seem to have made people panicky, as though I had just run through their living room naked, screaming bloody murder, while they were eating a quiet dinner with their perfect family. "I'm not going to lie. It would make me nervous to be engaged to a man who, in well over three years, still hasn't managed to get a divorce. Is it near impossible to do in Canada?" Well, yes and no. It depends on the people getting divorced, where you are getting divorced, whether children are factored into the equation, and whether you own a home and have your own business. In this case, yes, it did take almost three years. And, thankfully for you, you have no reason to be nervous, because my fiancé didn't propose *to you*. The divorce papers are finally signed! So, I guess I'm not a mistress anymore?

"Wow, talk about protesting too much … you're not engaged, you're 'the other woman' if he's still married, sorry. And I think what your so-called acquaintance wrote stung because it hit a little too close to home, hmm? You can put a nice spin on it if you want and claim to not care, but your friend only wrote the exact, literal truth—you have two kids by two different men that you have not been married to, and one of them is still married to someone else. It obviously bothers you so much that you have to write an entire article about how much it doesn't bother you. Maybe you should explore within yourself why that is," wrote another.

Why is it that everyone thinks there's something I need to explore within myself? And I didn't write an entire article about what my friend wrote. It was two sentences. Let me, right now, explore what's inside of me. Okay, I've thought about it, and I have nothing to report except the bowl of Special K I ate this morning and perhaps a bladder that will soon need emptying.

Not all posters are still using landlines for phones, nor apparently do they all have to get up off the couch to change the channel on their black-and-white television, meaning they're not stuck back in the age when women stayed home, barefoot and pregnant. Some are more forward-thinking, thankfully. But the beauty and ugliness of mommy blogging is that there is such a wide range of strong opinion that it's often inexplicable, like the Bermuda Triangle, it's so mysterious how people's minds work.

"I'm really quite baffled by most of these comments. First of all, an engagement occurs when a couple decides to marry. That's it. It's not a legal contract, and there are no official requirements, such as setting a date, or being unmarried, or even separated. Whether or not married people should date or get engaged is a personal choice. These days, it's generally acceptable as long as a couple has separated and begun divorce proceedings, but, again, there's no requirement that an engagement must be socially acceptable to exist," wrote one on Mommyish.com. I love posters like this, who have my back, and understand that people make personal choices, not always choices to please society or family. "I take issue with labeling women as mistress or other such labels under any circumstances. How often are men called out as homewreckers? Um, never," wrote another. I, too, take issue with being called a mistress or the other woman. I am neither. That is a fact, just as it's a fact that I'm a brunette.

"Mostly I can't understand why anyone else cares," wrote another poster. "Personally I wanted DH and I to be married before having kids with all the legal protection that provides. I know other couples that feel differently. I figure to each their own," she wrote. Another chipped in: "I have no problem with people having kids out of wedlock, as long as they're well cared-for, obviously, but I don't get the long engagement thing. The marriage process isn't difficult, and it secures you many benefits. Basically, I feel if you aren't ready or think you can't afford to get married, don't get engaged." So, basically, anyone who can't afford a wedding—who can these days?—shouldn't get married unless they go to City Hall? While the marriage or wedding process may not be difficult, which I'm not sure is true, thus the term *bridezilla*, and all those reality bridal shows where everyone featured is so stressed out you just want to tell them to take an Ativan with a glass of champagne, I don't know one person who at some point in their marriage hasn't admitted that marriage is difficult and hard work. And, even though you seemed to back me up, which I appreciate, you still used the old-fashioned term *wedlock*.

Some Mob Mobs took issue with the fact that I refer to my fiancé as my husband, as if I were introducing *their* husband as my fiancé. "If you don't want to be married or don't believe in it, what's the point of calling him your husband? It makes no sense," was a typical comment. Well, listen, people: it's just easier to say he's my husband to strangers, or to say, "Speak to my husband about that" to the plumber or electrician. Also, who exactly am I hurting by calling the man in my life my husband? No one has ever dropped dead, had a heart attack, or even broken out in hives when I've introduced him as my husband ... at least not yet. No one, in real life, who knows me and hears me call my fiancé my husband blinks an eye.

"Maybe it's just me, because my husband and I had to jump past a lot of immigration hoops in order to do it, but it irritates me when someone refers to a person they're not technically married to as 'my husband' or 'my wife.' It took my husband and I two years and a near deportation to get permission to marry, so it irritates me when I hear my SIL call her boyfriend [her] husband," wrote one Mob Mom. Well, I'm sorry to have gotten on your nerves, and I'm sorry you also get irritated when your sister-in-law calls her boyfriend her husband, but shouldn't that be her choice? And just because *you* had to go through a lot of hoops to get married doesn't mean the rest of us should have to change the way we live or the language we use to describe our relationships. Being irritated over this is really an energy-waster in my opinion. There are much more serious things to get upset and irritated about, like being stuck in traffic, fixing a leaky roof, or filing taxes.

I had to jump through many hoops—including going to court—to get my driver's license re-instated after I didn't pay for a speeding ticket for almost a year, but that doesn't mean I'm going to stop driving. I wasn't *that* irritated.

"Of course, referring to someone as your husband/wife does not legally make them so. If I called my husband a cream puff, it wouldn't mean that he was a delicious pastry. But people reserve the right to call each other what they want. It never created confusion with anyone, as everyone who knew us understood the nature of our relationship, and those who didn't, well, there was no reason why it should cause confusion, unless they were seriously interested in nosing into our business. I didn't try to claim marital status on any paperwork or in any official way," wrote one. I loved this comment because it made me immediately think of cream puffs, and I *love* cream puffs. It also made me think, what if I called my fiancé my hamburger and fries, and he magically turned into a hamburger and fries? How awesome would that be?

And then the reality television portion of the blog program kicked in—grab your popcorn!—when posters who aren't married but also call their partners their husband jumped in, attacking others who don't like it when you call the man in your life your husband.

"Yeah, I'm going to go ahead and refer to *my* relationship any old way I want to. I understand you had to jump through hurdles to get married, but that really has no bearing on what I am allowed to call my lover. A piece of paper does not define a marriage in the ways it counts," wrote one commenter.

Exactly. Which is why there are so many damn divorces, because that piece of paper has no magical powers. It does not guarantee a long, healthy, and happy marriage. In fact, even a pre-nuptial agreement doesn't guarantee anything anymore.

I provoked others, apparently, because, as one wrote, "It annoys me when other people refer to each other as husband and wife when they're not legally married. If you're not legally married, it doesn't really matter how you feel. The law does not recognize feelings." What? The law doesn't recognize my feelings? I had no idea that was the case when I was in court trying to get back my driver's license!

After this, the comment thread turned into a discussion about whether or not a piece of paper defines a marriage. "Not emotionally, that's true. But it does count when it comes to benefits, property laws, health care, and whether or not your children are legitimate. My husband can make end-of-life care decisions for me. He's legally entitled to half of everything I own," wrote one. Another chimed in, "If you don't want to get married, fine. Whether or not to do so is everyone's personal choice, and the fact that *anyone* legally can't is terrible. But no matter how long you've been lovers, you don't have the same benefits your average married person does. It's just not a piece of paper, and calling it that devalues those who would kill to get married and can't. Marriage isn't a certificate. It's so much more than that." For some, yes. But not all. And, of course I believe that anyone who wants to get married should have that right.

There are, in fact—I knew it!—other mothers out there who got knocked up before marriage and have been called out on it in the most unnecessary way by judgmental mothers. (I often wonder how many babies are conceived while their parents were drunk, as my daughter was. She knows it and calls herself The Best Accident Mommy Ever Had.) "Speaking as someone who was eight months pregnant when she got married and, almost a year later, still hears whispers behind my back that my son is a 'bastard,' I'm not sure who you are preaching to. I speak from personal experience when I say that everyone who calls my son a bastard can kiss the very widest part of my ass," one wrote in response to an earlier commenter. Add my ass too to that list! It does seem somewhat hypocritical when people have children and raise them without that piece of paper, just because some people seem to think that a marriage certificate is better than a stock option worth hundreds of millions. It's not. In many ways, my relationships are just as permanent. I will be linked to each of my fiancés through each child until I die. And, as for my non-husband taking half of what's mine when I'm dead, well, I'm dead. I want to come back as a unicorn, so I'm not sure how this will affect whether I eventually get married or not. Plus, I have a will, which I think is even more important than a marriage certificate. What person doesn't know a family torn apart after someone dies and thinks they deserve more? Plus, I want to make my own decisions about what happens when I die. I don't want my fiancé to make those choices and he knows it. My children, I've made sure, will be well taken care of.

Another: "My husband and I have gone through three intercontinental moves in the nearly ten years we've been together. His dad had cancer. His sister got divorced. We were also told that children weren't a possibility, which was incorrect. We grieved anyway, because we both wanted children, and we believed a senile doctor. We went through various other family issues that are far too personal to discuss. My husband never actually proposed. He bought me a ring one day and that was it. I got pregnant and had quite a few difficulties. Did we feel married? Hell, yes. Were we? No." You go girl! It sounds like you have an amazing non-marriage, and I'm glad everything worked out for you.

I like people who understand that decisions sometimes get reversed. Not every choice is irrevocable. It's just like when I go out to dinner with my fiancé and I order something I think I want, but when his plate arrives, I realize that what he ordered was what I really wanted, so I make him trade with me. "People are allowed to change their mind. I didn't come to terms with the fact that marriage wasn't for me for a long time due to societal pressures and crap from my family. My partner and I went as far as buying rings and starting the early planning stages of getting married before we decided that it wasn't for us. We're still together, and we both still wear the ring sometimes. It just doesn't seem like an issue to us," contributed one poster on Mommyish.com.

And there are modern humans who, like me, are just a tad nervous. "Growing up, I watched 99 percent of the marriages around me fail spectacularly, and it gave me a genuine aversion to marriage. Together forever, no problems, but marriage ... So, after a lot of talking and compromising, my partner and I decided to get engaged as a way of saying to society, but also to ourselves, that we're committed to each other for the rest of our lives ... Sometimes people choose the engagement as the commitment because they don't believe in or trust marriage," wrote one.

I have contemplated marriage. Mostly, because I am a human and a female, and human females at some point in their lives think about marriage, just as human males, at some point, think about marriage (but more often sex). Others disagree with this. "The only thing she contemplated was, 'Do I want to wear this pretty diamond? Fuck, yeah, I do!'" wrote another on Mommyish.com. I love it when anonymous posters think they know me so well. Yes, that's exactly the only reason I accepted his proposal, because of the pretty diamond ring. It had nothing at all to do with the fact that, you know, I *love* him.

And some posters are really just, well, as smart as my fifteen-month-old. "I have had friends who refer to their significant other as husband and wife on FB, and it's confusing as hell, because I'd like to know if you're just referring to each other, or I need to send an actual gift." First, if you find *that* confusing, I'd love to give you a one-hundred-piece puzzle to see how long it will take you to put together. Plus, if they were good friends of yours, as opposed to someone you may have known briefly in high school twenty years ago and follow on Facebook, I'm sure it wouldn't be that confusing. If they were really close friends, I think they'd let you know if they were married or not. If they were that close to you, then wouldn't you also be invited to the wedding? How, and why, is it so confusing for you or why do you care so much?

Posters continued to be amazed by my thought process. "I do not understand the whole engaged but not getting married thing. Being engaged means being engaged to be married. So don't be surprised when people expect there to be a wedding. If you don't want to get married, just let him buy you a nice ring and just be together. It makes absolutely no sense to trash marriage and then go around calling your partner your husband, which he is not. You can feel as married as you want, it does not make it so … it makes no sense at all."

Well, it makes sense to me, and you're not marrying my fiancé or me, so it doesn't really matter if it makes sense to you. And, again, I never trashed marriage. But why don't we try to make sense of it all over a puzzle and some cream puffs, while we all stare at my sparkly diamond engagement ring?

Slut-Shaming

Not everyone has your (ahem) experiences with a partner. Some people see only the usual adult version until much later...

Poster #1: "Um, no, I just reread the article, and nowhere in it does Rebecca Eckler claim to be unfamiliar with penises in general. She says that she's only seen a baby penis once before, and that it looked weird, and that being unfamiliar with baby penises, she's nervous about it. Plenty of women who have lots of experience with adult penises have no experience with cleaning penises and being peed on while changing diapers. It is a new experience to her regardless of how many men she may have slept with in her life."

Poster #2: "It is relevant, because the poster above implied that everyone should be freaked out by the sight of a penis—like Rebecca—unless they've had lots of experience with them. The poster also said she hadn't seen a penis or balls until she met her husband, and suggests

---

A version of these comments appeared on Mommyish.com.

that Rebecca must be in the same boat, since she finds the penis so scary. I merely pointed out that Rebecca Eckler is not exactly new to penises, as she has written about her sexual dalliances quite openly. The fact that she slept with her current boyfriend on the first date, and felt the need to share this fact with the world, suggests that she's better acquainted with the penis than this article would have you believe."

Poster #3: "Who cares who she slept with and when? How is that relevant? She never claimed to have never seen a penis before."

Poster #4: "I generally don't like Ms. Eckler's posts, and I choose not to read them, because we have differing opinions. This does not make her a bad person in any way. Yes, most of her articles you can spot a mile off, so if you know you're not going to like it, don't read it. Don't waste your time reading something that will anger you, and then waste more time writing vitriolic responses. Do something better with your time ... Details of Ms. Eckler's love life have nothing to do with this article at all. That's like saying that you don't respect a scientist's discoveries or a politician's ideas because you heard they had sex on a first date—plain ridiculous."

Poster #5: "Not everyone has your (ahem) experiences with a partner. Some people see only the usual adult version until much later with our own [children]. (I thought there was something wrong with our first son until my husband who has younger brothers reassured me.)"

Unstructured
Play

*I wonder whether the author knows
anything at all about early childhood development.
If we were going to write an article, we would sure
know the definition of the topic first, right?*

find it ironic that, from the day your baby is born, mothers and experts will tell you over and over and over that babies need routine, routine, routine. Then suddenly one day, they start lecturing you that children need unstructured play, which is the exact *opposite* of routine. You can't win. And no matter what you do, you can be sure the Mob Moms will give you a hard time. If, for example, you mention that your child takes activities outside of school, they go all Mob Mom on you, saying you're *over-scheduling* your children. But scheduling unstructured play doesn't make it structured at all. It just means that your children are going to be playing on their technology devices, texting friends, video chatting, or showing you YouTube videos of dogs smoking cigarettes. Welcome to the modern world!

When I wrote a piece for Mommyish.com about how I thought that unstructured play had gone the way of the dinosaurs, and also that I didn't understand exactly what unstructured play means, the Mom Mob raked me over the coals. From one short sentence—"I don't even know what unstructured play means these days"—Mob Moms jumped on me for having the mental capacity of an amoeba.

"Would it really have been that difficult for the author to Google 'unstructured play?'" wrote one Mob Mom on Mommyish.com. She continued, "This seems like she is intentionally trying to come off as ignorant." Another poster followed up, agreeing: "Great point! Google! There are too many tools out there to remain so ignorant on a simple topic. I wonder whether the author knows anything at all about early childhood development. If we were going to write an article, we would sure know the definition of the topic first, right?"

This Mob Mom, like so many others, just had to add an insult. "Definition of Ms. Eckler: Ignorant. May the Lord have mercy on her children and stepchildren." Well, thank you, Mob Mom, for praying for my children. I appreciate it. Just because you look up a definition doesn't mean everything is explained. For example, I looked up the definition of *mom* and found this: a "female who gave birth." So, obviously, those females who adopted, used a surrogate, or are foster mothers, under the definition of *mom* in my dictionary (which I did use Google for) leaves out a whole lot of women raising children who are mothers. So why should I rely on a Google search to figure out what unstructured play means? I know what it *means*, because I really don't have the intelligence of an ant. I just don't know what it means *in this day and age*. Perhaps I should have spelled that out a little more clearly.

When I was a child in the eighties, I would ride my bike down the street to my friends' houses. When the time came, I could actually hear my mother call me to come home for dinner. I guess that was unstructured play, but hello! That's not what people mean now when they use the term. Times have changed!

Every time I read the news, there are stories about rape, kidnapping, murder, and kids doing drugs, which is why it's so hard for me to read newspapers these days. So would I let my nine-year-old, in the major metropolitan city I live in, go outside for a few hours of unstructured play without worrying? Seriously, when was the last time you saw kids playing hockey on the street, calling out "Car!" In the residential area I live in, with wide streets, I've seen boys playing hockey on the street just one time in the five-plus years I've lived there. You may not like it, but that's the way it is. A playground used to be safe. Now they are covered in needles and used condoms. The mommy blogosphere used to be a nice playground, a place to bond, commiserate, and have a picnic with strangers. Now it, too, is like a playground covered in condoms and needles, at least in the comment section.

That's not to say I keep my daughter locked in the basement, that is, unless she's practicing her violin, and then I definitely lock her in the basement.

Nope. I would rather she was in a singing lesson, at swim practice, or in a play. In a previous piece I wrote for Mommyish .com, the Mom Mob was all over my ass for over-scheduling my daughter. Well, it's just not true that she's in some program every free moment of her life. She has play dates often. But even these play dates can be dangerous. Last time my daughter had an unstructured play date, she and her friend Googled Justin Beiber's phone number and called him (or the recorded message with his voice) ten times. It was a long-distance number, and, of course, mommy had to foot the bill. I'm telling you, unstructured play has cost me a lot of money. (And Justin Beiber, I'd like to be reimbursed!)

Plus, if I told my daughter it's time to go outside for some unstructured play, she'd look at me as if I'd grown a beard, since I don't think she's ever, in her ten years, heard those two words before.

My daughter loves the activities I've signed her up for. If she's in structured play, let's say, or taking part in her concert singing series, then I know she's not doing drugs, and also she's being supervised.

I believe that scheduling activities keeps kids out of trouble, while they also have fun experiencing new activities and meeting new friends. At least while they're young. My thirteen-year-old stepdaughter tells me what the girls who don't have structured play do in their unstructured time after school. You know what they do? They give blowjobs and smoke pot. And that's coming straight from the mouth of a thirteen-year-old. When I watch my stepdaughter during her unstructured play periods, she's texting friends on her phone even if another friend of hers is sitting right beside her. And that friend, too, is texting away. (This isn't always the case, but it happens often.) I think it is kind of rude, but I'm old, and that's what kids do now. In fact, usually my stepchildren's unstructured play does not include any movement away from the couch, or a hand that is not holding some sort of technological device. Nor does it include actual talking. But it doesn't bother me. It's just a sign of the times. And they're happy, so why should I shove them outside to play in the leaves? They're teenagers.

When it comes to my ten-year-old, and even my fifteen-month-old baby, there are so many options available, why not take advantage of them? So, there is barely any unstructured play in my daughter's life, because we are too busy with structured play to schedule in unstructured play. So what? "Listen," wrote another Mob Mom, "I'm glad your thirteen-year-old is not using crack or giving out blowjobs yet, but you don't grow complacent just because you don't think she has the time. I was very scheduled and did many activities in high school and still found the time to have sex and smoke pot. I had to work harder for it, but I made it happen." Another poster also commented in the same vein. "Interestingly enough, my man was a star soccer player. Year round, recruited as a freshman … Ended up with a drug problem … so, yeah … I don't get the crack and the BJs thing either."

I never said my children would never do crack or give blowjobs. I may be ignorant about what unstructured play is nowadays but I, too, was once a teenager. (If you are reading this, Rowan, *you better fucking not smoke pot or crack ever! Or give blowjobs until you are at least twenty-five! And don't ask me what a blowjob is.*) But, my daughter is only ten, and I do think keeping her busy is better than the alternative. But, apparently, to Mob Moms, I'm perpetuating a terrible, terrible stereotype, as if I had written, "Men are only doctors. Women are only nurses."

"I don't buy that good kids who are kept busy don't get in trouble. I came from an upper-middle class family, took guitar and swimming lessons, Hebrew school twice a week, ballet as a little girl, read constantly, was in the gifted class, etc. … I'm also in recovery and spent a few years getting well-acquainted with heroin withdrawal … It's actually quite classist to envision the kid without dance classes left to roam urban environments as being a step away from crack and blowjobs." Point taken. But I've also always believed that children are a crapshoot. Who doesn't know alcoholic moms who have respectful and top-of-the-class students? Or (nearly) perfect mothers—because *no* mother is perfect—who raised her children with morals, ate meals together every night, sent them to the best school, and yet they still ended up in rehab? But, for now, I'm still the boss of my daughter and son, and while I believe that free time is a good thing, I also think scheduled activities are even better.

I mentioned in my piece that in no way am I a helicopter mom. That, too, didn't sit well with the Mob Moms. "The fact that you won't let your kid walk down the street in your own neighborhood without fearing rapists or shootings tells me you are overprotective," wrote one. I'm am so not overprotective, but surely I can't be the only mother who worries whenever their child leaves the house, and sighs with relief when she returns home safely, even if I don't have crack dealers in the park near my house or gangs in my neighborhood. There are other things to worry about, like the drivers who, more often than not, do not stop at stop signs. Every parent I know in real life sometimes is uncomfortable about letting their kids walk down the street to a friend's house, but they still let them do it, and make them call when they arrive. Real Moms worry about their children. Forever.

At least one mother agreed with me. (I'll send you flowers if you give me your address.) "Rebecca," she wrote, "I might be on your side with this one (!). I personally don't think that putting your kid into activities, even lots of them every day, is harmful, so long as they enjoy themselves. You're right. Ballet, art, soccer, and whatever other activities kids are into these days (Slavic drumming, perhaps?) are enriching, social, and they *do* involve play." This mother continued, "And while I believe, of course, in unstructured play, as in kids just hanging out and playing, I'm not a subscriber to the philosophy that there's a danger to over-scheduling, so long as it co-exists with some unstructured play (or maybe 'free time' is what you mean), and your kid is happy overall."

Yes, readers, my kid is happy overall, so you can stop worrying about her. And, maybe I didn't know what unstructured play really meant these days, because what it means is just, as the above commenter pointed out, free time. I may be an idiot for not understanding the phrase in its current usage. So sue me. But did you know what gluten-free was ten years ago? Or what kale chips were? Or anything about Botox?

Remember, our parents didn't use the term *play dates* when we were kids. I still refuse to Google *unstructured play*. But I am planning to Google *Slavic drumming*. My daughter may have just enough time in her structured schedule to sign up for that. Or maybe I will. You're never too young—or too old—to have structured play.

Snip, Snip ... Again!

What an incredibly horrible person you are.
My favorite is where you needed sperm so bad,
you banged him three days after surgery.

Maybe I am slightly obsessed with penises. There are worse things to be obsessed about. For example, there are people who have a foot fetish, and others who like watching pregnant women having sex on the Internet. And there's that woman who is so obsessed with Barbie toys that she's had plastic surgery to make herself look like the doll. These people really exist. I don't judge, but I do find it strange.

My fiancé got a vasectomy reversal so we could have a child together. Nothing says love more than a man willing to get a vasectomy reversal for you. The operation cost $5,000, and it took more than three hours. The doctor was a friend of mine, so I knew my fiancé would be in good hands. Or his penis would be.

"I'm scarred for life," my fiancé told me when I first asked him, not long after we met, how long it took for him to feel better after his original vasectomy. He had undergone the procedure eleven years earlier, after having two children with his ex-wife. Men can be such babies, as any woman knows who has dealt with a man cold. They get the tiniest of sniffles and next thing you know they can't get out of bed, and you're bringing them soup like they're another one of your children. But my fiancé's vasectomy reversal worked brilliantly: I have proof in the form of our little terror, now just more than a year-and-a-half old.

I played nurse for my fiancé after his operation, bringing him ice and food while he lay in bed for about a week. I don't doubt he was in pain, because he was constantly moaning about being in pain. Yet, even though we weren't supposed to have sex for three weeks, according to the doctor, a medical professional, my fiancé wanted to have sex three days after his operation. So, really, how much pain could he have been in? Of course, I never will know, because I don't have a penis, and I didn't get a vasectomy reversal. Just as men can't comprehend what a contraction feels like, no matter how hard we pull their chest hairs and scream, I can't fathom what it's like to have a procedure performed on a penis. Nor can I imagine what it's like to have a sex drive strong enough to override penis pain and a topnotch medical opinion.

"What an incredibly horrible person you are. My favorite is where you needed sperm so bad, you banged him three days after surgery," wrote a Mob Mom on Mommyish.com. Actually, technically, he banged *me*. All the while I was saying, "I don't think this is a good idea at all," as the bed shook. (Also, I didn't need his sperm so bad. There are places called sperm banks and other men who would have gladly slept with me. But I wanted my fiancé's sperm and him to be the father to our baby.)

At present, my fiancé and I are using that good old-fashioned pullout method of contraception, because he hates condoms, and I hate being on birth control. (It makes me kind of insane and, worse, bloated! And, trust me, I've tried different kinds, and they just don't mix well with my body or mind. They make me act like a moody bitch.) The pullout method, I know, isn't the greatest form of birth control, considering he has super sperm, and I am apparently very fertile, even at my ripe old age. We were pregnant practically before we were technically even allowed to have sex after his tubes were reconnected! And I worry every month about getting my period. But now that between us we have four children, we know we are done, done, done, unless we want another baby, but there's no room for another baby, unless that baby sleeps in the laundry room. So I told my fiancé that he was going to have to go back to the doctor to get his vasectomy reversal reversed. Yes, it's a mouthful. Try saying that ten times fast! He didn't like this much. I said, "But it's just a vasectomy. It will take you ten minutes!" which is how long a vasectomy takes with today's technology. Heck, I know men who go on their lunch break for a little snip, snip and go right back to the office. I had another male friend, who had to undergo a three-hour operation for prostate cancer, and he was out at a bar one week later, feeling fine. Sure, I was asking my fiancé to have yet another procedure done, which is a bigger deal than, let's say, asking him to take out the trash, give me a back rub, or take the dog for a walk. But, as I told him, we are really tempting fate by sticking to our present pullout birth control method, and I don't want a baby sleeping in our laundry room, even if it does smell like Bounce Spring Fresh Dryer Sheets.

There's no way in hell that I'm getting my tubes tied, because that would mean I'd have to be operated on. I've already been through two C-sections, and I'm seriously done with doctors operating on that part of my body. Plus, there's just something about the finality of it that makes me not want to do it, even though I know I don't want any more kids. Or do I? No, I don't.

So now we're at a standstill. I argue that I've had two C-sections, and he argues that he's had two operations on his penis. I told him I could go on the Pill, but I would be a miserable, moody fuck forever. He agreed in a split second that I should definitely not go on the Pill. After all, he wants to live with me.

I also don't want some birth control device stuck up me, because I am terrified that it will get stuck there forever, no matter how irrational this sounds, and I'll be the equivalent of the man who took Viagra and had to go to emergency, because he has had an erection continuously for sixty-nine days. I'd be the one going to emergency saying, "I, um, think my IUD is stuck and I can't get it out. I'm sure it's now infected, and I'm probably going to die!" I'm not the only one who worries about IUDs. I have a friend who's freaking out because she needs to get one for medical reasons.

So I've been pressing my fiancé for months to call the doctor who performed his vasectomy reversal to book an appointment for his second vasectomy. I even suggested he ask the doctor for a deal. (Get a vasectomy reversal and your second vasectomy is on the house, or at least 20 per-cent off!) But my fiancé always has some excuse. He can't do it this week because he has soccer practice. He can't do it that week because he promised to play poker with guys he hasn't seen in years. He can't do it another week because he may be out of town and can't commit. He can't do it *ever* because soccer practice is all year long, and his schedule is busy until the year 2025! Don't get me wrong, I feel for the guy. But even he admits that a vasectomy isn't that bad. Ten minutes for the procedure, followed by a couple uncomfortable days and some down time.

Of course, the Mob Moms think that I'm the most awful, selfish person in the world for even suggesting that he should get another vasectomy. You'd think I was asking him to run over hot coals, get my name tattooed across his chest, and then forcing him to eat twenty hotdogs in less than one minute.

"I got snipped because I don't want kids," wrote one Mob Dad in the comment section of Mommyish.com. "If I were your fiancé, I would have told you to go to the beach with a sledgehammer and pound sand up your ass." (Excuse me while I take a moment to wonder what this comment even means. I also wonder: What is the maximum depth of rudeness and obnoxiousness?) But thank goodness that this man has a vasectomy.

Another wrote, "Personally, I think Eckler should be the one to get snipped. The world doesn't need any more like her running around." Gee, thanks, and we haven't even met! Catch me if you can, because I'm a pretty fast runner.

Some Mob Moms agreed that birth control is a problem, but they still didn't let me off the hook. "I get what a pain birth control options are. I really do," wrote one commenter. "But to think that one partner has the right to demand that the other in the relationship do something as drastic as a reverse vasectomy/re-vasectomy is really crappy to me. You won't let him demand that you get an IUD. What gives you the right to demand that of him? Shouldn't this kind of significant stuff be decided on together?" First, I didn't demand he do it. I requested it bluntly. And I did tell him I would go on the Pill, but he would have to live with my moodiness, and he didn't like that option.

Not every significant issue in a relationship can be decided together, or there wouldn't be such a high divorce rate. Sometimes, someone has to take charge or take one for the team, or be the bigger person. Sometimes, there is no compromise. All I did was tell him to call and book an appointment. And that, I think, is a perfectly good solution to our issue, because if that doesn't happen, then we may just have another baby, who will have to sleep in the laundry room that smells of Bounce Spring Fresh Dryer Sheets. With three children, plus being the bonus father to my daughter, my fiancé definitely doesn't want another child. I had to carry our baby for nine months, so asking him to endure two days in a little bit of discomfort after a ten-minute operation doesn't make me a demanding woman, in my opinion. It makes me a woman who doesn't want a baby who could only sleep in the laundry room. I can, of course, be demanding about other things, but that's not the point.

Mob Moms didn't agree. "What? You can't get your tubes tied? Yes, you are demanding. Consider yourself blessed that this man puts up with your shit," wrote another. Well, I can tell you, he would rather put up with my shit than deal with yet another baby's shit. And, of course, it wouldn't be a mommy blog without name-calling. "The writer of this article is an asshole. Get over yourself, lady. Get your damn tubes tied, and do something for *him* for once. He gave up his vasectomy in order for you to have another child, and you're being selfish. Ugh! You baby!"

Hold up! I'm not being a baby. I'm trying not to have another baby. And I do things for my fiancé all the time. I make and bring him coffee in the morning. I write him love poems. If I see something in a store that I know he would like, I buy it for him. I take his children shopping for clothes. And, excuse me, but he didn't give up his vasectomy in order for *me* to have another child. He gave up his vasectomy so *we* could have a child. It's not like I held a gun to his head when he made the appointment for the procedure. If he didn't want to have another child, I think he would have told me.

With Mom Mobs, there is no sisterhood with significant issues, and that pisses me off, because I think there should be a sisterhood in the blogosphere, especially when it comes to parenting. I'm not saying that all women should side with other women just because we have vaginas, but so many women, after reading this post, wanted my fiancé to *leave me*. Why is that? Why don't trolls on the Internet ever seem to want other people to be happy? Take this comment on Mommyish.com, for example: "What a controlling and selfish person. Women like this give women a bad name. Take responsibility for yourself and exert some self-control. Get your tubes tied! As for your fiancé? He should run fast and far away!" I think I did take responsibility by reminding him to call the fucking doctor already. And why would you want me to be a single mother again? Why do you want him to run from me? You have no idea what my relationship is like, just as I have no idea what happens in your house. Perhaps your spouse, if you have one, should run fast and far away from you. Not that I'd know. And how do I give women a bad name? Because I asked my partner to do something for us, something that takes less time than a facial?

But, as always, I seem to learn something from the posts I write, and not just that so many mothers have strong, judgmental, and outrageous opinions about my fiancé's penis. I loved the commenter on Mommyish.com who wrote, "Dude, it's not his penis the doctors are fiddling with. It's his *balls*. That was the one detail in your post that bothered me." See, commenters will call you out on the littlest thing, or clarify the one little detail that I got wrong. I, of course, didn't actually watch the operation, so balls, penis, whatever. He got the vasectomy reversal. But I did get a chuckle out of this. Next time I write about vasectomies, I'll get it right, I promise.

My fiancé *will* be getting another vasectomy. Not because I'm demanding it, but because I'm asking him to get one and he loves me. I also promised him that this wonderful doctor would take tender care of his penis—oops! I mean *balls*. And, of course, I also promised my fiancé that I'd play nurse for him afterwards. His balls most definitely will be in good hands then. And if he doesn't make the appointment, then I am going to tell him I'm going on the Pill, tomorrow, which will turn me into the Wicked Witch of the West, but not as nice. I'm positive he'll be on the phone with the doctor in a split second.

But *She* Got One!
The Modern Birthday Party

*I have to admit, if a friend called me
up to gripe about a gift I bought my child,
I'd think they had more than a few screws loose
and seriously reconsider that relationship. I'm not
saying that to be snarky or insult the writer, I just
think that sounds incredibly nutty. I'm trying
to imagine that phone call, and I really can't.
I'd think the caller was mentally ill.*

My daughter attended a birthday party for a nine-year-old friend who received an iPhone from her parents, which she got to open in front of all the other kids at the party. My daughter came home from the party, and guess what she asked for? She wanted a new Monster High doll. Not. She, of course, wanted an iPhone, too. After listening to my daughter go on and on for three days about how she wants an iPhone because her friend got one, I did what any mother would do. I called the mother of the aforementioned birthday girl to give her hell.

"I'm going to fucking kill you," I told this mother. "Ever since you gave your daughter an iPhone, my daughter won't shut up about getting one. Thanks a lot!" As I wrote in my post for Mommyish.com, I don't have a problem with parents buying their kid whatever they damn well please. But I do have a problem, now, with unveiling gifts at a party, especially when it comes to expensive gifts that every other kid wants, and then my daughter comes home begging for one, too.

When my daughter turned nine, her father and I got her a MacBook Air laptop computer. Over the top? Not sure. Don't care, especially since I won't let her touch mine. But I do know that we didn't give it to her at her birthday party, in front of all the other children. We handed it to her at home, the day before her birthday, saying, "You'd better not break this. We're not getting you another one. Happy Birthday!"

"Get in line," the mother of the birthday girl responded, laughing, when I told her I was going to kill her. Apparently, I wasn't the first mother to complain. Of course, I was kidding around with this mother. I was pissed about the iPhone—but mostly at my daughter for constantly begging for one. As for the mother, she's a friend. As if I would actually pick up the phone and threaten to kill some mother who *wasn't* a friend, or anyone for that matter. Please. But Mob Moms have no tolerance for clowning around.

Thankfully, my daughter forgot about the iPhone about a week after the party, as I knew she would. And my poor friend was still fielding calls from other mothers. I wanted to (and I think I did) laugh in her face and say, "See. Ha, ha, ha. It's not always great to be a trendsetter!"

Of course, Mob Moms didn't like the fact that I called this mother to complain about her gift. Mob Mobs can be so sensitive and humorless. "I don't choose my child's gifts based on the parenting styles of others," wrote a Mob Mom. "I have to admit, if a friend called me up to gripe about a gift I bought my child, I'd think they had more than a few screws loose and seriously reconsider that relationship. I'm not saying that to be snarky or insult the writer, I just think that sounds incredibly nutty. I'm trying to imagine that phone call, and I really can't. I'd think the caller was mentally ill." Well, I would think it was nutty, too, if it wasn't done in jest. Again, because the commenters didn't read or comprehend it the first time, I was calling a friend, who already thinks I have a few loose screws, thanks very much, but for entirely different reasons that have nothing to do with birthday presents.

In any case, my issue was not what my friend bought her daughter, but the pain I endured in the days that followed the party, when my daughter tried to explain why she needed her very own, very expensive phone. "Who are you going to call?" I would ask her. "You," she answered. "But you can use the home phone or email me from your computer or iPad," I told her. She talked to her father, and he also asked her whom she was planning to call. "You!" she told him. "Because I love you!" When she tried to pull the "Because I love you" line with me, I answered, "Whatever. You're not getting a phone. But I love you too!" See? I do not bow down to my child's every desire.

"Rebecca, my friend went through something similar with her son and wanting the iPad, so he could read on it!" another mom wrote on Mommyish.com. I love children's attempts to manipulate grownups. They're just so adorable. "I need the iPhone so I can call you! Because I love you so much, Mommy!" Right. As for the kid who needed the iPad, his mom and dad bought him something else, but tucked into an envelope with it was a brand new … library card! Now I wonder about this. I fully support libraries and think everyone should have a library card. But this seems a bit cruel. Still, many of us do things to our children for our own amusement. For example, I sometimes make my daughter say the words *birth certificate*, because she can't say them properly and it gives me a chuckle. I have also held a slice of lemon to my baby's mouth to see his reaction when he tastes it.

Turns out there are a lot of parents fucking around with their children when it comes to gifts. Which, depending on your sensibilities, can either be hilarious or just plain mean. "My parents did the opposite," wrote another mom, responding to the last poster. "They would give a nice gift in a box of something no kid would want, so I would desperately pretend to be happy with underwear or cereal or something, and then find a present I had asked for or wanted. I fell for that for an embarrassingly long time." I should totally do that with my kids, at least once, to see their reaction. I get good ideas sometimes from mommy blog readers. So thank you for that!

"Yeah, my parents thoroughly enjoyed doing that to us too," wrote another. "Now they wonder why none of their children want anything to do with them. Hope that glee is worth it. I know you're going to reply with something about spoiled brats, but there is no value in crushing a child's spirit. You aren't teaching them anything by doing that, and if it gives you some sort of sick satisfaction, you need therapy. Desperately." Ouch! And again with the therapy! Anyone who doesn't agree with another mother's way of parenting apparently needs therapy, which makes me think I should have become a therapist. I would never be out of work.

I'm not sure how the thread became so vicious, but, hey! At least they weren't attacking me, which is always a pleasant turn of events. "The glee is almost as good as the amusement I get from reading this post about the incredible depths of your inner turmoil and your crusade to save the innocent from improper gift-giving." Wait ... that *was* antagonistic. I'm not on a crusade to save the "innocent from improper gift-giving." I just made a phone call to a friend. I'm not going door-to-door making parents sign a petition for improper gift-giving. Now that would be nutty.

But others attacked the poster whose parents had, I guess, a twisted sense of humor. "Your spirit was crushed by not getting luxurious presents, and now you're punishing your parents by not having anything to do with them? That seems really over-the-top … Can you clarify exactly what your parents did that was so bad that's comparable to giving your child a library card instead of an iPad? I have a hard time understanding what is so spirit-crushing about not getting all the gadgets and toys that you want, and instead getting something useful like underwear or an iPad." Okay, even I would be upset as a child with getting *underwear*, especially as a birthday gift, even if it was useful. (Unless I was under the age of two, in which case, mind you, I wouldn't need underwear.) However, do I think not speaking to your parents—ever—because they bought you something you didn't like, or didn't wrap the gift in an appropriate way, is possibly a little off-the-charts? Sort of. Yes.

Some of the other comments were funny, including this one, even if I didn't agree with her attacking the poster, who obviously still holds a major grudge against her parents. "It is pretty clear that *you* are the one who needs therapy for your bitter attitude. Now, you may have good reasons, if your parents were as evil as you claim, but that is no reason to drag everyone else down into your humorless pit. Off to crush some spirits, mojito style."

Yes, there is nothing like a few mojitos to lift someone's spirits. As a mommy blogger, you can definitely pick out the temperament of different posters. The poster who complained about the gifts and refuses to speak to her parents is definitely a Debbie Downer.

An amazing number of people think they know every aspect of my life, all gleaned by reading my 800-word blog posts. In the same way that they actually misunderstand me, we are probably misunderstanding the poster's rage at her parents. There has to be a lot more going on there than crappy gifts. There must be, unless she genuinely is a spoiled brat. But getting back to my phone call to the iPhone girl's mom, it turns out (not surprisingly!) that Mob Moms have clear rules about when it's appropriate to call out another mother, and when not to. Unfortunately, I'm not privy to these rules, which they seem to make up on the fly. Or they're keeping them a secret from me, like purposely leaving me out of a party.

"What I don't understand are all these parents ringing up to give the mother a piece of their mind. Why? So she can turn back time and undo it? I understand mentioning your frustration at your own child's insistence in passing, but to specifically call up a parent and complain about a gift they got their own child, because your child doesn't have one, is ridiculous. Can people not just mind their own business anymore?" I don't know. By even commenting, doesn't that make you a hypocrite? You're not minding your own business when you tell me and others to mind ours. You're actually going out of your way to *not* mind your own business. And I didn't call my friend only to complain that my daughter now wanted an iPhone. I also called to say hi.

And, of course, there are the Mob Moms who just have to say, "Part of being a parent is to …" Man! If I got a dollar for the number of times I've read that sentence in comment sections after my posts, I'd be a thousandaire. "Yeah, I don't get that either," agreed another poster. "Unless it was done in a joking way (which this may have been), I don't see what the point is …" (Wait for it!) "… part of being a parent is having to say no once in a while, especially if a friend gets something much cooler than what your kid has. I don't agree with the big unveiling at the birthday party, but the birthday kid's mom is parenting her own kid, not the author's." Obviously, and also, thank goodness. I kind of like my own daughter. And yes! I did call the other mother in a joking way! She, at least, laughed.

If anything, putting aside the whole business of what kind of gift you choose to give your child, when, and in front of whom, I wish we could all agree that present-opening at children's birthday parties, or any birthday party, is often a giant bore. But, no, commenters engaged in a frenzied debate over whether or not to open gifts at a party, as if it were something to be extremely concerned about, like electing the next president, or watching your child go off to war.

"Really, all these moms bemoaning a kid actually opening gifts at a party? OMG! The humanity! Is this the continuation of the mentality of 'let's give them all a trophy so no one's feelings get hurt?' Guess what? In life, everyone does *not* get a trophy, you are not *all* the best at everything. At twenty, or thirty, or forty, your kid is going to want things they cannot have, and they are going to have to deal with it. I fear a future of grown-up children who cannot handle these truly harsh realities of life, like being denied an iPhone," wrote one. Well, in my daughter's defense, her feelings weren't hurt at all that her friend got an iPhone before she did. She just wanted her own damn phone. And aren't you taking this a tad too far? I just mentioned that I didn't like unveiling expensive presents at a party, not that I'm on a crusade to stop them. I'm far too lazy for that. I have kids to raise, you know, and a manicure appointment to make.

But the post on Mommyish.com really did create a kerfuffle over whether or not it's a bad idea to open birthday presents at a party. It went on and on. The commenters who like it when people open gifts are really, really keen about it. Check out this comment: "Personally, I still think it's a great idea … When you pick out a gift for someone and go to the trouble to wrap it and give it to them, it's awesome to be able to see their expression when they open it … It gives the recipient valuable practice in graciously accepting gifts and thanking the gift-giver, even if the present is the most hideous hand-knitted Santa sweater you've ever seen, lovingly created by your half-blind Great Aunt Myrtle ... We also have an epidemic of kids who can't handle seeing someone else get something (an award, trophy, present, whatever), unless they get one, too. Kids need to learn that it's not always going to be about you, and you're not always going to get the present. When it's your birthday, it will be your turn. But when it's not your birthday, you need to learn how to graciously watch and share in the celebration, while the birthday kid opens his presents, without throwing a hissy fit because you want one, too."

Wow, serious much? Really, my daughter has never thrown a hissy fit at a friend's birthday party, and the last birthday party my daughter was invited to (three days ago), I went out and picked out a very specific gift, based on what the birthday girl loves (dogs). Her mother took the present from me, and the kid didn't even seem to *care* about any of the gifts. I wasn't offended at all. I can't remember the last time a kid actually opened a gift I gave her in front of me. I think of children's birthday gifts as a way to even out the score. Like, "Hey! You're taking my kid to trampoline to celebrate your kid's birthday? Great. Here's her gift in return for babysitting my daughter for three hours and feeding her lunch!" I still have no idea if my daughter's friend ever opened the present I bought for her. I probably never will. Do I care? No.

Of course, there had to be one troll who wrote, "What the fuck does a nine-year-old need a MacBook Air for?" Well, it's for something called homework! And also to show me funny videos on YouTube, and play "Dumb Ways to Die." All my daughter's homework is now online, and "Dumb Ways to Die" is a hilarious game, and, as I said earlier, I won't let her touch my computer. And for all the sanctimonious mamas who called me out for calling a friend, not to complain about the gift she gave her daughter in front of everyone, but to complain about my daughter wanting an iPhone after the party, did they not read the most important part? Which is that I said no to my daughter despite her attempted manipulation and begging. Is that not a huge triumph for a parent? Could the Mob Moms not at least acknowledge that I did a good thing as a parent? Apparently, the answer is a big NO, wrapped, I hope, in fancy tissue paper with a bow.

Designer Jeans

I understand how cute the jeans are,
but do you know how fast kids grow? She'll
be wearing them for two months and then
outgrow them. I'd say to save the money
for something else, like her education.

I blame it on being a first-time mother. What did I know? I was not born a mother; I became one when I had a baby. No one is born a mother. I thought the designer jeans for my then two-year-old daughter were adorable. How could I not? I didn't even know they made True Religion jeans for practically babies when I happened to come upon a pair that I couldn't resist buying. After my purchase, I blogged about the $140 pair of jeans I had just bought. I asked readers, "Would you spend $140 on a pair of jeans for a two-year-old?" I was, albeit after the fact, looking for guidance and perhaps to assuage my guilt for spending so much money.

This just happened to be one of my first and most controversial blogs on parenting. I posted it on my own blog, Ninepounddictator.com, which I no longer write. It was after I wrote this post, and saw the hundreds of comments come in, that I thought, "Hmm. Other mothers don't always think the same way I do. That's strange!" I also realized that this parenting gig has high stakes, and that, sadly, moms can be the worst critics of one another. It's the Judgmental Mother Syndrome all over again. A lot of mommy blog readers, and writers, suffer from this. Some doctor or scientist will start working on a cure for it, I'm sure, as soon as they find a cure for diabetes and cancer. Judgmental moms seem to be an epidemic.

Did I need to buy my daughter this pair of expensive designer jeans? No, of course not. But I *so* needed to, in the way that women need another black cocktail dress, the kind of black dress that is almost identical to the dozens of other black dresses hanging in their closet.

Some mothers attacked me as if I were spending my daughter's future college money at a casino slot machine. Or, make that, spending *their* hard-earned money in a casino. What I was actually thinking when I saw the jeans in an American store was, "Oh, my God! How cute are these? I need to get them!"

"I understand how cute the jeans are, but do you know how fast kids grow? She'll be wearing them for two months and then outgrow them. I'd say to save the money for something else, like her education," wrote one. Well, I didn't know how fast kids grow. She was my first. I know now! Which is why I'm only too happy to accept hand-me-downs for my son and buy him eight-dollar snow pants. And I wish I had read her comment before I purchased the jeans, though I'm not sure it would have stopped me, they were that adorable.

"Wow, I'd never tell someone how to run their life, and you've probably just posted this to rock the boat, but in my opinion $140 for a pair of toddler jeans is just plain gross," contributed another mother. "American excess (gluttony) at its finest." I can see where this poster was coming from. How many of us Canadians, when we sit down at an American chain like The Cheesecake Factory, are appalled by the quantity of food on our plates? Before you can even finish your drink, which comes in pint-size glasses at least, the server is asking if you want a refill. Meanwhile you're grinding your teeth, trying not to say loudly so everyone in the restaurant can hear, "Um, this one meal could feed a family of four! What do you do with the leftovers?" And people are so shocked that there is an obesity problem in North America.

I admitted that it was idiotic to buy a pair of designer jeans for a two-year-old, but maniacal mothers jumped all over me anyway, as if I had just tricked them into investing in a Ponzi scheme.

"First time commenter. I stumbled upon this blog a few weeks back and now I've become addicted. I'm not quite sure why. Perhaps I enjoy reading about a hip mother. But $140 for a pair of jeans is ridiculous. I understand they are True Religion, and it's all about the brand name. But Rowan will never know the difference, and she will just grow out of them in a few weeks. Either way, she's lucky that when she is older and becomes a fashionista, she has a mom who understands and will buy her what she wants," wrote one. I was glad that this poster was addicted to my blog. But, um, no: I am not that hip, and I don't buy my daughter expensive clothes regularly, if ever, nowadays. (Luckily, she has an amazing grandmother, who is way more hip when it comes to children's clothes than I am, and splurges on her only granddaughter.) But message boards, as this poster mentioned, can be addictive, especially nowadays when comments are fierce and often more of a draw than the blog itself. And I have never bought her everything she wants, and never will.

Another suggested that "expensive jeans are only expensive because they are expressly created to make women's flawed bums look better, right? And your daughter already has a perfect little baby bum, so why the need for the expensive jeans?" Good point. My daughter's baby butt was perfect! And they would look even more perfect in the designer jeans!

But, no, I didn't make her try them on—I couldn't find her in the store—and watch her walk out of the changing room and exclaim, "Those really lift your butt cheeks, babe!"

Another commenter was worried about the message it sends to, I suppose, other two-year-olds. This mother wrote, "No way would I spend that money on jeans for my baby girl. No way. Not because it's out of our budget range, but because of the message it sends, that you're a better person if you have the right brand of jeans on. I want my girl to feel confident in herself from within. I want to instill that in her before she's faced with all the BS she'll get in school about wearing the right brands, or you're not cool because your jeans are from the Gap, not Sevens. Why start it now? Why encourage it now? Do enjoy your blog though!" There's no way I could be mad at this poster, because, after all, she enjoys my blog!

Still, I want to say my daughter could not have cared less about what brand of jeans they were. She didn't know what a brand is. She was too busy hiding behind the racks of clothing, and jumping out and scaring other customers to care, and, truthfully, I never had the talk with her about brand names versus non-brand names, and still haven't, eight years later. What normal adult believes that wearing a brand makes you a better person? What mother doesn't want to instill confidence in their children? At that time, our talks centered more around, "If you have to go to the washroom you have to tell me before, not as you are peeing." In fact, flash forward eight years, and now, at age ten, my daughter still doesn't care about brands, but she does know when she needs to take a bathroom break, at least.

Amazingly, there were just as many commenters who thought that buying a toddler designer jeans was an excellent idea, as there were opposed to brand-name shopping, which kind of balances things out.

"Wow. People are sure assholes. Jealous much? Buy whatever you want for her, and use whatever means necessary to justify it. I do. I bought myself some clothes from Victoria's Secret, and justified it by saying I had been so good lately and working so hard. So what if she doesn't know the brand name? You will, and that's all that matters. Also, what's the point in working hard and earning lots of money, if you can't use it to spoil those around you? None," wrote one. I understand completely women buying themselves nice gifts for being good and working hard, because I do it all the time. But, trust me, it wasn't as if I was going to parade my daughter around in these designer jeans, with a sign around her neck reading, "Look at my designer jeans!"

"Live life! That's what it's for!" wrote one mom, even though the jeans weren't for me. Another mother added, "Why not? If they're cute? Besides, I always justify expensive kids' clothes by thinking that I will save them for my next baby, or pass them down to someone else." I hadn't planned at that point on having another child, but I did plan on eventually framing the jeans, because they were so damn adorable, or at least dressing one of her stuffed animals in them, so I would have them forever. Now I am so lucky to have a friend who only bought designer clothes for her son, just a year older than mine, because I get all his hand-me-downs.

Other commenters had the green-eyed monster, which made me laugh. "Is it bad that at twenty-six, I'm insanely jealous of a two-year-old's jeans? Work it Rowan!" wrote one. Trust me, I've always been jealous of my daughter's wardrobe, and I'm forty! I really can't wait until she's my size and I can borrow her clothes!

I also discovered that I'm not plugged into small-fry fashions: apparently there are a lot of expensive designer jeans for toddlers, and I purchased the wrong brand. "I can't believe how mean-spirited some people are. As for the jeans, does Blue Cult do infant wear? Much hipper than True Religion," wrote another commenter. I'll look into it, but I definitely won't write about it!

But then my post about toddler jeans turned into something completely different, which, in the mommy blogosphere, is an all-too-common occurrence. "Ladies," wrote one. "You have opened up a can of worms! My cousin last year almost got engaged. Why almost? Because she refused to wear the engagement ring. The fiancé makes more than $200 grand a year, and he collects cars as a hobby. So she expected a $20K ring. But he didn't think a ring was important enough to cost more than $10 grand. Now, honestly, does it matter, and why? What does the price tag show? His love? Her commitment? Priorities? Who says how much we should spend on different items?"

I'm not sure about this woman's cousin, and I'm not a couples therapist (I could get you some names), but how does one go from an article about toddler jeans to a cousin who refuses to wear an engagement ring because she didn't think it was expensive enough? I just have to shrug when this happens. Often the comments make no sense in relation to the post. Sometimes, I think, posters just need to vent, and when all their friends or their pets get sick of hearing them complain, they turn to message boards. And why not?

As for those $140 jeans? Well, my daughter wore them once—for about three seconds. Not because she didn't fit into them, but because she hated wearing any sort of pants or jeans. I never saw that coming. She wore only dresses or skirts for the next three years. But it wasn't a complete waste of money. A good friend's daughter really loved the jeans, which I had passed on to her. And I saved a lot of money on any kind of jeans or pants for the next three years, after learning that my daughter hated wearing them, which means I actually saved money in the long run, right? (Yeah, I can pretty much justify anything.)

My favorite comment, which also happened to be one of the wisest, was, "Hate to beat this topic to death, but I don't think you should do it. I mean, why spend money on designer jeans for a kid when you can spend it on yourself?" Good point. Very, very good point. I just wish this commenter had been shopping with me at the time. I could have used her sound advice.

part six

Can We Please
Just Admit It?

School Concerts:
A Necessary Evil

*I completely agree with your feelings on
school concerts. I don't care about any children
other than my own. Not even a little. However,
I suffer through it, because it results in me seeing
my child perform. And every other parent in
the room is doing the same thing.*

The only time I lock my daughter in the basement is when she brings home a musical instrument from school. I know. I know. I'm supposed to be proud that she can sort of eke out the song "Twinkle Twinkle" on her violin. I'm supposed to be super-proud that she can play "Three Blind Mice" on the recorder. I'm really not, which is why I not only lock her in the basement, but I also got the basement sound-proofed! I'm not kidding. Can't we mothers all agree that a child's first attempts to play a musical instrument are super-painful to listen to? Like you kind of want to take that violin bow and stab yourself in the eye or hide it somewhere high where it can't be found? Or shove that recorder under your couch pillows and be all, "I'm not sure where it is. Sorry. You'll just have to practice later! Like when mommy goes to the gym or grocery shopping. I'll find it just before I leave, I promise!"

Even my ten-year-old is smart enough to know she is not a prodigy on either the violin or recorder, although she is a talented singer. She laughs when I say, "Take it down to the basement, babe!" when she brings home a musical instrument. I'm pretty objective when it comes even to my own children. Yes, I think it's important to learn how to read music, but unless you're dedicated to an instrument, you will never get good at it. So unless my daughter practices the recorder, violin, or piano for an hour every single day, I'm going to have to deal with ear-shattering noise when she practices! So, when writing about school concerts for Mommyish.com, I admitted that I really hate them. What's more, I hate the fact that I'm supposed to actually look forward to them.

Now, at the start of the school year, my first call is to the junior school administrator who tells me when the Christmas concert is. My second call is to my travel agent to book plane tickets, so I can miss the school concert. Parenting is all about planning, whether it's to get your child to school on time, book a dentist appointment, or skip the school concert.

I remember one of my friends asking me a couple years ago how my daughter's school concert went. "Brutal," I answered. "It was brutal." I felt as if I had been locked in an auditorium for fourteen hours with someone breathing down my neck, while also fighting off a migraine, which made my eyelids tremble. To this day, I can hear the ringing in my ears from the sound of screeching recorders and other off-key string instruments, which is weird, because I was also falling asleep. Don't even get me started about the band. I told my daughter that if she dared bring home a band instrument, I wouldn't let her in the door. Her stepsister once brought home a tuba from school, and let me just ask, "Why do they have to play anything?" (She was pretty good, but I was especially disgusted when she had to clean up all her spit that gathered in the tuba. Talk about gross!)

Part of the problem is that school concerts are so damn long. It was great when my daughter was in grade one, because generally the school organizes concert performances starting with the younger grades, and the older grades come on later. So when she was in grade one, I could watch her perform, and then sneak the heck out of there. But by the time she was in grade four, I knew I'd have to stay for practically the two full hours, just to see her class contribute to the entertainment. You know what is entertaining at school concerts? When I see the one kid in the class who refuses to sing and instead is focused on picking his nose. Now *that's* entertainment. I have to ask, and I want your brutally honest answer: "Do you care if you see or hear anyone else perform but your *own* child or children (and—maybe—the child of a relative or a good friend who is also performing)?"

"I completely agree with your feelings on school concerts. I don't care about any children other than my own. Not even a little. However, I suffer through it, because it results in me seeing my child perform. And every other parent in the room is doing the same thing," admitted one commenter on Mommyish.com. So can we all agree that school concerts or holiday performances are a beautiful and yet unbearable event? Well, apparently not.

For me, attending a school concert is like being in a restaurant, hating your meal, but being too lazy or reticent, when the server asks, "How's your food?" to actually tell the truth. For Mob Moms, however, school concerts are the happiest moments of their lives, or so it seems, and they mean something and are life lessons. "A concert," wrote one, "is to give students a goal to work towards, to encourage them to practice … and perfect their performance, and then to experience performing something they worked hard on in front of an audience. That is a valuable life experience, not something fluffy. Kids need to see that working on something pays off, and that adults support this."

This is most likely true, but are Mob Moms tone deaf? Even if we all agree that performing in front of an audience is a positive experience for children, can we not also admit that they sound like cats in heat? And that's being kind. Even the vicious raccoons fighting in my backyard sound like a celestial harp by comparison.

"It can be upsetting for the last group of kids to come out to a nearly empty audience or watch adults leave," wrote another on Mommyish.com. "Plus it's disruptive." No, you know what's disruptive? Having to take my daughter to school, only to come back forty-five minutes later for the concert, drive around to find a parking spot, and then sit in a room while my work is not being done, six-year-olds are playing their damn recorders, and I'm trying to daydream until my child hits the stage. *That's* disruptive.

And how come Mob Moms can't admit that we're not at the fucking Met, and that their children are not all that talented? I'm listening in a gymnasium for God's sake! "Nice example you set for your kid. 'I am allowed to be rude if I find something boring,'" wrote one. Well, as I said, they're not all boring. The nose-pickers are hilarious. The mothers in the audience trying to encourage their stage-struck kids to sing by waving their hands manically over their heads are not boring—they're hilarious. And sometimes, if you are extremely lucky, you'll have a great parent friend to whisper to during the performance, until your kid's class hits the stage. The most entertaining school concert I ever attended was super-enjoyable, not because my daughter was singing or playing the recorder, or whatever it is they were trying to accomplish on stage, but because I ran into a male friend whose kids also go to my daughter's school. We got to hang out, which was great, but even better, his ex-wife had just returned from rehab for the third time, and he shared some great stories. I know, right?

Stories about rehab and coke-addicted mothers are so much more entertaining than what may be "Have Yourself a Merry Christmas," or *could be* "Yellow Submarine," but you really have no fucking clue, because the kids on stage can be that bad. Instead of making the kids perform eighteen mediocre, at best, songs, why not have them play or sing three really good songs? Better yet, teach them to hip hop dance or something more modern than the recorder.

"It's like two hours out of your entire year, tops. Forget about yourself for a few minutes," wrote another. Mob Moms love saying this almost as much as they love using the term *Real Moms*. "If you can't suffer through the horror of listening to other kids sing to hear your own, then God bless you. I wish that was my biggest problem," another mom chipped in. And another: "It's only two hours out of your time." Mob Moms will say something like this about everything from hosting birthday parties to trick-or-treating, to helping kids with homework. It's always, "It's just two hours …" but when you say that about every aspect of parenting, those two hours here and those two hours there add up to be roughly 624 hours in a year. And if you are a working mother, and really can't get more time off, losing that time at the office adds to your stress and guilt if you can't make it or have to rush back to the office. And even if it *is* only two hours out of my life, it feels like eighteen! School functions are endless. Honestly, I now think of my daughter's school as a lifestyle, because there are a million things I'm invited to attend each week.

One poster wrote, "Our schools used to have a finale where the whole school performed. The reason? To keep parents from leaving after their kid performed." See, teachers are onto mothers like me. Or they, too, know that it can be brutal for parents. So they have to manipulate us to stay, which is understandable and admirably cunning.

"My mother and father never made it to any of my school shows or plays during the day. I can't say that I feel all that deprived, to be honest," wrote one. See? Contrary to some Mob Moms, I don't think I'm depriving my child either, not when we're lying on a fabulous, sun-drenched beach, or parasailing on calm blue water, because I booked our vacation to start the day before the concert. The last thing on our minds is that we are missing the school concert.

Some Mob Moms shared my opinion. "*Kudos!* I was so itching to write this article, but you beat me to it! Can I tell you I think that you expressed the sentiment of *most* if not all parents? And truth be told, the feeling of, OMG! This again! usually strikes after you've endured several performances. Yes, in the beginning, kids' concerts are totally adorable, and, yes, as a parent, what you want most to do is see your kid perform and then jet. Last year, my huzza and I sat fidgeting in our seats for the last hour of the concert when our daughter and her classmates were no longer on stage. It was painful," wrote one cute poster. I know, in real life—that is, not hidden behind a computer screen—most of us would have on our faces expressions of suppressed horror, or at least, boredom, but we hide this behind a plastic smile, because, God forbid, we don't look like we're watching and hearing Beyoncé perform. This poster continued, "I think there has to be a better way, like maybe concerts should last no longer than an hour. Or maybe serve the parents cocktails? I kid. *Something.*" Oh, I do not *kid*! I say, "Give me two shots of tequila when I walk in, even if it's at 10 A.M., and then I'll definitely enjoy the show!" And, hey! Maybe schools should consider having a cash bar in the back before the start of a student concert. It could be justified as a way to raise money for charity. I'm sure many more mothers and fathers would enjoy themselves if drinks were an option, and some charity would benefit. It's a win-win!

A few moms in the blogosphere actually seem to care about the negative reaction my articles sometimes generate, which is super-sweet. "Rebecca, I really hope people receive your article nicely this week, because (a) I'm tired of watching the hateful messages on so many articles on this site, and (b) you are absolutely right! It's not just Christmas concerts either. Dance recitals, piano recitals, it's all the same. I'll go. I'll stay the whole time (I don't really agree with showing up late or leaving early). I'll applaud your kid and mine, but I'll be replaying scenes from *Pulp Fiction* in my head the entire time." Right? *Pulp Fiction* is an amazing movie. Good choice! "I also agree with Rebecca, just not the way she went about it. I think this is one of those situations where you keep how you *really* feel to yourself. I can think of lots of instances where how I react, and how I'd like to react, are completely different." But isn't mommy blogging a way for mothers to commiserate with one another about unrealistic parenting expectations, showing up to a school concert and loving it, for one? Why not just admit that you hate them, too? It doesn't make you a less loving mom. It makes you a human who isn't tone deaf. Plus, the argument that you should keep how you feel to yourself, well, there goes the entire concept of blogging. If I can't complain about school concerts in a blog, then I can't complain about how expensive gas is either. I should, obviously, put on my plastic "I'm so into this!" smile, and keep how I feel to myself. And, of course, I'm writing my thoughts on a blog, not telling my daughter how I hate concerts (although she is well aware of this, and doesn't seem to care). I'm not yelling out, "You suck!" after each class performs. I'm sitting there, quietly popping Advils, trying not to fall asleep, and guessing what song they are performing up there, like most others in the audience.

Hilariously, even teachers hate school concerts. "I am a music teacher and I hate the recitals just as much as the parents. Either don't go, or if you do ... stay till the end. It's two hours out of your life, suck it up. Leaving mid-performance, or *talking* during the entire performance, is just plain rude," wrote one. But if you admit to being both a music teacher and hating school concerts, and even suggest we don't go, then why do you expect us to look forward them?

Another woman wrote: "I think it must be a Christmas/ Hanukkah miracle! I actually agree with you, Rebecca. Even as a kid I *hated* sitting through the performances of others, and as an adult I find them mind-numbingly boring ... I'm pretty sure anyone who's ever sat through a kids' holiday concert would have to agree with your basic message."

I'm glad some posters shared my opinion that children's concerts are a horrid, but necessary evil. I was also surprised to learn how many adults play the recorder. I, for one, have never been to a dinner party where the host has pulled out a recorder to entertain guests. I have a friend whose husband can ride a unicycle, but that's not quite the same thing. "The recorder has been around for a long time. It was just re-popularized for use in the public schools by Carl Off, because it's fairly easy for kids with developing motor skills. But there's a vast repertoire of recorder music (mostly from the Baroque period and earlier), and I know a lot of adults, like myself and my husband, who get a great deal of joy from both playing and listening to the recorder," wrote a recorder-lover on Mommyish.com. Please, then, come to one of my child's concerts, and see if you still feel the same. But at least I now know whom to blame for forcing kids to learn the recorder: that man is Carl Off, apparently. These days, children learn motor skills by playing Xbox games. Another adult recorder-lover wrote, "Professionals play handcrafted wooden recorders, which come in several sizes and registers, and actually require a great deal of skill and training to play." Well, my daughter is no professional. But it is interesting to know that there are adults who love the recorder, when I thought it was just a cheap way for kids to learn music.

So, if I accidentally—oops!—book a trip somewhere warm for the day before my daughter's school concert, I swear, it was an honest mistake on my part. Not. "I just love the time of year when people can forget their differences to complain about the painfulness of school concerts," wrote a fellow sufferer on Mommyish.com. Couldn't have said it better myself. (P.S. If I'm there, meet me in the back of the auditorium! I'll have a flask of spiked eggnog.) And now that I have a second baby, I may just have enough time to convince the school that concerts wouldn't be so horrible for parents … if there were a cash bar.

Waiting Times.
Kill Me Now

Nice try at heading off criticism
regarding over-scheduling your child.
Frankly, this is a big-ass White Whine.

I have counted the hours I have to wait around for my daughter while she's at her extracurricular programs. I was so bored waiting for her one evening when she was at ballet, I actually calculated how many hours I spend waiting ... *while waiting*. That's how bored I was.

On Monday evenings, I wait one hour during her singing lesson. On Thursdays, I wait an hour and a half for her play practice. On Friday nights, I wait an hour and a half for her ballet classes, and on Sundays I wait another hour for her second ballet class of the week. That's five hours a week—almost an entire workday—that I generally sit in my car outside whatever studio she is at, praying my friends will be around to talk to me, or playing Boggle on my iPad. In one month, that's twenty hours I could be productive, and even though trying to beat my last high score on Boggle could be considered productive, it's not really. But trying to get an all-time high score at Boggle is all my chauffeur/mommy brain can handle after a long day and fighting traffic while driving her to these programs, and making sure she has her dance outfits or song books before we leave the house.

Of course, it turned out that the Mob Moms who read my post on Mommyish.com didn't care that I had to spend so much time waiting. They just thought that my daughter was over-programmed. She's not. She enjoys all these extracurricular activities and never complains about going. I'm the one who complains, not because she wants to do these things, but because I'm fucking bored waiting for the programs to end.

The problem is that most of these activities are only an hour long. Yes, I could sit and listen to her sing, but trust me, listening to a group of children sing the same songs over and over again, as they practice for the Big Performance, gets tedious, to say the least. By the time the actual play or concert comes around, I know pretty much every single song, and every single line from memory. I could be a fucking understudy in the play *High School Musical Two*, if the opportunity ever arose.

At her ballet lessons, they shut the curtains because, apparently, it's distracting for the kids if their parents watch. Which is a-okay with me. There's nothing more painful than watching a group of wannabe ballerinas practice flexing their feet over and over again for sixty minutes.

I suppose I could go for a walk, but usually it's cold and dark when her activities begin. I could read a book, but as many mothers can appreciate, my brain stops working at about 3 P.M. With only an hour, I can't even go grocery shopping. Rather, I don't want to. Why? Because I'm too friggin' tired! I may call friends or flip through a fashion magazine, but in the back of my head I'm just counting down the minutes, even seconds, until my daughter walks out.

Waiting for your child's activity to end is like having a newborn and going on endless walks. You have nowhere you need to go, so you end up at a drugstore just killing time, and maybe buying another tube of toothpaste to give yourself the feeling that you've accomplished something. There's no point in dropping off my daughter and then going home because, by the time I get home, I have to leave to pick her up again. Waiting for her makes me feel as if I'm wasting time. About all I have to show for it is my score in Boggle. (My high score now is 166.)

Mob Moms commenting on Mommyish.com often complain that my writing reads like I just ripped it off, meaning that I don't put any time or thought into it, which is their way of coming up with something—anything—about me to criticize. They wouldn't be Mob Moms if they couldn't come up with an insult: if it's not the topic of the post, it has to be the writing. Let me just say, for the benefit of all aspiring writers and mommy bloggers, it's much harder to make a post read like I'm just talking to a friend than it is to write something serious. (I know because I've written hundreds of serious journalistic pieces as well.) But blogs are different. Blogs are mostly supposed to be breezy, as if I'm conversing with my best friend. That's my style. But when this post about waiting around, bored out of my fucking mind, was uploaded, the first comment I got was, "You don't pen this column while you're waiting? Reads like it." Well, you have a good night, too!

A Mob Mom got into the whole, "You're over-programming your kid! You're an awful parent!" spat. As another commenter wrote, "My brother is like you. He chooses to over-schedule his children and then complains about his family life being so busy and chaotic. There is an easy fix. Have your daughter choose one activity per semester and cut your waiting time in half." But I'm not complaining that my life is too busy and chaotic. I'm complaining about how I'm bored to tears when I'm waiting. I think, in fact, I would be a worse parent if

I deprived my child of activities she loves doing, just because Mommy doesn't like hanging around. Now that would be selfish and not putting my child first, which is what Mob Moms say they believe you should do always. So which is it?

When I tried to explain that my daughter's activities didn't affect how busy my life was, the effort was pointless, to say the least. "Nice try at heading off criticism regarding over-scheduling your child. Frankly, this is a big-ass White Whine," wrote one mom, after I explained that my life was not too chaotic because of my daughter's programs. Perhaps the post did come across as a whine, but so what? Am I not entitled to a little whine? If not, then mothers should never complain about their job, their marriage, their weight, their mortgages, their children who refuse to eat vegetables, or anything else, which kind of misses the whole point of blogging. Like commenters who vent, this mommy needs to vent, too.

One responded with a really weird interpretation of what she thought I had written, which I hadn't. She wrote: "(1) I [meaning me] can afford to pay the fees for multiple expensive activities. (2) I don't lose time from work having to ferry my child to her activities. (3) I have an iPad to entertain my spoiled self while I wait and then I complain about being bored. Why is it that other writers on this and other sites manage to write articles while privileged without sounding like people who need a time-out?" Here was more proof that Mob Moms read way, way too much into blogs. I had written about how much time is wasted, and how boring it is to wait for children while they are in dance class. Do you hate me because I have an iPad? Or do you not like it when I vent, because I chose to be a mother, and therefore should shut the hell up and stop complaining forever about anything? But I'm pretty sure other mothers have felt this about waiting for their children's activities to end. I can't be the only one. I know this because sometimes I talk to other mothers at these practices, and they, too, are constantly checking their watches, as if counting down the approach of midnight on New Year's Eve.

Another thing: as a mommy blogger, you can't mention anything you own—such as an iPad—without someone assuming you're as wealthy as the founders of fucking Facebook. How do you know how much my daughter's activities cost? Am I really that spoiled for having an iPad?

Waiting is like one big time-out; it can be that painful. It makes me sympathize with my son when he sits out his time-outs after he bites someone, except he screams, and I am just silently irritated.

Other Mommyish.com commenters offered suggestions, as if I couldn't possibly come up with my own. But I appreciated their efforts. "Try bringing a laptop (or loading some of the work-related apps onto your iPad) and do work or virtual chores. While waiting at my child's activities, I have done budgeting, to-do lists, created/edited documents and a host of other work, volunteer, and personal projects, while using my laptop and iPad. Working like this during wait time has saved me a lot of late nights and has allowed me to take on volunteer projects that I otherwise would not have had time for." Do you know what I thought when I read this mother's comment? I thought, Wow! You are one organized and busy mommy! Can you be my assistant? You sound fantastic! You're hired!

Other Mob Moms were concerned about my safety, which I thought was pretty fantastic, considering they don't know me. Some seem to worry about me more than my own mom. "For your sake and your child's, I want you to stop waiting outside in the car. Wait inside the facility your daughter is in or at a nearby coffee shop and read good, interesting books for a change. Waiting in a car on a lonely parking lot or on the street is perhaps not the safest and smartest thing to do.

There are just too many criminally minded and/or deranged people with loaded guns out there these days. Remember that your safety and security is paramount, and sitting alone in a car all these hours is perhaps not a good/great idea. Be safe!" That was really sweet, and I'm sure it's totally bad timing for me to make a joke, such as, "Someone *please* blow my brains out while I am waiting in the car alone. I'm so fucking bored!"

Others, of course, commented with my favorite line of all time when it comes to mommy blogging, aside from the term *Real Mom*. This line, as one commenter succinctly put it, is, "Wow, First World problems." Well, I suppose they are First World problems. I never said they weren't. But my job as a mommy blogger is not to write about Third World problems— there are newspapers and other blogs for that—but to write about what mothers go through in a humorous and relatable way, which often, as you can see, is difficult to accomplish, when so many people have so many conflicting opinions. And I know, like most mothers who follow the news, there are horrific things going on in the world. Just because I'm a light-hearted mommy blogger doesn't make me uncaring, or unaware of what most of the world's children go through. Don't most people in First World countries know that in countries across the globe, babies and children are dying every day? It truly breaks my heart. But are horrifying blogs about kids being murdered, abused, or suffering from horrible diseases what you were really expecting to read on a mostly fun and entertaining parenting blog? And, frankly, isn't motherhood endlessly fascinating? And isn't there always something to complain about, or discuss, even if we're not raising our kids in a Third World country?

The problem sometimes with mommy blogging is that I'm the only one who thinks it's funny! That's my First World problem! Of course, I definitely believe that it's important to stay updated on what's going on in the world, but aren't you reading my blog to hear how my son bit me so hard that I had teeth marks on my cheek for three days, how my daughter wrote the alphabet in ink on her newly painted wall, or how to pack for a family of six?

Another commenter stuck to the same theme: "Wow—talk about First World problems! I have a daughter the same age as yours, and I also have an infant son. Unlike you, however, I don't have a nanny, and my husband works several nights a week, so I have to bring an eight-month-old with me to soccer practice, piano lessons, and Girl Scouts. We could not afford to pay the fees for these activities by ourselves, but we have been fortunate to receive help from my daughter's grandparents (the gift of a class or registration fee in lieu of toys or clothes for Christmas, birthdays, etc.). It's sometimes quite a challenge to keep my son occupied during my daughter's activities, and, frankly, I would love the chance to zone out by reading a magazine or by playing a game by myself. Consider yourself lucky." Obviously, this mom was a regular follower—she knows all about me (or thinks she does). I can write something and have people throw out the fact that I have a nanny, as if that will cut back on my waiting time, and I didn't even mention in this post anything about my nanny. Mob Moms, while at the same time saying, "I hate Eckler's writing, you should fire her," clearly remember every single post I have ever written, like they all have photographic memories. *I* can't even remember what I write from one week to another.

One commenter actually wrote something like, "Why don't you get your nanny to chauffeur her?" Well, unfortunately, that isn't part of my nanny's job description, not to mention that she finishes work at five, doesn't have a driver's license, and, for that matter, doesn't know how to drive.

Other moms jumped down my throat for, of all things, having my daughter in singing lessons. One wrote, "I would really, really encourage you to re-think the hour-long weekly voice lessons … The basic idea, and I say this as a professional singer and voice teacher myself, is that a nine-year-old is too young and immature vocally to benefit much from intensive vocal training. In fact, while her vocal cords, which are still very delicate at the age of nine, are still developing, it could actually do much more harm than good if she's singing inappropriate literature that's too mature for her vocal maturity." So many mothers seem way too concerned about my parenting decisions. However, after reading this comment, I did talk to her singing teacher, who has taught children to sing for twenty years. He waved it off, saying that it has never been a problem, and he doesn't strain their voices beyond their years. I was reassured by his answer, although I wasn't really worried before I spoke to him, until Mob Moms commented. See? Sometimes I do heed the concern of Mob Moms.

Still, I didn't, as readers seem to assume, pick some random music teacher off Craigslist.com or the subway platform. I did some research before I signed my daughter up with this teacher. So, I wonder, why are mothers always so concerned about my daughter—and her vocal chords—as if I didn't give a crap about her at all?

Happily, not all mothers found fault in this post. "I can't believe people flipped out over this article! She invests in her daughter's future. She lets her daughter explore her interests and sharpen her skills. And she has the audacity to not *enjoy* spending twenty hours per month waiting around? OMG! Alert the authorities! Call CPS!" wrote one. (Please don't give them any ideas!) "Or, you know, admit that you wouldn't enjoy it either," this poster continued. "I spend sixteen hours per month invested in my daughter's activities. She has one hour of dance on Wednesday and another hour on Thursday. She has one hour of soccer practice on Monday and one hour for a soccer game on Saturday." Like me, this mother says her daughter's schedule is not overloaded, and her daughter is not exhausted. But she's right. I have the *audacity* to not enjoy spending twenty hours a month waiting around. It's as if I said I don't enjoy sweet potato fries. (I don't. And, trust me, I've been yelled at for not liking them. Some people are really offended by anyone who doesn't like sweet potato fries.) This poster added, "And I get bored out of my mind waiting for her." Thank you! I'm not the only one. It's okay to admit it. Don't worry. I'm certain you're a fabulous mother!

Another poster summed up my sentiments exactly: "Let's be serious. Any parent/guardian who has experienced a crowded dance studio has to have an idea of what I'm talking about. Forty parents, an array of kids coming and going, shuffling teachers ... while we sit at the table nearest our kids' studio and wait for the hour to be over. That's not serious work time. I read sometimes, but it's still hard to concentrate. I also write, but every time I open a document, I find some wide-eyed child reading over my shoulder. I can watch my daughter's practice, but there's only so many times I can watch passé, first position, plié, again. Same with soccer: drills and more drills. I am forever grateful that we have been blessed with the time and money to let her do these things ... But that doesn't change the fact that, as her mother, I can still get bored." Ta-da! An honest mother in the blogosphere! I don't want to make any assumptions, but do the mothers who don't get bored waiting for lessons to end also love watching "Thomas the Train" (fucking boring!), or taking their toddler to the park for the *third time* in one day (really fucking boring!). As this poster summed up, "Instead of lambasting me or the author of this article, why not admit that you might get bored, too?" Mob

Moms, however, rarely admit the truth, which is that some aspects of parenting are *really fucking boring*.

I'll end with one commenter who made me chuckle. She wrote, "Try knitting! It's freezing outside where I live, and you just can't have too many sweaters or scarves, ever. Lately, I've even been wearing multiple sweaters. Start with the scarves, though, way easier than a sweater. Scarves and sweaters for everyone!" See how a post about how boring it is to wait around for your child can lead to some interesting suggestions? I'm off to the knitting store, because it's cold where I live, too. Joking. I'm going to beat my high score at Boggle by the end of the year. And, then, perhaps, I *will* teach myself to knit. Although, frankly, I still may be so bored waiting, that I might try and stab myself with a knitting needle. It's probably safer I stick with my iPad.

I Love Kids
Who Swear!

She resorts to using the f-word in the second sentence of this blog. She uses it liberally in other pieces, too. A writer who resorts to such words in a published piece likely uses the word all the time at home.

'm so glad when one of my posts inspires a laugh of recognition. Once this laughter would have been shared only with my close friends, but now I have a potentially unlimited audience to crack up. A lot of readers saw their own experience reflected in a post I wrote about swearing toddlers on Mommyish.com.

My son's first word was "fuck." Actually, what he meant was "truck," but in his baby babble it sounded remarkably like "fruck," which is what he calls his toy cars. "Fruck! Fruck! Fruck!" he'll say when he sees a truck on the road. To anyone, say, sitting beside us at a restaurant when he's playing with his toy "fruck," it sounds like he's saying, "fuck." So I hang my head in humiliation, wanting to tape his mouth shut, because I'm assuming, probably correctly, that everyone around me thinks he picked it up from me. He *could* have picked it up from me, because I tend to use the f-bomb a lot when I'm driving.

While I'm embarrassed when he appears to swear in public, I'm also biting my lower lip and taking a deep breath to stop from laughing. I mean, it is unfortunate that "fruck" was his first word, but also super-memorable. I'm one of those immature adults who laughs uncontrollably when a toddler says a bad word.

Kids who swear crack me up. They are just too awesome for words. One of my friend's kids had to go to the hospital when he was three, when a hot drink was spilled on him accidentally. When the doctor asked how it felt, my friend's toddler said, "It hurt like a bitch." I can so completely picture my friend's adorable son saying this, and each and every time I think of it, it brings a smile to my face.

I can't help but love seeing the appalled look on people's faces when my son says, "fruck." Usually, I admit, I'm the one egging him on, whispering in his ear, "What's that?" pointing at a truck, just so I can hear him say, "fruck!" in public, or when I need a good laugh.

Eight-year-olds swearing in public? Not so funny. Fifteen-month-olds swearing in public? Hilarious.

Mob Moms contributed some awesome stories to my post on Mommyish.com about my son's potty mouth. Some were sympathetic, too.

"My daughter used to pronounce truck like 'cock,'" wrote one. "So a walk around town would inevitably lead to the following: 'Look Mommy! Big cock!'" Yeah, I bet that kid fed many men's egos without knowing it, during that phase.

"My son's name is Asher," wrote another. "Sometimes Ash. Here's hoping he masters the *sh* sound early on, or he's going to be introducing himself as 'Ass.'" Ah, don't worry about it. People will love it! And you'll love seeing their reaction, even if you might want to hide your head in your armpit. But you'll also probably laugh, or others will. And Asher is a fantastic name!

"My now two-year-old son pronounced truck as 'cunt' for several months. Riotous laughter would ensue every time he pointed out a 'big, big cunt,' or a 'red fire cunt.' And then there was the time that I pointed out how dirty a truck was, just to hear him repeat that back to me," contributed another, who also finds it fun to encourage her toddler to swear. Really. I'd rather do that than almost anything.

"Apparently, when I was a toddler my mother and her friend were shucking corn for Thanksgiving, or something. I was like, 'Mommy, what are you doing?' And she replied, 'Shucking corn.' To which I replied, 'I want to fuck,'" wrote another. See? It's not the birthday parties or their first smiles we parents really remember. It's things like their first swear word!

"My daughter got to go on a boat ride when she was around two. She refused to call it a boat, though; she insisted on calling it a ship. She wanted to tell everyone she saw, 'I get to go on a ship.' What it came out as was, 'I go shit. I go shit!'" wrote another.

And yet another: "My cousin is a super-prim-and-proper church lady with never a hair out of place. I'll never forget the day her precious, perfectly dressed two-year-old tripped on the steps leading up to their house, fell down, picked herself up, shook herself off, and exclaimed, 'Well, God *damn*!' at the top of her little her lungs in front of all of us (who were gathered for a baby shower). I almost pissed my pants."

What is truly awful about thinking it's funny when kids swear is that it is pretty hard to get them to stop, because every time the little angel, who is not yet two feet tall, says "fuck," how can you not laugh? It's like an adult speaking after inhaling helium. It's funny! And, trust me, toddlers love seeing and making you laugh, and so they will say the bad word over and over again, until they finally catch on to the proper pronunciation. And that will be a sad, sad day.

"When my son used to say 'fork,' it sounded like 'fuck.' We had some friends over, and my son was asking for a 'fork,' and they gave us the oddest look because it sounded like he was asking for a 'fuck'!" added another on Mommyish.com.

The comment section became a hilarious place, where commenters competed to top one another with their favorite toddler swear-word stories. "My little brother was notorious for mispronouncing words," wrote one. "My personal favorite? His favorite song as a baby was Tom Jones' 'Sex Bomb.' It was the *only* thing that would automatically make him fall asleep, so my mom had it on repeat … until he started running around singing, 'sex bum, sex bum, I have a sex bum' … Many an awkward eyebrow was raised at my mother when we were out with him as a toddler." Well, I would rather that than my son, who will fall asleep only to Christmas carols.

Apparently, I got off easy with my son's habit of mispronouncing "truck." "You know what's worse?" asked a commenter. "When he pronounces that *tr* as a hard *c*. 'Cucks.' Add in baby mumble? Everywhere we went, 'Cock! Big cock! I want see da cock!' Not to mention 'blueberries' = 'boobies.' That's a fun one in the grocery store!"

"My older daughter couldn't say 'sit.' She spent six months telling everyone to 'shit down,'" added another.

At least all of us moms seem to agree that we need to rein in our swearing. I know I do, or should. I have one rule: I'm allowed to swear only when I'm in the car or in the house. Not all moms had funny stories to contribute. Some just wanted to wash my mouth out with Tabasco sauce, like I was the one saying "fuck" every second in public. Naturally they blamed me for my son's potty mouth.

"You expect us to believe that your son didn't learn the f-word from you? Please. Your articles are littered with the f-word," wrote one. Well, I may use a lot of "fucks" in my writing, but since my son is so young and not that bright just yet, seeing as he was eating *dog food from the dog bowl* last night, I doubt he is reading my blog. And then there's the fact that he was trying to say "truck," so there's that, too.

But Mob Moms continued to argue with each other over whether or not it was me who was responsible for my son's unintentional swearing. "She resorts to using the f-word in the second sentence of this blog. She uses it liberally in other pieces, too. A writer who resorts to such words in a published piece likely uses the word all the time at home," wrote one of my many critics. To which another responded, "Please. Writing something down for a blog post on a site for adults is completely different from how one speaks out loud, or around family. My husband has the *worst* potty mouth. Except around kids or polite company, when he wouldn't even dream of uttering those words."

And then one poster commented on a family member who was seventeen years old and had a speech impediment, and when she said "shirt," it sounded like "shit." "It's led to some awkward moments ... but she thinks it's funniest of all!" That's because she's probably very confident, which is obviously a good trait! But, inevitably, another Mob Mom wrote in, "I'm a speech pathologist. She [meaning the seventeen-year-old] should really see about getting this cleared up. She's probably going to have a hard time being taken seriously as an adult, applying for jobs and whatnot, if she continues to misarticulate words." To which another commenter wrote, "What makes you think she hasn't already seen a speech therapist? One of my good friends has a really bad stutter and she's just learned to embrace it. Believe me, she has had tons of speech therapy." Plus, I hate the word *whatnot*.

Some people who post on mommy blogs seem to think other parents are morons, and that because they are mothers, they try to mask their judgment, as seen above, in feigned concern and helpfulness. The girl they were writing about was seventeen! She's a young woman! She has a speech impediment, knows it, and can even laugh about it. Does the self-described speech therapist seriously think the girl, or her parents, haven't long been onto this? Why do Mob Moms automatically assume that we're not doing what's best for our kids, and that they could, and would, do better?

In the meanwhile, I'll probably keep egging my little guy on to point out trucks.

After all, I'm supposed to enjoy every single aspect of parenting, especially the milestones. And his first word, even though it sounded like "fuck," is a milestone. *Right?* And I have a feeling that this phase isn't going to last that much longer. So, now, I think I'll go shit him in his stroller, and we'll take a long walk looking for fucks!

Grade Five Math:
Suck It!

*Sorry, any functioning adult should be able
to do grade five math. This isn't a woman thing.
It's an ignorance thing, and it is not something to be
proud of. Nor is your attempt to conflate your
ignorance with your femininity.*

FML, I thought, when I first met my daughter's grade five math teacher during curriculum night at her school, which I blogged about. My daughter's self-confessed math-nut math teacher said to us parents: "And moms? You should not be waving off your daughters' math homework, and telling them to go ask their dads for help. You should be learning it with them!" Right! While I'm at it, I'll also learn to fly a fucking plane and magically become a supermodel. Exactly! It's so not happening.

I stopped understanding my daughter's math homework two years ago, when she was in grade three. That's because in the old days, when I learned math, we just had to memorize the fucking answers. We didn't also have to write out an explanation of how we got the right answer.

I have never been good with numbers. I still have to count on my fingers or use my phone's calculator to figure out the tip at a restaurant. I love restaurants that already add the tip onto the bill, because it takes me as long to figure out the tip than it did to eat my meal. I wanted to say to my daughter's math teacher that it was highly doubtful, in fact, totally not going to happen, that I would be learning math along with her, and that she, the teacher, would have to suck it up. I already did grade five math, woman! I did my time! Not only do I know, at my age, what I'm good at (typing quickly, tree pose), and what I'm bad at (math, cooking, not losing my ATM card weekly), but I also have a career, a baby, a fiancé, two stepchildren, friends, family, a yappy dog, and a daughter to chauffeur around. Where would I find the time, even if I wanted to, to learn math all over again? My brain hurts just thinking about it. It just makes me want to take a long nap.

I also was offended because this teacher assumed that most of us moms wave off the math homework. I mean, it's true that I do. In fact, I would ask a stranger on the bus to help my daughter, if it meant she wouldn't ask me for math help. (In fact, my daughter did do this to a man sitting beside her on an airplane once. He was more than happy to help, while I fell asleep.) But not all of us do this, right?

"You're offended that your child's teacher thinks you should be able to do fifth-grade math and that, in this culture, you might not want to send the message that math is a boy thing by passing it off to daddy? I mean, I'm not about to multiply two-digit numbers without a calculator in my daily life either, but taking the time to do it to show my daughter that women can be competent at math seems like a good idea," wrote one poster on Mommyish.com. It is a good idea if you go in thinking that women are not good at math. But I just happen to be a woman who also sucks ass at math. I don't suck at math because I'm a woman. I suck at math because I suck at math. The fact that I have a vagina doesn't, excuse the pun, enter the equation.

Many were sympathetic to my plight, not because of the gender stereotype, but because they too are bad at math. "I think most parents have trouble helping their kids with it when it gets advanced because, really, why would you remember stuff like algebra? You don't do it anymore, so you forget it," wrote one. Well, apparently, some Mob Moms are also math teachers, or should have been, or act like they are. "You don't remember it anymore?" one woman responded to the above poster. "I'm a housewife and while algebra isn't a part of literally every single day, it is something I use on a regular basis. Probably upwards of four to five days a week." Seriously? Are you kidding me? Like when?

Like a number of commenters, I, too, just couldn't help but wonder why and how this housewife uses algebra so often. "Curious," wrote one. "What situations are causing you to use algebra?" Another reader asked, "When do you use algebra? I never even took calculus, so I know I don't need that in real life. Of course, I want my son to do well in school, and I'll be very happy if he's good at math, but that doesn't mean I'm going to stress over the fact that I can't do it. If he ever saw how I struggle over it, that sure wouldn't be a break in any stereotypes that girls can't do math."

Another asked the poster who professed to use math almost daily, "In what ways do you use algebra with that frequency?"

Another wrote, "Trig is good for playing pool. That's the extent of my higher math in real life knowledge ... and I'm a grad student in a statistics-heavy field." It seems a lot of people only use math to win at pool. "Yup," wrote another, "that is the most important thing I learned in eighth-grade math—how to figure out where I need to aim a pool ball or putt a golf ball in order to sink it." So maybe, instead of learning math with my daughter from her textbooks or online math tutorials, I'll just take her to a pool hall or golf range. I'm willing to learn golf with her. Math? Nope. And who knew there were so many uses for math? Perhaps the housewife Mob Mom who professes to use math every day is at some pool hall every day … or golfing.

Even posters who use math regularly agreed with my sentiments.

"I use basic arithmetic, percentages, and basic geometry (I'm a quilter, otherwise I'd never use geometry) on a regular basis, but I do it all with the aid of a calculator. There's no way I could do long division on paper, never mind anything above sixth-grade level. I learned enough algebra in high school to pass the tests, and then promptly forgot it. I do think it's asking a bit much to expect parents to be as proficient at math as the math teacher, even at a fifth-grade level," commented one. Right, because if I were really into math, I would be a math teacher, a rocket scientist, or a doctor.

"If I had a time machine, one of the many things I would do [is] go hit my seventh-grade math teacher in the head with a smart phone," someone else, who obviously still has anger issues on the subject, wrote in the comments column.

Others, of course, were less sympathetic to my point of view. And some inevitably speculated that I have the brain of the fly that keeps soaring into a light bulb, zapping myself over and over again. "Sorry, any functioning adult should be able to do grade five math. This isn't a woman thing. It's an ignorance thing, and is not something to be proud of. Nor is your attempt to conflate your ignorance with your femininity." Again: I didn't say I hate math because I have a vagina. I hate math because, really, I don't get it. Also, why can't we pawn off some of the homework on Daddy?

"Look around the room," I wanted to tell the math teacher on the night I first met her. "There are, like, three men here for curriculum night, and the rest of us are mommies. Is it not apparent that we women, in real life, already take an interest in our child's education, or otherwise we wouldn't be here! Why aren't you asking where the dads are? Can we not ask our men to do anything, because we mothers have to do it all?" That seems to me to be a stereotype.

"Whatever, I'm on Eckler's side here. *Of course*, the idea that boys can do math and girls are always bad at it is a poor message to send, but she doesn't have to learn the math in order to refute that message. I am legitimately terrible in math, always was, and, yeah, sorry, I wouldn't be able to do fifth-grade math with the shit they're teaching them now. That doesn't mean it's not valuable. It just means I wouldn't be able to help my hypothetical child out in that subject," wrote another on Mommyish.com.

The housewife who uses algebra upwards of four times a week never did explain herself. This isn't surprising. Posters disappear into the ether sometimes, when they are attacked or questioned by other posters. Perhaps she was lying, or she was so busy doing algebra, golfing, or playing pool that she didn't have time to respond to the numerous people who were eager to hear her answer. We will never find out. It will be one of life's all-time mysteries.

But I don't think anyone can question another parent's devotion to their children, just because they can't help out with math. I especially don't think the math teacher can make that judgment. I'm glad this woman is my daughter's teacher, because she does, according to my daughter, make math exciting and fun. She is setting a great example and my daughter loves it. But will I be sitting there beside her trying to understand her math questions and how she came up with the answers? Nope. I may sit next to her reading *People* magazine, just so she knows that I care that she studies her math homework. But, as I said, I did my time, thanks very much. And, I admit, when it comes to math, I'm not smarter than a fifth grader … or even a third grader.

No, I'm Not Pregnant.
I Had the Damn Baby

There are only two situations where you can ask if a woman is pregnant: (1) if you can see parts of the baby coming out of her vagina; and (2) if you think you had a hand in putting the baby there.

Because, you know, we live in modern times, I thought that pretty much everyone in the entire world, especially women, would have learned never to say to another female anything along the lines of, "So when are you due?" or worse, "Congratulations! You're pregnant!" when maybe you just had a big lunch ... or already had the damn baby.

Shortly after I gave birth to my son, Holt, I attended a function at my daughter's school, where not one, not two, but *three* mothers said to me, "You look like you're ready to pop!" And, "You must be due any day now!" And, "You must so be ready to get that out of you!" What could I say, except, "I sure am!" Except I didn't say that at all. Why? Because I had given birth a week earlier! In the split second after I told each of these mothers that I already had the baby, each one changed her tune and expression to, "You look great!" And even, "You can't even tell you had the baby, your body is practically back to normal!" Really? *Really?* Because, literally, fifteen seconds earlier, they thought I was still pregnant and ready to pop it out of me!

I gain a daunting amount of weight when I'm pregnant, so much that even one of my very best friends in the entire world thought I was still pregnant after I gave birth. I went into labor a week earlier than my scheduled C-section, so the baby was delivered a week early. I didn't even have the chance to pack an overnight bag, let alone call my friends to tell them the news. So one of my closest friends stopped by my house, as a surprise, after I was released from the hospital with my newborn, the day before I was originally scheduled to go in for my C-section. I opened the door, and she handed me some flowers and said, "Good luck tomorrow." I was like, "Good luck for what again?" She looked at me incredulously. I looked at her questioningly. Finally she said, "You're having a baby tomorrow," in a tone that suggested I had lost all my brain cells after watching too many episodes of "The Real Housewives" (which, admittedly, I have, and so has she). I finally responded, "I had the baby six days ago." She laughed, not believing me. "I swear," I said. "I have proof!" And I led her to my baby, who was sleeping in a basket on the kitchen floor. "Wow. Is that really yours?" she asked. "Nah, I just borrowed it," I told her.

The point is that even one of my closest friends still thought I was pregnant when I answered the door, and I see her at least twice a week. I actually wondered if I had gained *more* weight, even though I had popped out the baby days earlier, and had been eating nothing but air since the second he came out of me.

I never ask women, even if I pretty much know they *are* knocked up, if they are pregnant, for exactly this reason. Perhaps they just gained weight, even if that weight looks like a basketball tucked under their shirt. I usually ask, "What's new?" and then wait until they tell me they are pregnant. Only then will I say, "That's so exciting! Yay!"

This was one post in which most commenters on Mommyish.com actually sympathized with me. As one wrote, "There are only two situations where you can ask if a woman is pregnant: (1) if you can see parts of the baby coming out of her vagina; and (2) if you think you had a hand in putting the baby there." So true. *So true.* And funny!

"I've had this happen a few times since the birth of my second kiddo," wrote another mom. "What I always find ridiculous about the situation is that I end up consoling the person who asked, because they are completely mortified, when all I really want to do is punch them." I agree completely. It is uncomfortable for both the person who is not pregnant, but may look it, and the person who congratulated her on her pregnancy (or rather, non-pregnancy). It's best for both parties to change the subject immediately to the weather or what Lindsay Lohan is up to these days.

Another poster explained, "I also had this happen. A week after giving birth, I went to a store and was asked how far along I was. 'Oh, I had the baby last week,' I answered. 'Oh, wow! You still totally look like you're pregnant,' the clerk said, a shocked look on her face. (Thank you. Because I don't already feel fat and unattractive. I just needed that extra slam.)" Who's with me that this sales clerk needs to be fired? Okay, maybe not fired, but maybe she needs a punch in the face? Okay, maybe not a punch in the face either, but karma is a bitch, and if this sales clerk ever ends up pregnant, hopefully at least one person will tell her, "Congratulations! You're pregnant!" five months after she has given birth. There should be a handbook for store employees telling them that when they see a woman who may be overweight, or possibly pregnant, they should never ask when the baby is due, even if they are going into labor in the store. Just call an ambulance and maybe give the woman in labor a discount card for when she comes back.

But that's not the worst. "I had two people within the space of five minutes congratulate me on my recent baby (then eight days old, which they knew, because they asked her age) and the baby I had on the way," wrote another. Yeah, sorry! I'm not a celebrity: the weight hangs around for more than a day or two after the baby's out. That, and, is it even possible to get pregnant after giving birth eight days earlier? Is that medically achievable? It seems unlikely, especially as no woman I know wants to have sex right after having a baby.

Some posters thought I shouldn't care. Not care that people still thought I was pregnant when I was not? I cared! I am a woman who was insecure about the seventy pounds I had gained while I was still sleep-deprived and recovering from a C-section. Excuse me for being a little sensitive! And I don't know one woman in the real world who doesn't complain about the weight she needs to lose after she's had a baby, or at least feels unattractive and insecure about it. But, apparently, there are some. They are just hidden behind their computer screens, or, most likely, lying.

"Who cares, since you knew you looked pregnant anyways? And those preschool moms knew you were pregnant and couldn't tell you had popped, so they were nice enough to ask you a friendly question, but it's horribly rude even though you admit you were still looking pregnant? Try a belly bandit if you have another baby. I can't believe all you commenters also find this offensive. At least you had a healthy baby. Lose the weight if you want; if not, chill out if someone does not know whether your due date is past. This has happened to me too, and it's not offensive. I had the opposite problem as the author, not so hungry while pregnant, craved sugar for energy after my second child. Got fat. What offends me more in public is when strangers hit on me, or bums make up stories about why they need $2. I'm busy shopping with three kids and don't have time for that BS. Better not visit China if you can't deal with people sharing their observations about your appearance. Maybe my travels there are the reason I have more tolerance for the little questions that bother the author and commenters?" wrote one Mommyish.com commenter. You had to travel to China to learn tolerance? What were you like before?

It sounds like this poster has a lack of tolerance or, rather, none at all. She doesn't have the time for a homeless person who asks for money? Or strangers hitting on her? Man, I would have loved a stranger to hit on me while I was, or still looked, pregnant. I would have loved a homeless person asking me for two dollars to hit on me then. In fact, I would have given the homeless person twenty dollars just to tell me I was still attractive!

And I'm not quite sure what China has to do with it—something about people's perspectives?—so I'm not even going to bother. But posters should never assume that we bloggers also see the big picture. In this case, unfortunately, the big picture was, um, all of me, and especially my ass. And mothers? If you do accidentally say to another mother who is not pregnant, "Congratulations!" you better react to their probably horrified reaction with an Academy Award-worthy apology, or duck, because they just might want to punch you. But the smartest course is to use plain common sense and keep your mouth shut, until that woman shares with you that she is, indeed, pregnant. That way, no one gets hurt.

Sharing Your Unborn Baby's Name Is a Really Bad Idea

*I proudly share my baby names. Because,
unlike you, I have a mind of my own, and I don't
care what others think. I don't spend my time trying
to impress or please other people ... Your name choice
is retarded. But if you were confident and secure
in yourself, it wouldn't matter.*

once wrote a post about how sharing your unborn baby's name is a really bad idea. Many mommy blog readers, I think, feel isolated and are searching for a place to network. They're looking for support and friendship. This is one post I wrote where I found a mostly supportive and witty readership.

I was hesitant when I was pregnant with my second child about sharing his name. In fact, as I wrote in a piece for Mommyish.com, I was downright scared. I was afraid that I was just asking for trouble. I'm not sure why people, including good friends, feel the need to throw in their opinion if you tell them your baby's name before its birth, but, alas, they do. You will get funny looks or, even worse, people will say things such as, "Why did you pick *that* name?" Or, "Really? *That's* the name?" However, if you wait until after the baby is born, people understand it's a done deal, so there's no point in their saying anything other than, "What a great name!" or, at least, "Cute baby!"

When I was pregnant with my second child, before I knew the gender, I had a couple of girl's names picked out. One was Blu. I also had the name Jupiter picked out. I just love it. Thankfully, I learned I was having a boy, because around that time Beyoncé had a baby girl whom she named Blu, and there is nothing worse than having to tell people that no, you had picked that name way before (name of celebrity) had named their baby. For the rest of your life, if your baby and some celebrity's child share the same name, you will find yourself saying, "Actually, I didn't copy (name of celebrity). My baby came out first. First! (Name of celebrity) copied me!"

I named my son Holt. In another post for Mommyish.com, I complained that people must think I'm a total moron because, where I live, there is a department store called Holt Renfrew. Even after he was born, to this present day, I still get cracks from people, like, "Oh, you must really love shopping at Holt Renfrew!" As if I would name my child after a fucking department store. It would be the equivalent of naming your baby Target or Nordstrom. And who the hell would do that? Who really loves a department store so much they would name their child after it, except, maybe, an honest-to-goodness shopaholic? Holt is actually a family name. (Reminder: It's a done deal, people!) When my grandfather came over to Canada from Poland, he couldn't get a job because his last name was Burnholtz, which at that time was too Jewish-sounding. I wanted to bring back the name Holt, in honor of both my grandfather's last name, and my grandmother Helen's first name.

But, really, if I'm at the gym and about to hop on a bike, I really don't have the time or energy to explain the back story to my son's name. So now, when someone makes a crack about the store, I just say, "It's a family name," which shuts them up. Or, sometimes, I pretend I don't speak or understand English. This also works remarkably well.

Frankly I'm not sure why people make jokes like this, considering some of the names they give their kids. When someone makes fun of the name Holt, I'm thinking, "You named your child after a bottle of wine, which, by the way, is delicious, but also really hard to spell." But I just nod and smile, as if I were stoned and then hypnotized. In the real world, you have to be courteous. In the real world, unlike the blogosphere, people who don't like the name you choose for your child, or any other aspect of parenting, may engage in some harsh behind-the-back talk (which you won't be privy to), whereas posters in the blogosphere want you to read their harsh opinions.

Now, I'm not opposed to any name (except if you name your child Twitter, or Hitler. Then I think you have it coming). In any case, when I was pregnant with Holt, and people would ask if I had his name picked out, I would say direly, "Yes, but it's a done deal, so you have to like it, and even if you don't, I want you to pretend you do, okay?" Only after they agreed to my terms, and pinky promised, would I then share the name I had chosen.

Not all commenters were as sympathetic about this as I hoped they would be. (I never seem to learn!) "But if you live in a country with a popular department store that bears the same name as the one you chose for your son, you had to figure that some people would crack stupid jokes about it. Sure, I get that it's annoying, but you seem really, really ragey about something that is pretty predictable," wrote one. The truth is, I never once thought about the department store when I came up with his name, so I wasn't predicting it at all. I only thought about it after others reminded me there was this department store. (I shop more online now.) And I wasn't enraged. I was aggravated. Total difference.

"There's no point in giving a kid an unusual name. For one thing, you can't make them special by doing that. For another, any name will eventually become common (but that doesn't help the poor kid, and the hell he or she will go through, a hell the well-meaning parents are largely spared)," wrote another. I don't really think my son, Holt, will go through hell because of his name. He'll probably go through hell because of our judgmental society.

But a lot of commenters had the same issue I did, which made me happy, happy, happy! "I regret telling my husband's grandma our baby's name because every time I see her, I'm asked, 'Are you still going to name him *that?*'" wrote one. "Or, 'It's not too late to give that baby a real name' ... This isn't a new reaction from her either. She doesn't like my husband's sister's name, and, even though she is twenty-five years old now, she still complains about her name." Dear God, I thought after reading this comment. Do people really hold a grudge for that long over a name? It must be exhausting! But mommy blogs work two ways: readers get a glimpse into my life, and I, along with millions of other people, get insight into other people's lives. Which is why mommy blogging, or reading mommy blogs, can be so very voyeuristic, and therefore addictive.

Even non-mothers appreciated this post, which is interesting, because it made me wonder why people who are not mothers read parenting blogs. Maybe it's research, or preparation for motherhood, which isn't a bad idea. These mothers need to know these days how bitchy some mothers can be, so they won't be so shocked when they find themselves constantly judged, something I was never prepared for. "I don't have children yet, but if I ever do, I will not be sharing the name I choose until the very last minute possible if I can avoid it. The reason for this is the same as for many: Too many people with opinions and judgments around me, and it will just tick me off. Based on my experience with friends, you don't really want to tick off a pregnant lady." Too true. Especially one like me. When I was pregnant, I would literally want to kick the customer in front of me while waiting in line at the bakery for my fourth chocolate croissant of the day.

Another poster wrote, "When my partner and I decided to name our son Gabriel, most people loved it, except for the mother-in-law. She said, 'You can't call him that, I don't like it, and other kids will call him Gabby!' I've never heard of a Gabriel being called Gabby before. It pissed me off for weeks. If you can't be constructive in your objection to a baby name, just keep your bloody mouth shut!" Amen. And don't you find it shocking that family members are so invested in your child's name, as if they were carrying them? (By the way, I adore the name Gabriel or Gabe.)

I love commenters who admit they weren't exactly in the right state of mind when they came up with the name for their baby, just as I wasn't in the right state of mind when my daughter was conceived (otherwise known as her being the Best Accident I Ever Had). "We picked out Ripley for our daughter while we were a bit inebriated and watching [the film] *Alien* over a year before we got pregnant. Once we sobered up, we realized we really loved the name and it was something that we could actually agree on … But when people would ask, we'd say, 'We're naming her after one of the first really strong female leads in cinema.' Sort of a concise way to say, 'Yes, we thought about it. Yes, this name means something,'" wrote another.

And another, "When I was pregnant and told my boy-friend's family I planned on naming our son Rocco, his father kept saying, 'That sounds like a dog's name. I know a dog named Rocco.' I'm sure he was hoping I'd go with another name, but it annoyed me that he kept repeating it. Then a perfect stranger (the sandwich-maker at Subway) asked what

I was going to name him, and when I replied, she looked disgusted and said, 'Is that a family name you feel you need to preserve?' I couldn't believe how rude people were. After his birth, the only comments we get are '*I love it!*' It's even grown on his grandfather ..." Let me just say, no matter what you name your child, someone will mention that they know of some dog with the same name. It's par for the course when it comes to choosing a baby name. And, by the way, Rocco was on my list of names for my son, too!

Other posters wrote about how awful their experience was in sharing baby names before the birth. "I've changed my unborn baby's name 40× maybe, because of people's reactions ... it hurts and it keeps us awake at night. It's not just something simple. It really hurts my feelings when people say, 'Oh ... that's special' (sarcastic). I seriously cried when my mom nagged me for days about my choice, it's so annoying. So now I have a name, and I'm keeping it a secret from everyone, and they'll just have to see when they receive a card in the mailbox," wrote a poster, whom I just wanted to hug and also ask, How did you come up with so many names? And, what name did you eventually choose?

Even if you come up with a common name, you will get negative comments, as shown by the following mom on Mommyish.com: "Yes, we told everybody who asked. At first, I was going to say that since we chose a classic name (Elizabeth), nobody said anything, but then I remembered just about every person said, 'That's a long name for a little girl!' Yes, but she will only be a little girl for a short period of time. Besides, there are a ton of nicknames for Elizabeth! So you are right, everybody has an opinion." I just love being right. It's so much better than being wrong.

You might think that there was nothing much for the Mob Moms to attack in a blog as non-provocative, in my opinion, as this one was. You would be wrong! "At first," wrote one, "I was just thinking you like weird names because yours is so blah and generic, but now I legitimately think your brain has fallen out. Jupiter? Jupiter??? And I proudly share my baby names. Because, unlike you, I have a mind of my own, and I don't care what others think. I don't spend my time trying to impress or please other people … Your name choice is retarded. But if you were confident and secure in yourself, it wouldn't matter." I have so many issues with this poster that I. Can't. Even. But I'll try. First, please don't use the word *retarded*. No further explanation needed. Secondly, I was and am confident with my choices, but who the hell wants to put up with other people's opinions, especially when it comes to naming your own baby, and their opinion wasn't solicited in the first place? And that was my point. I can be both annoyed and have a mind of my own, because I am an awesome multi-tasker. Finally, you are literally the one and only person, in my entire life, who has said my name is blah and generic, and quite frankly, it's a lot rude.

Another etiquette-challenged poster chipped in with this: "I can still tell you that your baby's name is stupid after it's born." Sure you can. But, really, why would you want to do that? If you do want to, you may want to ask yourself, "What kind of person am I?" Because *who does that*? Just because you can doesn't mean you should. "I agree with a previous comment, it's only a bad idea if you care what other people think. And I don't. People want to know what we're naming our son, I'll tell them. They don't like it, it's their problem," posted another commenter. Yes, but are you *human*? Does it not at least annoy you when people make mean, or uncalled-for remarks about your child's name? I'd love to bottle up some of your patience for myself.

Another Mommyish.com poster had a great idea. She wrote, "Of course it doesn't matter. But what I'm trying to avoid is the negativity generated by the loudmouths. I just don't want or need it. Why give them a chance to nitpick? Plus, it's just fun when the nosy ones are annoyed at my non-answer." Brilliant! Instead of being pregnant and annoyed, throw it back to the other person with a non-answer and let them be annoyed. Genius! And, as I mentioned already, you're just plain screwed if your baby ends up with the same name as a celebrity's baby, even if you gave birth first. It happens more often than you'd think. As one commented, "I wanted to name my daughter Elliot or Parker, but my boyfriend was set against it. So we decided on Harper. Of course, within six months after her birth, at least three celebrities named their daughters Harper." The commenter added a sad face to her comment. And I feel for her :(. And I'm sure her boyfriend will never hear the end of it.

Amazingly, a lot of mothers admitted that, like me, they like offbeat and unusual names. "I tend to find names I like in fantasy novels or video games, same goes for my husband. In fact, our name for a boy is from one of my favorite games of all time that I grew up playing since I was about six years old, but I know if I told my family and friends I was naming my kid after a video game character, there would be backlash like nobody's business," wrote one. It was interesting, to say the least, to see how many people name their children after characters in video games. Another added, "Just reading this now ... and wanted to share that *both* of my kids, both boys, are named after video games! I have a Colgan (after Culgan) and a Ridley. We didn't want family names, and wanted something different. So, we went with my husband's love of video games to decide." I like it, even though I have no idea what video games these names came from!

We got my daughter's name from Brooke Shields' daughter, after my then-fiancé saw it in *US Weekly*. Deciding on a baby's name that both you and your partner can agree on is a whole other blog. But, trust me, if someone shares their baby's name before they are born, just nod and say enthusiastically that you love the baby's name, even if you detest it. Remember, it's not *your* baby. You won't be calling their name out to come down for dinner or to do their homework. Also, as one poster mentioned, you really don't want to tick off a pregnant woman. As for the name Jupiter, I suppose all Mob Moms will be happy I had a boy, because Jupiter would be way too unique for them. But I still think the name is out of this world. I'll save the name Jupiter for when, or if, I get another dog. It's too beautiful to go to waste. No one ever says a dog's name is dumb.

Overnight Camp

Wow, Rebecca! I applaud you.
This is probably one of the first articles
that I like from you, but that aside, you
give some very solid wisdom here.

There's more to parenting than reading bedtime stories, childproofing, and filling sippy cups. Part of parenting is letting go, no matter how painful that can be. I posted a blog on Mommyish.com about overnight camp. I was talking to a mother after school ended in the spring, and she asked what my daughter was doing for the summer. I told her she was going to overnight camp. The mother asked for how long. "For a month," I answered. This mother's mouth dropped in horror, as if I had told her I had genital herpes (which, for the record, I don't), or as if I had just told her, "Yeah. I hate my kid. I'm going to spend my time in a drunken stupor for all of July, from the moment that camp bus takes off until the moment it brings her home."

This mother said she could *never* send her nine-year-old to overnight camp, because her daughter didn't know how to shower on her own, and also because, "I'm not ready for her to be gone that long from me." It's so hard to not be judgmental as a mother sometimes. But you have to at least try to hide your disapproval (which means controlling your facial expression and avoiding eye-rolling) because that's the polite, normal thing to do when having a conversation with actual humans. I *wanted* to tell this mother, "Well, you may not be ready, but your daughter probably is. In fact, she probably would enjoy some time away from you, if you're still bathing her and she's almost ten!" But I didn't say that. I kept my trap shut. I wasn't ready when my daughter started walking, but she was! I'm sure I won't be ready when she heads off to college, but I'm sure she will be.

I don't really care if you send your kids to overnight camp or not. I do care, however, about the pathetic excuses sometimes offered for not sending them, especially if the kids really want to go to overnight camp. Not being able to afford camp is a reasonable explanation. "I'm not ready for her to leave me," is not. Neither is, "She can't shower on her own yet." I first sent my daughter to overnight camp when she was seven. The first time, she came back wearing exactly the same outfit she left in, just backwards and inside out, and I highly doubt, from the stench of her, that she showered at all.

I miss my daughter terribly when she's off at camp. But she loves it. In fact, that's where she learned to shower on her own! Camp is the best place for kids to learn to shower, eat different food, and try new things, like waterskiing, because there are other children around who they watch and learn from. (Although I was slightly taken aback when she came home and told me her favorite food was now ham, since we are Jewish and all. Then again, she learned how to water-ski!) My daughter, generally, leans to the shy side. But when she got off that bus from camp, she was outgoing, funny, and confident, like a comedian. I *loved* the new her. I loved the old her, too, but the new her knew fun hand games and jokes, so of course I wanted to keep her even more.

When they're at camp, no news is good news, so, although you have no idea what your kid may be doing, you know they are in safe hands. I say, let the counselors worry about her jumping off rocks or wearing a life jacket. Let them worry, stress, and get frustrated getting her into bed. I do it eleven months of the year. Mommy needs a break!

The point of my overnight post was that overnight camp is not about parents. It's about children, and the memories they will make, like the first time I got felt up. (That came much later!) But that was at overnight camp! Ah, memories! And the lifelong friendships they will form. I couldn't see how this post could offend anyone, but some Mob Mom always finds a way. Obviously, the Internet is a great place for anonymously judgmental people to hang out, as if it were their own sinister private club. You can say things to mommy bloggers anonymously that you'd never dare to say to a friend, and if you did say them to a friend, you'd probably lose that friend forever, and I wouldn't blame them for never returning your calls.

"This post is wrapped up in a big package of 'everyone is wrecking their kids by not conforming to your personal wealthy WASP traditions.' I honestly can't stand the judgmental tone behind this article. There are a million right and wrong ways to raise children and even if you disagree with how someone is parenting, it doesn't make you right," wrote one. Exactly. It doesn't make me right. It doesn't make you right, either. I sometimes don't know if Mob Moms actually read the blogs or just get their thrills by posting rude comments. Maybe it's like the high a gambling addict gets. Nowhere did I argue that sending your child to camp was the only right thing to do, nor do I think I made any judgment, but somehow Mob Moms feel entitled to make things up out of thin air, by suggesting, for example, that I'm a WASP or that I think you're wrecking your kids by not sending them to camp. Another added, "It's tremendously judgmental and sanctimonious. She can't get why someone wouldn't send her kid to camp? Just because Ms. Eckler values her free time more than spending time with her kids doesn't mean I'm a helicopter mom. Maybe Eckler can get that. Geez." Oh, I get it all right. You sound angry. That's okay. I don't live with you. And I don't value my free time more than spending it with my kids. I value it equally. Obviously, I love my children, but I would never have uttered, "I love my daughter. That's why I'm sending her to camp!" Because if I dared to use that as justification for my parenting choice, Mob Moms would instantly assume, wrongly, that what I'm saying is, "If you don't send your kids to camp, you don't love your children as much as I do."

Another Mob Mom didn't get camp or children who can't shower on their own. "Any nine-year-old child who cannot shower on their own should be checked by doctors for mental impairment. Having other nine-year-olds teach you is just creepy. Dear heavens, I was in puberty by that age!" Again, just because you had begun puberty doesn't mean every nine-year-old has done the same. And what exactly did you do at school when you had to change for gym? Mob Moms think they are always right. They offend not just me, but other posters as well. They insult our children when they say, "They should be checked out by a doctor." Right. Because my doctor is going to really care that my daughter can't always get all the shampoo out of her hair, and it's so wrong to ask someone—a friend at camp or a parent at home—for help. When did asking for help become a bad thing? Would you tell your child not to ask for help from a teacher?

But then a beautiful thing happened. After the Mob Mom remarked that any nine-year-old who couldn't shower should be checked out for mental impairment, the posters turned on *her*, which was great (and totally deserved!). Let the Mob Moms go after one another, so I can get a break, and make myself a snack to nibble on while watching the action! The hilarious part is that they didn't go after each other about overnight camp, which is what I wrote about, but about grooming! It all started with a commenter who wrote, "I was way too disturbed by the fact that there is a nine-year-old out there who cannot shower without her parents' help to finish reading this article. How and why?" Well, that just got things going! Even my daughter, at age ten, needs help sometimes getting all the shampoo out. Everyone with hard-to-deal-with hair had to jump in. "I have very long hair with tight ringlets. At nine, I struggled getting all the shampoo out, so I used to have a shower, shampoo my hair, rinse it to the best of my childhood ability, then my Mum would finish rinsing it out. I don't think that's so terrible," wrote one. Another added, "I always wonder about people who condemn the family of any child over the age of six who can't control 100 percent of their grooming, especially when it comes to hair. Like, do all their kids have just the finest, most stick-straight, utilitarian haircuts in the universe?" Another wrote, "My mom had to brush my butt-length, extremely thick and curly hair until I was thirteen and hacked it all off. It was literally too hard for me to brush on my own."

So, somehow my post on overnight camp not only offended some mothers, but it also went into a direction I could never see coming—hair! This happens on mommy blogs more often than you'd think. You could be writing about report cards, and then somehow the discussion turns to breastfeeding, or you could be writing about breastfeeding, and posters will start talking about biting kids in daycare. I'm not sure how this happens, but when it does, I love it, because the Mob Moms are no longer criticizing me. They're not even discussing my post. They're going after each other in a way you'd never see on the street. Am I a bad person for actually liking this? Don't answer! But somehow my blog post about camp was now about hair. "I'm sorry that everyone isn't completely fucking destroying their hair to conform to what you think is cute," wrote another mom. "I can 150 percent promise you that, if you'd seen my hair unbrushed for several days as a child, you'd change your tune on a dime, because—Newsflash!—not everyone's hair looks like cute bed head or windswept straight/wavy hair if they leave it alone."

Some mothers were supportive of my post, sort of, if not of their families. "That sounds *just like* my sister-in-law. My niece will be sixteen this year, and her mom won't even let her get on the bus to school by herself in the mornings. One would think a teenage girl would be embarrassed by this. But this girl still crawls into bed between her parents every night … I mean, my sister-in-law still talks to her in a baby talk and insists on picking her clothes out every morning, and sitting in the bathroom with her while she takes a shower 'in case she falls,'" wrote another commenter on Mommyish.com. Yeah, I don't see this girl going off to overnight camp ever. But, again, let's not judge! And some kids, I learned from posters, do have helicopter moms—moms who refused to unleash them—and the results were not ideal. "Kids *need* time away from their parents," wrote one. "I have a cousin whose mother couldn't stand the idea of her being so far away, even to the point that my cousin was accepted to an excellent college to major in dance, and had to turn it down for a closer and far inferior college because her mother wasn't willing to have her go out of state. And now, not only is my cousin like a twenty-one-year-old child because she never developed any self-reliance, but she resents the hell out of her mother, and only spends time with her when she's forced to."

There are still some understanding moms in the blogo-sphere, as shown by this commenter who brought the dis-cussion back to the original topic: "Wow, Rebecca! I applaud you. This is probably one of the first articles that I like from you, but that aside, you give some very solid wisdom here. It's not about whether *you're* ready to let your baby fly. It's about when *they* are ready. And even if they're not entirely ready because they're unsure about testing their wings, it's almost a guarantee that they will have gotten past their initial fears by the end of a week. Bravo :)." I'll take that ovation now. And maybe get my daughter to help brush my hair. Or maybe even start a blog on grooming, because it seems to be a very popular discussion-starter. Nonetheless, there is a phrase I've heard. It says that children are only rented: You don't own them forever. And it's best to be prepared for that. One way is to send them off to overnight camp with some really good conditioner.

Just Another Day in
the Mommy Blogosphere

*You don't need to worry about
whether or not I have kids, I certainly
don't give a flying fuck about yours.*

Commenter #1: "He's not her husband. He's some other woman's husband. Eckler is just the whore on the side."

Commenter #2: "Could you make a more inappropriate comment?"

Commenter #1: "And trust me, honey, that was mild compared to what other women have to say about her."

Commenter #2: "I'm not a new reader, this isn't news to me. But that doesn't make it okay. (In fact, I notice that on this particular post, you are the only one.) The truth is, you are not only slut-shaming Eckler for a way of life that is not your own, and truthfully you probably don't even know the whole story, but on top of that, you're being a bitter woman over … what? Because she has money? Because you are bitter at her fiancé/boyfriend/fuck buddy? *Who cares? It's none of your business.* Because she's paid

---

This comment thread first appeared on Mommyish.com.

to write for a blog site? Because she has met celebrities? Because she doesn't believe in marriage—*for herself?* Many of her posts make me roll my eyes. But apparently no one taught you manners. Just because you're anonymous on the Internet, doesn't make it right to make those kinds of comments. Look, you don't have to get over your Eckler hate. But letting yourself hide behind the anonymity of the Internet to be a nasty human being does no one any favors, most of all yourself."

Commenter #1: "Want me to find some rainbows and cotton candy for you?"

Commenter #2: "Aw, cliché troll has to keep trolling. At least, you used the right clichés to show you're still a child. Enjoy!"

Commenter #1: "And yet you keep responding like the stupid bitch you are. Get off your fucking mastodon and quit griping that people on the interwebs aren't nice enough for you. Cunt. How's that for inappropriate?"

Commenter #2: "I get an email every time you respond to me. You don't have an account, so you're taking the time to come back and check and see if I have commented. What's your excuse? Seriously. Get over it. Move on. Obviously, from post one, you've been looking for the drama. All I tried to point out was that you acted without manners, and instead of graciously realizing that perhaps you were a little rude, you exploded into troll mode. I hope to God you ended up on a parent-themed site by accident … I'm not trying to say my shit smells like roses. I'm trying to say that you are acting immature and, per-haps, if you are truly a mother, as being on a parenting-themed blog suggests, you should consider how you are acting and whether or not you would approve [of] your own children acting in the same way. In person."

Commenter #1: "You may get emails, but you don't have to take such precious time out of your life to respond. You bitch about letting it go, yet here you are. Fucking hypocrite … Strangers aren't being nice on the Internet. Seriously? If strangers online are all you have to worry about, you must have an extremely boring life. You don't need to worry about whether or not I have kids, I certainly don't give a flying fuck about yours. Now you can go back to sucking the dick of that mastodon. I have better shit to do in my spare time."

Epilogue

After reading the manuscript for this book, one of my friends suggested that I stop mommy blogging entirely because of all the nasty, outrageous, insane, and rude comments my blogs have attracted. I have a thicker skin than she does. I may soon be ready to stop mommy blogging, but not because of the commenters. I feel that I'm not finished yet. I'm still in uncharted territory, testing my way post by post, grappling not only with judgmental mothers, but also with the question of how much to share about my life, and especially about my children's lives as they get older. I admit I never anticipated how judgmental moms could be, no matter how trivial the topic. Even when I'm writing about how hard it is to fit in time for a shower, the Mob Moms have to have their say. At the same time, I know most mothers are trying really, really hard to do what's best for their children and their family.

I have worked hard to be myself when writing my blogs. I don't pretend to be a perfect mother. I am however comfortable with my parenting choices. On the one hand, I don't want to be known *only* as a mommy blogger. On the other hand, I sort of want to continue blogging because mommy bloggers often help one another through this journey of parenting in the modern world. Mommy blogs have created freedom for women, especially new mothers, to share the experiences they may not be comfortable discussing with a friend, relative, or their spouse. This, surely, is a good thing. And, sometimes, mothers' comments—not all which are included in this book—amaze me. Many talented writers have shared their insights and offered sound advice on my blogs.

Parenting is a beautiful, if sometimes unpleasant, undertaking. There's no probation period once you give birth. It's often forgotten that a mother is born along with her baby. This is where mommy blogs are helpful, because you realize that others are going through the same challenges that you face. The Internet means that advice can be found within seconds, right at your fingertips. I have shared laughs and triumphs with other mothers in the blogosphere. As well, I've learned that what one Mob Mom thinks is just plain wrong, other moms find thought-provoking and will often indicate that they have been through the same ordeal.

In this book, I have focused mostly on the maniacal mothers who post vicious, yet unintentionally witty comments, precisely because they are so vicious and so unintentionally humorous. I try to remember, however, that even the seemingly most offensive Mob Mom may just have stumbled on my blog on a miserable day. And while I may come down hard on judgmental Mob Moms, I know I have occasionally been guilty of committing some of the same offenses, even if I don't realize it. (Although I would never call anyone a douche, and I don't ever feel the need to get in the last word, and I would never insult a child.)

Even though I may want to hang myself after reading some of the more egregious comments, and I wonder what the heck is happening in society to make people so nasty, I also think it's better that everyone has their say, no matter how vulgarly or disrespectfully they express themselves. (I definitely don't want censorship for anything other than hate literature.) I rely—and my advice for other mommy bloggers is that they do the same—on my motherly instinct and common sense to sort out sound advice and supportive readers from the kind of comments that should simply be ignored because of their stupidity.

I've always liked making mountains out of the tiniest parenting molehills, but perhaps it's time to move onto something new. The genre sheltered under the umbrella title Mommy Blogger has exploded. The parenting platform will become larger and larger as parenting magazines and books add online components and message boards and there's a good possibility that commenters will become even more nasty. Setting up a mommy blog is amazingly simple to do. Unfortunately, in some cases, it's just as simple for anonymous posters to chip in, too, with delightful opinions such as, "I hope you die in a plane crash."

But, as a mommy blogger, you learn to take the good with the bad. Almost four million people now identify themselves as mommy bloggers in North America: Obviously, you aren't going to please them all. That's just the way it is. But I do worry for the future of our children. If mothers can be so mean now, what will happen in ten years, when our children, especially our girls, become parents? Will mothers get even more judgmental and Mob Mom-ish? I don't want to think about it. Or is being a judgmental mom just a fad? "It is not until you become a mother that your judgment slowly turns to compassion and understanding," Erma Bombeck once said.

Oh, if only she were on mommy blogs! I think she'd feel differently these days. But here's hoping!

And who knows? Maybe one day my kids will be writing missives about my parenting. But now I'm going to shut off my computer and give my children a big hug and a kiss. Our happiest, most memorable moments as mothers come, not from being attached to our computers, reading, commenting, or even writing about our children—although these all can be entertaining diversions in our free time or at that boring office job—but from actually spending quality time with our children … in person.

XO
Rebecca

Acknowledgments

Thank you to: Sarah Scott of Barlow Books, simply, and most importantly, for believing; and Jonathan Webb, for being a perfect editor. For Joanna Track, you're a Good Egg in every way. Thank you Sarah "Strategy" Miniaci. A massive shout out to the team at Mommyish.com, where I have had the privilege to write and have some extra fun being a mother. You gals are, in my daughter's words, "totally awesome!" And thank you, especially, to all my readers. I wish for you to have love in your heart and peace in your mind.

About the Author

Rebecca Eckler is one of Canada's best-known journalists and authors. She is the international best-selling author of *Knocked Up*, *Wiped!*, and *Toddlers Gone Wild*, as well as the author of the international bestseller *How to Raise a Boyfriend*. She has been a columnist at *The National Post* and *The Globe and Mail*, and her work has appeared in *The New York Times* and *Los Angeles Times*. She writes for numerous magazines and parenting blogs across North America. *The Mommy Mob* is her ninth book. She lives in Toronto with her ten year-old daughter, Rowan, and one-year-old son, Holt.